Women, Men and Everyday Talk

Also by Jennifer Coates

LANGUAGE AND GENDER: A Reader
LANGUAGE AND GENDER: A Reader (2nd edition) (*co-editor*)
MEN TALK: Stories in the Making of Masculinities
THE SEMANTICS OF THE MODAL AUXILIARIES
THE SOCIOLINGUISTICS OF NARRATIVE (*co-editor*)
WOMEN IN THEIR SPEECH COMMUNITIES (*co-editor*)
WOMEN, MEN AND LANGUAGE
WOMEN'S STUDIES: An Introduction (*co-editor*)
WOMEN TALK: Conversation between Women Friends

Women, Men and Everyday Talk

Jennifer Coates
University of Roehampton, UK

First published 2013 by
PALGRAVE MACMILLAN

Palgrave Macmillan in the UK is an imprint of Macmillan Publishers Limited, registered in England, company number 785998, of Houndmills, Basingstoke, Hampshire RG21 6XS.

Palgrave Macmillan in the US is a division of St Martin's Press LLC, 175 Fifth Avenue, New York, NY 10010.

Palgrave Macmillan is the global academic imprint of the above companies and has companies and representatives throughout the world.

Palgrave® and Macmillan® are registered trademarks in the United States, the United Kingdom, Europe and other countries

ISBN: 978–0–230–36869–9 (hardback)
ISBN: 978–0–230–36870–5 (paperback)

This book is printed on paper suitable for recycling and made from fully managed and sustained forest sources. Logging, pulping and manufacturing processes are expected to conform to the environmental regulations of the country of origin.

A catalogue record for this book is available from the British Library.

A catalogue record for this book is available from the Library of Congress.

Contents

List of Illustrations

Tables

Figure

Acknowledgements

The chapters in this collection of papers and lectures written over the last 20 years rely on data collected over the years from same-sex friendship groups. I am very grateful to all the women and girls, men and boys who allowed their conversations to be recorded, transcribed and used for analysis in my research. I am also grateful to those women and girls who allowed me to interview them about women's talk and female friendship. I am grateful to colleagues and students who have made data available to me, and to those who helped with transcribing the data. Apart from those in Chapter 4, the names of all participants have been changed. (For a more detailed acknowledgement of those who contributed to my research in a variety of ways, see the full Acknowledgements in *Women Talk* (1996) and *Men Talk* (2003).)

The research which is the subject of the chapters in this book was supported by the following grant-giving bodies: Melbourne University, Australia (Arts Faculty Visiting Fellowship); University of Canterbury, Christchurch, New Zealand (Erskine Fellowship); the British Academy (small grant); the Arts and Humanities Research Board (Research Leave); the English Department, University of Roehampton (Study Leave).

I would like to say a big thank-you to Annabelle Mooney, Pia Pichler and Satori Soden, who have read and commented on the revised versions of these chapters and who have been unstinting in their support. Thanks also to Olivia Middleton at Palgrave Macmillan for encouraging me to put together this collection of papers on language and gender. Special thanks go to Margaret Gottschalk for her ongoing support and for tolerating my neglect of her when I was absorbed in the book (and to William Coates and Simon Gottschalk for technical help). Finally, I'd like to express my gratitude to Blue Mountain coffee shop in East Dulwich for providing the perfect environment for reading, writing and revising, together with excellent coffee!

Jennifer Coates
London, 12.12.12

List of Sources

Note: All the papers published in this collection have been revised and updated specifically for this book.

Chapter 1 Women's Stories: The Role of Narrative in Friendly Talk

This chapter began life as an Inaugural Lecture, given at Roehampton Institute London on 20 May 1996. A revised version appeared as Chapter 5 of *Women Talk: Conversation between Women Friends* (Oxford: Blackwell, 1996: 94–116) and was entitled '"D'You Know What My Mother Did Recently?": Telling Our Stories'.

Chapter 2 'So I Mean I Probably...': Hedges and Hedging in Women's Talk

This chapter first appeared as Chapter 7 of *Women Talk: Conversation between Women Friends* (Oxford: Blackwell, 1996: 152–173). It was revised for the conference on Modality in Contemporary English held in Verona in September 2001, and appeared in the collected papers as 'The Role of Epistemic Modality in the Talk of Women Friends' in Roberta Facchinetti, Manfred Krug and Frank Palmer (eds) *Modality in Contemporary English* (Berlin: Mouton de Gruyter, 2003: 331–347).

Chapter 3 Competing Discourses of Femininity

This chapter first appeared as Chapter 10 of *Women Talk: Conversation between Women Friends* (Oxford: Blackwell, 1996: 232–262). A revised version appeared as 'Competing Versions of Femininity' in Helga Kotthoff and Ruth Wodak (eds) *Communicating Gender in Context* (Amsterdam: John Benjamins, 1997: 285–314).

Chapter 4 Changing Femininities: The Talk of Teenage Girls

This chapter began life as a plenary presentation at the Third Berkeley Women and Language Conference in April 1994; it subsequently appeared under the title 'Discourse, Gender and Subjectivity: The Talk of Teenage Girls' in the conference proceedings: Mary Bucholtz, A.C. Liang, Laurel A. Sutton and Caitlin Hines (eds) *Cultural Performances* (Berkeley, CA: Berkeley Women and Language Group, 1994: 116–132). Finally, a revised version appeared in Mary Bucholtz, A.C. Liang and Laurel A. Sutton (eds) *Reinventing Identities: The Gendered Self in Discourse* (Oxford: Oxford University Press, 1999: 123–144).

Chapter 5 Women Behaving Badly: Female Speakers Backstage

This chapter was first published in the *Journal of Sociolinguistics* (3 (1), 1999: 67–82) under the title 'Women Behaving Badly: Female Speakers Backstage'. The version printed here is a revised version of 'Small Talk and Subversion: Female Speakers Backstage', published in Justine Coupland (ed.) *Small Talk* (London: Longman, 2000: 241–263).

Chapter 6 One-at-a-Time: The Organisation of Men's Talk

This chapter was originally published in Sally Johnson and Ulrike Meinhof (eds) *Language and Masculinity* (Oxford: Blackwell, 1997: 107–129).

Chapter 7 'So I Thought "Bollocks to It"': Men, Stories and Masculinities

This chapter began life as a plenary lecture given at the Language and Gender Symposium held at Victoria University, Wellington, New Zealand, in October 1999. It was subsequently published in Janet Holmes (ed.) *Gendered Speech in Social Context* (Wellington: Victoria University Press, 2000: 11–38). (A longer version was published as Chapter 3 of *Men Talk: Stories in the Making of Masculinities* (Oxford: Blackwell, 2003: 40–81).)

Chapter 8 'My Mind Is with You': Story Sequences in the Talk of Male Friends

This chapter first appeared in *Narrative Inquiry* (11 (1), 2001: 81–101) and later as Chapter 4 of *Men Talk: Stories in the Making of Masculinities* (Oxford: Blackwell, 2003: 82–106).

Chapter 9 'Everyone Was Convinced That We Were Closet Fags': The Role of Heterosexuality in the Construction of Hegemonic Masculinity

This chapter originated as a keynote lecture at the symposium 'Love Is a Many Splendored Thing: Language, Love and Sexuality', Kingston University, April 2002. It was later published in Helen Sauntson and Sakis Kyratzis (eds) *Language, Sexualities and Desires: Cross-Cultural Perspectives* (Basingstoke, UK: Palgrave Macmillan, 2007: 41–67).

Chapter 10 Language, Gender and Career

This chapter had its origins in a research group on Women and Career convened by Julia Evetts at Nottingham University. I gave a paper based on my research as a plenary lecture at the conference on Language and Gender held at Loughborough University in May 1992, and this was published in 1995 in Sara Mills (ed.) *Language and Gender: Interdisciplinary Perspectives* (London: Longman, 1995: 13–30). The version appearing in this collection is based on a shorter version of the paper, which first appeared in Julia Evetts (ed.) *Women and Career: Themes and Issues in Advanced Industrial Societies* (London: Longman, 1994: 72–86).

Chapter 11 Having a Laugh: Gender and Humour in Everyday Talk

I first gave a (shorter) version of this paper at the 2nd European Workshop on Humour Studies, University of Bologna, April 2004, under the title 'Having a Laugh: Humour and the Construction of Gendered Identities'. This then mutated into a lecture which I gave as a plenary at the IATEFL annual conference, Harrogate, in April 2006. It has since been written up and is due to be published in Delia Chiaro and Raffaella Baccolini (eds) *Gender and Humor: Interdisciplinary and International Perspectives* (London: Routledge).

Chapter 12 Turn-Taking Patterns in Deaf Conversation (with Rachel Sutton-Spence)

This chapter was originally published in *Journal of Sociolinguistics* (4 (4), 2001: 507–529).

Chapter 13 The Rise and Fall (and Rise) of Mars and Venus in Language and Gender Research

This previously unpublished paper was first given as the Richard Hoggart Lecture 2009, at Goldsmiths College, University of London (December 2009).

Transcription Conventions

(A) Narrative

Stories are presented in numbered lines, each line corresponding to one of the narrator's breath-groups or intonation units (see Chafe 1980). This means that lines will typically consist of a grammatical phrase or clause. Falling final intonation is represented with a full stop, rising final intonation with a question mark.

(B) Conversational data

The transcription conventions used for the conversational data are given below. Where conversation involves a great deal of overlap, stave notation is used: contributions within a stave are to be read simultaneously, like instruments in a musical stave. Any word, or portion of a word, appearing vertically above or below any other word, is to be read as occurring at the same time as that word. This system allows the reader to see how the utterances of the different participants relate to each other.

1. a slash (/) indicates the end of a tone group or chunk of talk, e.g.:

   she pushes him to the limit/

2. a question mark indicates the end of a chunk of talk which I am analysing as a question, e.g.:

   do you know anyone who's pregnant?

3. a hyphen indicates an incomplete word or utterance, e.g.:

   he's got this twi- he's got this nervous twitch/
   I was- I was- I was stopped by a train/

4. pauses are indicated by a full stop (short pause – less than 0.5 seconds) or a dash (longer pause) or by figures in round brackets (representing seconds), e.g.:

   certain children . I really like/
   [he] left a video (2.0) in a video recorder/

5. a horizontal line marks the beginning of a stave and indicates that the lines enclosed by the lines are to be read simultaneously (like a musical score), e.g.:

A: the squidgy stuff that they put on pizzas=
B: =Mozarell[a/
C: [Mozarella/

---

6. an extended square bracket indicates the start of overlap between utterances, e.g.:

A: and they have newspapers and [stuff/
B: [yes very good/

7. an equals sign at the end of one speaker's utterance and at the start of the next utterance indicates the absence of a discernible gap, e.g.:

A: because they're supposed to be=
B: =adults/

8. double round parentheses indicate that there is doubt about the accuracy of the transcription:

what's that ((mean))/ gayist/
((it's something with nuclear-)) yes/ atomic/

9. where material is impossible to make out, it is represented as follows, ((xx)), e.g.:

you're ((xx)) – you're prejudiced/

10. angled brackets give clarificatory information about underlined material, e.g.:

why doesn't that creep – start to go wild/ <LAUGHING>
I can't help it <WHINEY VOICE>

11. capital letters are used for words/syllables uttered with emphasis:

it's in MExico/
you know he IS a little star/

12. the symbol % encloses words or phrases that are spoken very quietly, e.g.:

%bloody hell%

13. the symbol *.hh* indicates that the speaker takes a sharp intake of breath:

    .hh I wish I'd got a camera/ <LAUGHING>

14. the symbol [...] indicates that material has been omitted, e.g.:

    Tom [...] says there's a German word to describe that/

Introduction

This book brings together some of my papers on language and gender written between the mid-1980s and today. Most of these papers have been published before, but some only existed as lecture notes. The book will provide an overview of the development of language and gender studies over the last 30 years, with particular emphasis on conversational data and on single-sex friendship groups.

The theme running throughout the book will be that gender plays a significant role in the construction of the linguistic landscape of our everyday lives. While battles have raged over the last 20 years about the dangers of over-simplifying gender – in particular, the danger of seeing gender in crude binary terms – language use is inevitably influenced by contemporary gender ideologies. These ideologies shape our understanding of what it means to be a woman or a man today: when we speak, we perform gender in ways that are congruent with these ideologies.

I became interested in language and gender after Dick Leith asked me to teach an option on the subject as part of the undergraduate linguistics course at Edge Hill College in 1976. At the time, I was working on my PhD thesis at Lancaster University, a study of the English modal auxiliaries. Sociolinguistics was relatively new to me (I belonged to a Liverpool University reading group and we had just read William Labov's *Sociolinguistic Patterns* (1972), which made a big impact). But as a feminist, engaged in feminist activities on Merseyside, the language and gender field immediately made sense to me.

The option at Edge Hill was a great success, so I continued to teach it in subsequent years. I became more and more frustrated with the paucity of research in the area and the problems of students getting access to relevant material (which was often published in obscure journals).

In about 1979, a publisher's representative visited Edge Hill and handed out forms to teaching staff, asking us to name areas where there was a need for new books. I started to fill one in, about the gap in the market for a language and gender book – then stopped and decided I would not give the idea to this publisher but would write a book myself. Geoffrey Leech, my supervisor at Lancaster University, was the editor of a series at Longman, and he gave me an introduction to the staff at Longman concerned with linguistics, who gave me a contract. The next four years were devoted to reading everything I could that had any bearing on gender and language. This resulted in two things: a book, and me becoming more politicized as I gained a greater understanding of the way language is implicated in the construction of gender and in the maintenance of hegemonic discourses of gender normativity. (The observant reader will spot the anachronisms here: I could not have articulated a sentence like the previous one in 1980 because these ideas had still not been assimilated into socio-cultural linguistics.[1] But in an inchoate way this was what I sensed.)

Women, Men and Language was published in 1986 and brought together everything I could glean about gendered patterns of language around the world (though what was available at the time was inevitably skewed to English-speaking cultures). While I was writing the book, I became increasingly embarrassed by the fact that I had done no original research on the topic myself. As a result, in 1982 I began to record my own women's group (the Oxton 'ladies') and then slowly recruited other all-female friendship groups, to build up a database of women's friendly talk. (For a fuller account of this period, see Coates 1996: 2–6.)

In 1984 I moved to London and started work in the English Department of the University of Roehampton (at that point known as Roehampton Institute). I joined Deborah Cameron there, and together we taught the English Language component of the undergraduate English degree. When we first met, we realised that we had in common a strong interest in language and gender, and that we were both critical of the status quo in language and gender research. Accordingly, we wrote a paper – 'Some problems in the sociolinguistic explanation of sex difference' – which was presented at the fifth Sociolinguistics Symposium at Liverpool University in 1984, and subsequently published in *Language and Communication* (5(3), 1985). We later revised the paper and it became the first chapter of our co-edited book, *Women in Their Speech Communities* (Longman, 1989).

At the same time, I was working hard on transcribing the audio-tapes of all-female talk I had collected. The first paper in which I drew on this material was given rather subversively (in February 1987) to the Philological Society at one of their wonderful old-fashioned meetings at which one ate cucumber sandwiches and at which Professor Robins (the Chair) invariably dozed off, before asking astute questions at the end! This paper – 'Epistemic Modality and Spoken Discourse' – was subsequently published in the *Transactions of the Philological Society* 1987. It makes the overt claim that modality may be just as satisfactorily analysed by micro-analysis of a small stretch of talk as by macro-analysis involving millions of words of computer corpora. But more surreptitiously it takes examples from two conversations – one all-male (from the Survey of English Usage, now ICE-GB) and one all-female, from my database, and suggests that female speakers may exploit epistemic modality more than men, to discuss more sensitive topics. Soon afterwards I wrote my first paper wholly devoted to an analysis of all-female talk, 'Gossip Revisited: Language in All-Female Groups', which was published in 1989 in *Women in Their Speech Communities* (reprinted in Cheshire and Trudgill 1998 and in Coates and Pichler 2011).

During the early 1990s I continued to collect and transcribe audiotaped material from groups of women and girls; I conducted ethnographic interviews with women friends about friendship and language; I presented papers at conferences and published in journals and edited collections. In 1994 I was invited to Melbourne University as an Arts Faculty Visiting Fellow: this gave me the opportunity to consolidate my findings on women's friendly talk and to start writing. *Women Talk* was published in 1996.

When I went to give papers at university linguistics societies around the country, I was sometimes asked why I had not included all-male talk in my research project. I was initially reluctant to embark on such a project, as I felt my research on the conversation of women friends benefitted from my insider knowledge, that is, that I am a woman who loves nothing better than talking to women friends. But after a lot of thought, I was persuaded to do some research into the talk of all-male friendship groups, and began to collect conversational data in the late 1980s. This resulted in the book *Men Talk* (2003).

The paragraphs preceding this have described my journey from part-time lecturer at Edge Hill College teaching language and gender in the late 1970s, to becoming a full-time teacher and researcher at the University of Roehampton focusing on talk in same-sex friendship groups. This description omits a crucial aspect of the journey: how I framed my analysis of gendered language. Since I started working in the language and gender field, theoretical approaches to language and gender have changed enormously. The papers which appear in this collection reflect the evolution of the field and fortuitously provide an overview of the development of theoretical frameworks in language and gender studies over the last 30 years.

The early years of language and gender research were dominated by two main theoretical frameworks: the Dominance approach and the Difference approach. To some extent, the data you were working with decided which approach was appropriate. I observed that much of the language and gender literature (though it is important to remember that there wasn't very much) was based on observations of mixed talk, that is, talk involving both women and men. As early as 1975 Robin Lakoff had written about the unassertiveness of women's speech, and her description of what she called 'Women's Language' with its list of components – such as hedges, tag questions, speaking in italics – has been hugely influential. I felt that it was unsatisfactory to make generalisations from informal observations (which is what Lakoff had done) or only from mixed talk (which is what later commentators had done) where male dominance was such a major factor. I decided that I would focus on women, on the informal talk of women interacting with friends. Unsurprisingly, I adopted the Difference or Two Cultures approach, an approach which makes the naïve assumption that women and men can be treated as two separate (and homogeneous) subcultures, but which has the strength of allowing women's conversational practices to be valued in their own right. While I was clear that we lived in a male-dominated society, I was also clear that the dominance approach would not help me to analyse and discuss the all-female conversations I had collected.

My early work in the language and gender field, then, focused on women, and looked at both the interactional patterns of all-female talk, but also at more overtly political issues such as the difficulties of women in the professions, who came up against gender discrimination as they tried to progress in their careers. (Chapters 1–5 all come from my work on the talk of all-female friendship groups; Chapter 10 is a paper written on the topic of women and career.)

As the Difference approach came under challenge, language and gender researchers were forced to develop more sophisticated ways of thinking about language in general and language and gender in particular. Linguists adopting the Difference approach had investigated linguistic features such as minimal responses, tag questions, hedges and directives. Now, we began to work with larger chunks of language, above the level of word or sentence, and we accepted the claim that what was conventionally referred to as 'language' can more realistically be seen as a heterogeneous collection of discourses (see Gavey 1989; Lee 1992). We also came to understand that there is not one fixed, unchanging femininity or masculinity, but multiple (and often conflicting) femininities and masculinities. Chapters 3, 4 and 7 arose from my growing interest in this new approach. It enabled me to talk about the multiple 'selves' women express in their talk with each other (Chapter 3), to examine how the discursive repertoire of a group of teenage girls changed as they got older (Chapter 4), and to explore the range of masculinities performed in men's friendly talk with each other (Chapter 7).

Socio-cultural linguists increasingly viewed talk as performative and gender as constantly in the process of formation (see Butler 1990). Instead of showing how gender correlated with the use of particular linguistic features, such as hedges or questions, I aimed to show how speakers draw on the linguistic resources available to them to accomplish gender. This more dynamic social constructionist approach informs all my later work.

Most recently, my work has been influenced by Queer Linguistics. This developed under the influence of Queer Theory, and put LGBT speakers and heteronormativity under the spotlight (thus queering the socio-cultural landscape). One of the major insights of Queer Linguistics is that gender cannot be discussed without acknowledging that it is intimately linked to sexuality. So, dominant versions of femininity and masculinity are intrinsically heterosexual. (Chapter 9 explores the struggles of male speakers to perform a masculinity that is clearly heterosexual and to avoid the accusation of being gay.)

Besides my overarching interest in gender and in the multiple ways gendered identities emerge in interaction, there are two other key strands present in this book: turn-taking patterns in conversation, and conversational narrative. Chapters 6 and 12 both focus on turn-taking strategies, in all-male talk and in the talk of Deaf friends respectively. As these chapters show, I have explored the varying use of one-at-a time and collaborative patterns of turn-taking in single-sex talk, and have established that, for educated white speakers at least, collaborative patterns are preferred by women interactants, and one-at-a-time patterns are preferred by men. I became interested in the talk of Deaf friends (in collaboration with Rachel Sutton-Spence) because we wanted to test the hypothesis that a group of Deaf women friends (using British Sign Language) would not use the collaborative turn-taking patterns typical of hearing women, for the simple reason that Deaf interactants are not able to see everyone in a group at the same time. To our surprise, we found that Deaf women friends do indeed draw on collaborative turn-taking patterns, even though participants could not all see each other or be seen at a given moment, demonstrating that sometimes just being in the talk, even if not seen, was the most important factor.

Story-telling is a key component of everyday conversation. When I started to transcribe the audio-tapes that constituted my database, I realised that the conversations I'd recorded consisted of two main components: story-telling and discussion. Stories typically involve just one speaker, the narrator, while discussions typically involve all participants. I became interested in the role of story-telling in the talk of close friends. Through the exchange of stories, we share in the construction and reconstruction of our personal identities, our 'selves'. Several chapters in this collection explore the links between story-telling and the construction of identities, with Chapter 1 drawing on all-female talk, and Chapters 7 and 8 on all-male talk. Chapter 8 is concerned with the ways in which speakers construct stories in sequence, and the importance of this practice in signalling speakers' understanding of each other. The achievement of a sequence of stories is a powerful demonstration of friendship and is simultaneously a powerful demonstration of the way identities are crucially co-constructed in interaction with others.

Two papers in this collection are the result of projects I became involved in with other academics. In 1991 I was asked to join a group at Nottingham University led by Professor Julia Evetts, working on the links between gender and career. This led to my writing the paper which appears as Chapter 10. A very different stimulus was provided by Delia Chiaro of the University of Bologna, who invited me to take part in a workshop on Gender and Humour, held in May 2004. I presented a paper at this workshop, the written version of which appears here as Chapter 11.

The book is divided into four parts. The first two are devoted to talk in same-sex friendship groups: women's talk is the subject of Chapters 1–5, and men's talk of Chapters 6–9. The chapters in the third part focus on gendered language in three very different contexts. The context in the first of these (Chapter 10) is the workplace: I explore women's struggle to find a voice in the professions. The second (Chapter 11) encompasses a wide range of social contexts as it explores the links between humour in everyday talk and gender. The social context for the third chapter in this part (Chapter 12) was a room at Bristol University fitted with video recorders to record the talk of Deaf friends. The two friendship groups who participated in the research knew each other well, so despite the more public surroundings, the talk was highly informal. All twelve of these chapters rely heavily on the conversational data collected by me over the years, on data collected by my students, and also on data collected by others working in the field. In each part the chapters are arranged chronologically, so readers can observe the ways in which my ideas developed. The final chapter, Chapter 13, is more theoretical, with a particular focus on the role of binaries in language and gender research since its inception. This chapter was written the most recently (and has never been published before). It provides an overview of language and gender research over the last 30 years and thus provides a fitting conclusion to the book.

It has been a great pleasure to revisit my work in the language and gender field and to have the opportunity to revise a selected number of papers for this collection. I hope readers will enjoy reading the papers in this collection as much as I have enjoyed writing and revising them.

Jennifer Coates
London, 12.12.12

Note

1. For more on socio-cultural linguistics, see Bucholtz and Hall, who define the term as follows: 'the broad interdisciplinary field concerned with the intersection of language, culture and society' (2005: 585).

Part I

Language in All-Female Groups

1
Women's Stories: The Role of Narrative in Friendly Talk [1996]

In this chapter, I shall look in some detail at eight stories[1] told in conversation by women friends to each other. My aim is to show what women's stories are like in terms of structure and content and to tease out the role of narrative in friendly conversation. In a book on Women's Folklore, the authors commented that researchers have concentrated on male public performance and have ignored 'folklore that is more collaborative and enacted in the privacy of the domestic sphere or as part of ordinary conversation' (Jordan and Kalcik 1985: ix). Ordinary conversation is what I am interested in – the spontaneous conversation of people who know each other well – and in this chapter I shall focus on the stories women friends tell each other 'in the privacy of the domestic sphere', as part of their everyday talk.

Story-telling plays a central role in friendly conversation between women, as it does for most people, whatever their background. The writer Ursula Le Guin (1992: 39) argues that 'Narrative is a central function of language'. She also claims that narrative is 'an immensely flexible technology, or life-strategy, which if used with skill and resourcefulness presents each of us with that most fascinating of all serials, The Story of My Life' (1992: 42). Her account rings very true for me. My oldest friend and I always begin our weekends together (we live 60 miles apart and meet once every two or three months) by asking 'Who's going to tell their story first?' By 'story' we mean an autobiographical account of everything that has happened to us in the weeks or months since we last saw each other. The fact that we have spoken on the phone in between is ignored. What counts is the face-to-face, blow-by-blow account. In other words, we tell each other the latest episode of the Story of My Life. The reason this friend is precious to me is that she actually wants to hear my story, just as I genuinely want to hear hers. Through the exchange of stories, we share in the construction and reconstruction of our personal identities, our 'selves'. Doing this is part of what being friends entails.

In terms of their structure, stories differ significantly from the surrounding conversation in which they are embedded. When someone starts to tell a story, we listen to them in a way that is quite different from normal. Think of the quiet that descends on an infant school classroom when the teacher says 'Once upon a time...'. William Labov, who studied the language practices of Black adolescent males in New York City, was struck by the power of narrative to compel attention: 'they [narratives] will command the total attention of an audience in a remarkable way, creating a deep and attentive silence that is never found in academic or political discussion' (Labov 1972a: 396). A keyword here is 'audience'. In friendly conversation, the idea of participants functioning as an audience while someone speaks is nonsensical most of the time. In the conversations I've recorded, what is most noticeable is the noisy all-in-together quality of the talk. Story-telling is the exception. When someone starts to tell a story, the other conversational participants withdraw temporarily from active participation and give the story-teller privileged access to the floor.

A typical story

The stories women friends tell each other are about personal experience, their own or that of someone close to them. The following is a typical story told by a woman to her friend about buying a dress. Pat (all names have been changed) tells this story at a point in the conversation where she and Karen have started talking about their new dresses. (See pp. xiii–xv for transcription conventions.)

Sundresses

Well I saw those [dresses] um on Wednesday when I was up there,
and then my mother phoned me up and said,
"Oh I want to get a couple of these lengths which I've seen in Watford",
'cos she's going to America in a couple of weeks' time,
[...]
and she said "I want a couple of sundresses
and can you just run them up for me".
So I said, "Yeah, I saw them myself",
and I said, "Before you go and get them in John Lewis
go in St Albans market,

'cos I've seen dress lengths ready cut,
the lot . for four ninety nine".
And she said, "Oh I haven't got time to go in St Albans.
I've seen the ones I want anyway in John Lewis's
and I don't think there were much difference in price".
So I- and she was talking to me about them
and saying how nice they were,
and I said, "Yeah well I nearly bought myself one".
And then my Dad phoned up last night,
and he said, "Go and get yourself one,
we'll give you the money".
[...]
Didn't need asking twice.
But when I went up there
I was glad really,
'cos in- where they had the finished lengths they only had the prints
and I was going to get one of those.
[...]
God I've wanted a plain black sundress for twenty years.
Now I've got one.

At the heart of any story is a series of narrative clauses, that is, clauses containing a verb in the simple past. This story starts with the verbs *saw* and *phoned*, but the key verb is *said*: *she said ... so I said ... and he said*. The narrative core of this story is a dialogue between the narrator and first her mother, then her father. This dialogue is framed by the opening event, the narrator seeing the dress lengths in the market, and by the final triumphant *Now I've got one*. Notice that the narrator omits the key clause *and then I bought a sundress* – we are left to infer from the information given in lines 22–25 that this is what she did. The structure of this story is typical of oral narrative: clauses are organised in a temporal sequence which corresponds to the actual sequence of events. In other words, the basic structure is *A and then B and then C* ... . At the beginning of the story, the action is suspended from time to time to provide background information. Pat tells Karen when the story began – *on Wednesday* – and where – *up there* (line 1). She introduces the key players – herself and her mother – and explains why her mother wanted to buy the dress lengths – *'cos she's going to America* (line 4). Labov (1972b) calls this part of a story **orientation**, by which he means those parts of the narrative which answer the questions who? where? when? Comments which **evaluate** the events described, such as *didn't need asking twice* (line 21), tell the audience how the narrator intends the events to be interpreted. (Here, Pat lets Karen know that she was very happy with her father's offer.) The last two lines operate as a sort of **coda:** they bring the story to the end and re-orient us in the present.[2]

The language of oral narrative is much simpler than the conversation in which it is embedded. Most lines consist of one simple clause (e.g. *and then my Dad phoned up last night*) or of a simple clause with a chunk of direct speech as its direct object (e.g. *and he said, "Go and get yourself one"*). Clauses are linked by the simple coordinators *and* and *so,* with an occasional subordinating conjunction such as *when* or *because* introducing a subordinate clause. Women's stories are full of detail – the names of people and places are given (e.g. *Watford, St Albans, John Lewis* [a department store]). Women also fill their stories with people's voices: in Pat's story we hear the voices of Pat herself, her mother and her father. What each of them said is presented as direct speech. It does not matter whether these people actually said what they are represented as saying; the narrator animates her characters as part of the creative act of telling a story. There is an immediacy in direct speech which would be missing if the speaker's words were merely reported. Compare *and he said "Go and get yourself one, we'll give you the money"* with a possible reported version, *and he told me to go and get myself one, and said that he and Mum would pay for it.* Barbara Johnstone, in her analysis of the stories told by men and women in a medium-sized town in Indiana, USA, argues that this way of presenting what happened is typical of women's but not of men's stories: 'women's stories typically create a storyworld populated with specific named people engaged in interaction, while the storyworld created in men's stories is more often silent, and the characters are more often nameless' (Johnstone 1990: 68). As the other stories in this chapter will demonstrate, the representation of talk is a key component of women's stories. This is further evidence of the high value placed on talk by women.

The routines and rituals of everyday life: the topics of women's stories

What is the story 'Sundresses' about? It's really two stories in one: first, the narrator tells a story of agreeing to make her mother a couple of sundresses to take to America; secondly, she tells the story of buying one for herself after her father offers her the money for it. It's a story which affirms the importance of family ties: mothers turn to their daughters for assistance; parents treat a daughter to a dress. It is also a story which asserts the importance of everyday life – of going to the market, of making clothes, of talking to parents on the phone. This aspect of the story – its everyday quality – deserves attention. As I said at the beginning of the chapter, it is one of the strengths of ethnography that it validates everyday experience. This story and most of the others which will appear in this chapter are concerned with 'the routines, rhythms and rituals of everyday life' (Bell 1993: 298). As Margaret Yocom (1985) argues, the home is the context for women's story-telling. Yocom compares the competitive public arena where men's story-telling occurs with the private sphere 'with its intimacy and bonding' (Yocom 1985: 52), which is the setting for women's story-telling.

By contrast, the oral narratives of male speakers described in classic accounts by sociolinguists and folklorists are about danger and violence, conflict and conquest (see Abrahams 1983; Bauman 1986; Labov 1972b; Johnstone 1990, 1993). Bauman (1986: 36) describes the first-person narratives about practical jokes which he collected in Texas, USA, as 'a ludic exercise in dominance, control and display'. William Labov (1972b: 354) claims that his famous 'Danger of Death' question is a surefire way of getting at oral narrative, if used sensitively. He (or one of his co-workers) would ask 'Were you ever in a situation where you were in serious danger of being killed, where you said to yourself "This is it"?'[3] By contrast, the personal narratives told by women in conversation with their friends are not about dangerous or death-defying events. Perhaps this is another reason that women's talk has been undervalued: women's stories may be seen by folklorists working in the male tradition as boring, as unexciting. But it is self-evident that women friends would not continue to tell these stories to each other, year in, year out, if they found them uninteresting. We find such stories more than interesting – they fascinate us. Val told me in her interview that one of the things she values about her friend Cathy is her ability as a story-teller:

> She is the most vivid talker I've ever met ... it's better than- than observing it, getting it through her eyes. It's her skill with the language, she's really really really entertaining, and with this massive network of friends she's got who are always up to nefarious things ... I get every little detail, and it's like having a- a telescope into a completely alien world ... she can relay to me all this that's come up, and who did what and which brother ran off with which aunt, and I'm THERE, I can SEE it.

Women's personal narratives differ from men's both in the everyday nature of their settings and subject matter and in the absence of heroism. Women frequently tell stories which focus on things going wrong, rather than on achievement. But this isn't true of all their stories, as 'Sundresses' illustrates. Pat's story is, in its own way, a story of triumph – after 20 years she finally owns a black sundress. Her story invites her friend to share her triumph. The sharing of successes and failures, however minor by worldly (or masculine) standards, is of central importance in women's friendships. But triumph or achievement in women's stories tends to be restricted to the domestic environment: friends will be asked to share in celebrating achievements such as buying a dress, varnishing the kitchen table, buying a bargain of a Christmas tree, or to share in the achievements of those close to them – a daughter winning in an inter-school quiz, a father making a rabbit hutch (all examples from stories in the conversations). The centrality of such events in women's lives is reflected in their accounts of why their friends are precious to them.

Triumph

By contrast with the story about sundresses, the following story tells of one of those rare occasions when a triumph occurs in the world outside. But it is the narrator's mother who is presented as triumphing, not the narrator herself. (So, unlike the other stories quoted in this chapter, this story is a third-person narrative, with *she* as the main protagonist, rather than *I*.)

My mother and the jogger

She took- she's got these two Dobermans who are really unruly but very sweet.
She took them for a walk on the beach one day,
and this was at the height of the Rottweiler scare,
and this jogger's running along the beach at Liverpool,
and Rosy, her dog that she can't control,
decided to run along after the jogger
and bit him on the bottom.
And this man was going absolutely mad,
and my mother started off by being nice to him
and saying, "I'm terribly sorry, she's only a pup and she was just being playful" and so on,
and he got worse,

so the more she tried to placate him,
the more he decided he was gonna go to the police station and create a scene about it.
So she said, "Let me have a look",
and she strode over and pulled his- <LAUGHS> pulled his tracksuit bottoms down,
and said, "Don't be so bloody stupid, man, there's nothing wrong with you,
you're perfectly all right."
At which point he was so embarrassed he just jogged away. <LAUGHTER>

This is a story of achievement: it celebrates a woman who demonstrates agency, a woman who takes control. Moreover, this woman inverts the normal order of things, since at the end of the incident it is the man who is embarrassed and the woman who is triumphant. This is one of the reasons the story is so funny: it overturns normal expectations. But the mother, who appears in other stories, is presented as an eccentric – a woman capable of doing the outrageous: she is not necessarily a role model. The laughter with which this story is greeted arises not just from amusement and admiration, but also from shock.

Disaster

More typically, women's stories revolve around times when things went wrong. The following is an extract from a long story about being struck down with acute cystitis on a flight to Rome. The narrator, Anna, realised on the morning of the flight that she wasn't feeling well and suspected it was cystitis. She arranged for her colleague Shirley to get her something from the chemist's, which she took at the airport, and she also drank lots of water, because she remembered that this was important if you had cystitis.

Cystitis

So while we were waiting at the airport- our plane was delayed- I actually drank three litres of water.
We were there for like an hour and a quarter
and I just kept drinking and drinking and drinking.
We got on the plane and of course I couldn't stop going to the loo.

Then it got worse and worse and worse.
I spent the whole plane journey to Ro- to Rome in the toilet.
Three quarters of the way through the plane journey I- I literally couldn't leave I was in such pain.
Shirley came banging on the door.
"Are you all right? Are you all right?"
She was trying to get the air hostess to come and see to me
and Alitalia I will never fly again
they were just dreadful.
And she kept going up to these air hostesses saying, "My friend's in the toilet and she's ill.
Will you do something",
and they wouldn't do anything.
And finally we were coming in to land,
and by this time I was passing blood,
and I was really terrified out of my mind,
'cos I'm not a sickly person and I never get ill,
and if something like that happens it just freaks me out.
I was- I didn't know what to do.
So I had to go and sit down because we were about to land,
but it was like every two minutes I thought, "I've got to go to the- the toilet, I've got to",
so I was hysterical practically.
And finally we sat down coming in to land,
and there's a girl sitting on the other side of the gangway to me,
quite a pretty Italian girl,
and this air steward is bending down talking to her,
a male air steward chatting her up basically,
and he looks across at me.
He says, "What's the matter with you? Are you not very well?",
and I thought, "Finally getting through here",
and I said, "Yes I'm not".
And he said- and he said, "What's wrong?",
and he can hardly speak a word of English,
so I've got to try and explain,
and all the passengers are listening.
So I told the girl,
and she translated for him,
and he said to me, "Would you like to see a doctor when we land?
I can arrange for that if you want".
So I said, "Well OK,

but I don't want to be taken away in an ambulance or anything like that,
but yes, if you can arrange and radio ahead and and arrange for me to see a doctor, that'd be great".
He said, "Yes no problem".
He said, "There won't be an ambulance or anything".
Three minutes later we land,
and there are men running down the gangway towards me.
They- they bodily lift me out of my seat,
and there's the blue flashing light outside the plane.
I couldn't believe it.

This story is in the great tradition of funny stories women tell each other in which appalling things happen to them – the humour lies precisely in presenting oneself as at the mercy of incomprehensible forces. In Anna's case, the incomprehensible forces are, first, her own body (a potent source of humour for women) and, secondly, the unhelpful airline staff. Everything that happens in the story happens *to* her, and is outside her control. First, her illness forces her to spend most of the flight in the aeroplane toilet. This kind of excruciatingly humiliating and embarrassing detail is very much part of women's disaster narratives. Secondly, the air steward's poor English and general tactlessness mean that Anna is put in a position where she has to describe her symptoms knowing all the surrounding passengers can hear her. (This aspect of the story gains its humour from our culturally given understanding that you don't share the details of your malfunctioning urinary tract with strangers.) Finally, despite her having been given assurances to the contrary, she is whisked off in an ambulance, thus losing both her luggage and her companion. By the time Anna reached line 47 in the extract above, her two friends were helpless with laughter. Anna's friends' laughter is not callous: it arises from a heartfelt recognition of the world Anna describes, where women feel they are at the mercy of alien forces. Such stories underline the message that heroism is rarely an option for women: acting alone usually ends in disaster. (Anna's enforced separation from Shirley is portrayed as a significant factor in the continuing nightmare in the next part of the story.)

Frightening experiences

Research which looks at gender differences in personal narrative has found that women's stories are more often about experiences that are embarrassing or frightening than about personal skill or success (see Johnstone 1990: 66). This is precisely what I have found in the stories told by women in the course of conversation with friends. The cystitis story involves both embarrassment and fear, and so is particularly powerful. The following is a perhaps more typical story about a frightening experience, where a woman describes her walk home from the pub (the Talbot) at night. The group of friends have been talking about the (recent at the time) Yorkshire Ripper murder case,[4] and about women's fear of being alone, especially at night.

Walking home alone

I went to th- for a drink the other night on my own,
and met Janet and Paul.
And . when I was coming out through the Talbot to that back way,
a bloke in the car park sh- shouted across to me,
and he said, "Have you got a car?",
and I said, "er what?",
and he said- he said, "Have you got- Can you give me a lift up there?",
and I said, "I haven't got a car".
And I nipped up that back lane up the- the bo- up Talbot Road,
and all the way up I thought he was going to come,
'cos he went the other way up- up Rose Mount,
and I thought he was going to cut along . whatever that road's called.
And . my heart was in my mouth all the way up Poplar Road.
And what I did was I walked right next to the houses.
Normally I walk on the other side of the road,
but I thought, "If e- anyone comes near I'm just leap in this house
and batter on one of these doors,
'Let me in!'". <LAUGHTER>
But at the very top of the road there was a little kind of gap with-
where you have to cross over,
and I thought I'd had it. <LAUGHTER>

What is interesting about this story is that nothing happens – Meg, the narrator, gets home safely. But the point of the story (and it comes after another story told by her friend Sally on the same theme) is that the world outside is dangerous, especially at night, and that being alone is frightening. Even though nothing happens, you still have to negotiate all kinds of imagined dangers as you walk home. Notice again how direct speech is used to bring this story to life. The exchange in the car park introduces us to the unknown man, who makes a request that is experienced as threatening by the narrator. Her walk home is described both with detailed reference to place names (*Talbot Road, Rose Mount, Poplar Road*) and with her dramatisation of her thoughts and the words she imagines she would shout if anyone came near her: *"Let me in!"* It's noticeable that her friends laugh at the two points where she expresses her inner thoughts. Laughter here is a sign not just of amusement but also of recognition. Through their laughter, Meg's friends demonstrate a shared worldview: they too have experienced the feelings she describes.

Embarrassment

Embarrassment, like fear, is a common theme of women's stories. It is particularly common in the stories girls tell each other. This isn't surprising, given the tensions and dilemmas associated with that difficult rite of passage in British culture known as adolescence. The girls' conversations are full of laughter: much of this arises from their having fun, but some of it arises in the context of embarrassing stories which they tell each other. The laughter functions as a way of releasing tension. Becky, in the first of these stories, glosses the episode she describes as 'funny'. It is funny in that, both at the time it happened and when it is recounted as a story, the event reduces all the girls involved to hysterical laughter. But it is clearly also a story about embarrassment.

This first story is about an incident involving Becky, Claire and the school librarian which took place in school on a day when Hannah wasn't there (Claire's contributions are in italics):

Knicker stains

It was so funny when you weren't there one day.
Well we were in the library, right?
and we were in that corner where all the erm the picture books are.
Claire's putting on some lipstick,
I was putting on some lipstick,
and and and they said "oh what are you doing in that corner?",
and she said we were smoking ((xx)),
no I said we were checking for people who were smoking,
and he said- and he said "are you sure you weren't having a quick smoke yourself?",
and I said, "yes I must admit it",
and I meant to say, "Look at my nicotine stains",
and I held up my fingers like that,

and I said, "Look at my knicker stains".
((xx)) we were rolling about the tables.
It was so funny.

Notice how the evaluative clause *it was so funny* frames this story, appearing both as a prelude to the story and as the final line. The heart of the story consists of the narrative clauses in lines 6, 7, 9, 10, 12 and 13. Each of these contains a simple past tense verb (*said, held up*), and they are temporally ordered (we understand *and* to mean *and then* ...). The telling of this story is followed by chaotic talk and laughter, with Jessica saying that she had told the story to her mother, and her mother too had been reduced to hysterics, but had added a comment: 'she said that we weren't very good librarian monitors or whatever we were meant to be'. This functions as a rather delayed coda, and signals the end of the topic.

The story is about a funny (or embarrassing) slip of the tongue, and depends for its impact on Becky telling us what she *didn't* say: *Look at my nicotine stains*. The punch line, the wording she actually used, *Look at my knicker stains*, only has such an impact because we know what she was trying to say. Overtly the friends treat this as yet another ridiculous story which they can laugh over – it fits the tradition I mentioned earlier of a female protagonist finding herself in an impossible or humiliating or embarrassing position. But I don't think it's reading too much into this brief story to argue that it is also revealing about what is going on under the laughing surface of their talk. The girls are at a watershed in their lives, moving willingly or unwillingly from girlhood to womanhood. When they were younger, words like *knickers* were part of everyday playground currency, like *bum*, superficial coinage, always good for a laugh. Now, as social pressures force them to take notice of their bodies, as their bodies become the object of the adult male gaze, words like *knickers* are becoming fraught with sexual overtones and are losing their innocence. *Knicker stains* is an extraordinary slip of the tongue in the way it reveals the girls' anxiety about their changing bodies, and their fears of loss of control in all aspects of their lives. The impact of the slip of the tongue is also heightened by its co-occurrence with the direct command *look at*. It is inappropriate for less powerful speakers, like Becky, to issue commands to more powerful speakers, like the male librarian here. Becky's intended command *look at my nicotine stains* is only acceptable because it reinforces her powerless position, both as a pupil and as someone who has broken a school rule: by holding up her nicotine-stained fingers, she intended to incriminate herself. These words were meant to be part of a confession – she meant to admit her guilt and thus to acknowledge the librarian's power to punish her as he saw fit. But by transposing the object of this command from *nicotine stains* to *knicker stains*, Becky finds herself in the totally unacceptable position of giving a direct command to a high-status male, a command which tells him to do something with strong sexual overtones. It is not surprising that the girls seek refuge in laughter. It is hard to imagine any other escape route from this highly charged situation.

The next story, told by Claire two years later, when the girls are 15, narrates an experience which is explicitly described as 'embarrassing', when Claire visited a friend's house and saw her friend's brother naked.

I just saw everything
did I tell you about-
remember I t- I was- I went into the Stefanides' house,
and you know they've got a mirror up as you go into that- in the room up the stairs,
and I went in,
and I looked in the mirror,
and Mem was standing there naked,
[...]
and and Gina was cutting his toenails, <SCREAMING>
and I walked in,
and he was- and he had his leg up on the- on the sofa,
and I just saw everything. <LAUGHS>
[...]
I ran out.
I was- well I was really embarrassed.

Claire in fact produces the end of this story (lines 11 and 12) after some taunting from the others, in particular from Hannah, who says, *you loved it*. So, we see here girls of 15 demonstrating an awareness of a range of possible reactions, from *I loved it* to *I was really embarrassed*, and colluding with each other in arriving at the more appropriate, socially sanctioned one. The subject of this anecdote – a female seeing a naked male – raises a lot of questions. Representations of the naked female body are commonplace in our culture. Women's bodies are the subject of drawings and paintings, past and present; they also appear routinely in advertisements for products as disparate as motor cars and shampoo. This is without mentioning the many pornographic and semi-pornographic publications which explicitly trade in representations of naked women. Claire's story reminds us that the reverse situation – where the naked male body is exposed to the female gaze – has a very different meaning. It is men who have the power of the gaze, while it is women's role to be the object of the gaze. There is a profound asymmetry here, which helps to explain why a woman or girl seeing a naked man (or boy) is so transgressive: Claire feels she needs to deny the power of the gaze – *I ran out ... I was really embarrassed.* The detail of her story, however, particularly the line *I just saw everything,* suggests that this was only one of her responses, and that adolescent curiosity about the male body was another powerful force at work.

It is surely significant that in a relatively small corpus like this one, I have found a parallel story told by an adult woman to her friend. Here the accompanying emotions are more complex, though embarrassment is one of them. Karen tells this story to Pat (whose words are in italics).

Getting undressed

It was a couple of weeks ago,
I forget now which day it was,
but I was sitting in my living room
and without meaning to I was looking out into the garden
and I was looking straight into Lever's house,
that's the one up in Bentley Close on the corner,
and I saw him get undressed in his living room.
There's no reason why you shouldn't get undressed in your living room
  if you want to, *(yeah)*
and I thought "My God" *(yeah)*
"if I can see him"
he can see you,
and I don't always just get undressed in the living room. <LAUGH>

Again we have a narrative in which the central 'happening' is that a female sees an unclothed male. Notice how Karen, like Claire, disclaims any agency: she says she was looking into the garden *without meaning to.* In other words, she denies having the power of the gaze. What's more complex here is that Karen reveals that her chief anxiety arises not from her (unintentional) infringement of Lever's right to privacy, but from her anxiety about her *own* privacy. She infers that if she can see him, he can see her. This switches the focus directly onto women as the object of the male gaze. Karen wants to avoid this position. Karen's story is embedded in conversation about some trees she has just planted in her garden. When she tells Pat that she's planted 19 trees, Pat asks jokingly 'What are you doing? growing your own forest?' Karen's story functions as an explanation: the trees are to act as a screen, to prevent her from being overlooked. While Karen takes the appropriately modest position of desiring privacy, her comment in line 12 *and I don't always just get undressed in the living room* hints at more sophisticated (sexual?) activities and recasts her desire for privacy in a more adult, less fearful frame.

Collaboration in story-telling

I stated near the beginning of this chapter that telling a story gives a speaker special rights to the floor. This is true, but women friends prefer a way of talking which emphasises the collaborative and which is antipathetic to monologue. So, although story-tellers are granted a more privileged floor, this often lasts only for a brief period at the beginning of a story. Christine Cheepen calls this more collaborative form of story-telling 'dialogic': 'This dialogic form of story telling means that the distinction between "storyteller" and "audience" becomes blurred, because what is happening in such a situation is that the speakers are collaborating in a story-telling' (Cheepen 1988: 54). All the stories quoted in this chapter have been edited, and the editing has in large part consisted of suppressing the other voices, to make the stories more 'story-like'. I don't think this has falsified my analysis, but I now want to acknowledge the collaborative nature of women friends' talk, and from now on stories will include the other voices.

To show how women friends collaborate in story-telling, here's a longer and fuller version of the last story, 'Getting undressed' (Pat's words are again in italics).

Getting undressed

'cos you know how we said we were overlooked
th- that day we sat in there, *(yeah)*
I thought "Damn this",
and then the other day I was sel-
'cos that was the only thing wrong with it wasn't it?
yeah well I- it was a couple of weeks ago,
I forget now which day it was,
but I was sitting in my living room
and without meaning to I was looking out into the garden
and I was looking straight into Lever's house,
that's the one up in Bentley Close on the corner,
and I saw him get undressed in his living room.

There's no reason why you shouldn't get undressed in your living room if you want to, *(yeah)*
and I thought "My God" *(yeah)*
"if I can see him"
he can see you,
and I don't always just get undressed in the living room. <LAUGH>
You know I mean OK I'm sure he's not *peeping* peeping or anything,
but he- but it just-
you accidentally saw him
that's right
oh I don't blame you
I think it needs screening trees round it.

While Pat allows Karen to tell the narrative core of this story (lines 6–12) without intervention, once the key narrative clause has been reached – *and I saw him get undressed in his living room* – she joins in. From line 13 onwards the story is jointly constructed by the two friends, to the extent that Pat provides the verb *peeping* to complete Karen's *I'm sure he's not* ..., and it is Pat who recapitulates the main point: *you accidentally saw him,* and who provides a coda: *oh I don't blame you I think it needs screening trees round it.* This coda is very interesting: Pat now realises that Karen's reason for planting the trees is serious. Her earlier joking remark about growing a forest is no longer appropriate – she wants to emphasise that she sympathises with what Karen is doing, and that she sees her action as a sensible step to protect her privacy. The trees are no longer referred to as *a forest* but as *screening trees.*

In the stories they tell, women present an everyday world where their mundane activities are celebrated and where their problems and anxieties can be shared. They do not present themselves as heroes, and they are more often done to than doing. Barbara Johnstone argues that men's and women's stories depict strikingly different storyworlds: 'Women's stories tend to be "other oriented", underplaying the protagonists' personal roles and emphasizing social community and mutual dependence, while men's stories are "self-oriented", serving to build up their tellers' own personal images' (Johnstone 1990: 66). It is precisely those stories where women are on their own that are the most bleak: Meg's only hope as she walks home up the dark street ('Walking home alone') is that people living in the houses there will respond to her cries for help; Anna ('Cystitis') presents herself as unable to get the help she needs and as cut off from her friend. Apart from the mother in 'My mother and the jogger', in those stories where women do take action, such as

'Sundresses' and 'Getting undressed', the action is not foregrounded. Moreover, what happens is presented as *reactive* rather than *pro-active*. In other words, in these stories, the protagonist takes action in response to some other action. Pat buys herself a sundress after her father tells her to; Karen plants trees in her garden after realising she could be overlooked. Even in 'My mother and the jogger', the mother's action is reactive: she only pulls the jogger's tracksuit bottoms down to prove that he is unhurt after he refuses to accept her apologies for her dog.

Sharing pleasant experiences

One of the primary aims of women's story-telling is to share experience, and women use stories to share pleasant experiences with each other, as well as experiences that are more painful. I want to end this chapter with a story told by Mary which is a classic example of the way women relish the detail of everyday life, and which shows how women friends construct stories together. The basic story is very simple and can be summarised in one sentence: 'I got stopped by a train in the docks yesterday' (the road through the docklands is criss-crossed by train-lines). The narrative core of the story consists of five lines:

> I was stopped by a train.
> have you ever been stopped by a train in the docks?
> I got stopped by a train in the docks yesterday.
> I've never been stopped by a train before.
> It was lovely.

The first four lines are variations on the opening statement *I was stopped by a train*. This is a kind of summary or **abstract** (Labov 1972: 363–364) of the story and tells the listeners what is to come. The second line turns the statement into a question, a question which adds the important information that the event narrated took place *in the docks*. This question leads into her repeated statement *I got stopped by a train in the docks yesterday*, in which she orients the story in time by adding the adverb *yesterday*. Her incredulous tone is explained in the fourth line, where she tells her friends that this had never happened to her before. Every one of these four lines uses the same verb: *(was/got) stopped* followed by the same phrase: *by a train*. Three of the four lines have *I* as their (grammatical) subject. This kind of repetition occurs frequently in women's story-telling, as in their talk generally (see Coates 1996b). The fifth line breaks the pattern. This line – *It was lovely* – gives the narrator's viewpoint and thus gives meaning to the previous four lines. The audience now knows how to evaluate the story.

The story emerges at a point in conversation when Sally remarks how beautiful the docks look when it's sunny. At this point Mary asks whether any of her friends has ever been stopped by a train in the docks and Sally says *yes* (as Mary continues her story). As Mary elaborates on her basic story, Sally joins in, and the two friends construct the rest of the story together, with others present making minor contributions and minimal responses (*mhm* or *yeah*). The full extract is given below (Sally's words are in bold italics; minor contributions by others are in italics).

Grain trains in the docks

1 I was- I was- I was stopped by a train
((***xxxxxxxxxxxxxxxxxx***))

2 have you ever been stopped by a train in the docks?

3 [I got stopped by a train in the docks yesterday.
[***yes yes frequently***

4 [I've never been stopped [by a train before.
[***yes*** [***yeah***

5 [it was lovely
[***yeah***

6 'cos it was- it was go[ing across Duke- Duke Street [bridge
[*oh it's super* [*yes*

7 the [middle one
[***that's right yeah***

8 [that's right
and the guy just gets off [***((xx))***

9 [and walks
[***and ((sort of stops))***

10 and there's this bloke walking in front of the train=
yeah ***=that's-***

11 and you can hear this [clanging noise
[***yeah***

12 ['cos one of the chains is clanging on-
[***yeah***

13 and it sounds very romantic
yeah ***yes***

14 like it's like the far- the West

15 you know this clanking noise

16 and all it is- is- .hh is this bit of metal that's clanking along the ground

17 but I [didn't realise
[***oh it's LOVEL-***

18 but I've seen all these train tracks
((xxx))

19 [it's the grain trains [yes
it's the grain trains [***I think*** [***to go to the-***

20 [it was the bulk carriers
[*yes* *yes* *yes*

Mary's opening narrative tells of a single experience and uses the past tense. Sally, who has seen trains in the docks 'frequently', continues the story with the line *and the guy just gets off*, which Mary adds to: *and walks*. The story ceases to be about one single event in the past, and moves into a timeless present, using verbs like *gets off* and *walks* and *sounds*. In line 19 the two narrators sum up the experience they are describing: *it's the grain trains*, while in the last line Mary shifts her audience back into the specific past of her experience yesterday: *it was the bulk carriers*. This last line marks the end of the story both because it re-orients the story in the past, switching from *is* to *was*, to match the opening lines, and because at the same time it paraphrases the previous line, thus tying the (more general) middle section to the rest of the narrative.

This story, like the previous one, illustrates the way women friends construct stories together. The shared construction of talk is one of the chief characteristics of women's conversations, and this preference for collaboration is manifest in all aspects of women's friendly talk. Narrative is archetypally thought of as monologue, but as I've demonstrated with these two stories, women friends share in the telling of stories, transforming narrative from a solo to a polyphonic creative act.

Conclusion

I've looked at eight stories in this chapter, a small fraction of the stories told in the conversations in my corpus. For women friends, story-telling serves several functions. At the level of conversational organisation, stories are often used to introduce new topics. But more importantly, story-telling functions to bind these women friends together, through creating a shared world. 'In an important sense, a community of speakers is a group of people who share previous stories ... and who jointly tell new stories' (Johnstone 1990: 5). Women friends constitute such a community, and through our story-telling we create and re-create our identities and experiment with possible selves, in a context of mutuality and trust. Conversational narrative is our chief means of constructing the fictions that are our lives and of getting others to collude in them. But story-telling also allows us to 'order or re-order the givens of experience', and while stories undoubtedly reinforce the dominant culture, they also provide 'a relatively safe or innocuous place in which the reigning assumptions of a given culture can be criticized' (Miller 1990: 70). As we have seen in this chapter, the stories that women friends tell each other reinforce our sense of ourselves as objects, as powerless, as reactors rather than actors. But they also hint at alternative ways of being, at women as doers, observers as well as observed, who see ourselves as powerfully allied through our shared knowledge and our shared experiences.

Notes

1. I have edited some of these stories very slightly, to make them easier to read and to keep them to a manageable size.
2. The bold terms here come from Labov (1972b).
3. It's interesting to note that Peter Trudgill had to alter this part of his sociolinguistic interview when he carried out fieldwork in Norwich, England, because the 'Danger of Death' question was answered with 'No!' (Trudgill 1974). He substituted a question which asked interviewees whether they'd ever been in an *amusing* situation. So, the topics of stories relate to local culture as well as to social categories such as gender.
4. The Yorkshire Ripper was the name the British media gave to a serial killer who murdered at least 13 women in Yorkshire in the 1970s and 1980s.

2

'So I Mean I Probably ...': Hedges and Hedging in Women's Talk [2003]

In this chapter,[1] I explore the use of the linguistic devices known as 'hedges' by linguists. These are words and phrases like *maybe* and *sort of* and *I mean* which have the effect of damping down the force of what we say. The term is derived from the everyday usage of the word 'hedge', as in 'to hedge your bets', where 'hedge' means roughly 'to avoid taking decisive action'. When we hedge linguistically, we avoid saying something definite and so we keep our options open. Hedges encompass a wide range of linguistic forms, from the modal auxiliaries (*may, might, could*, etc.) and modal adverbs such as *perhaps, possibly* and *probably*, to discourse markers such as *I mean, I think* and *well*. These words and phrases, as I hope to demonstrate in the chapter, are a valuable resource for speakers.

There is evidence that women use hedges more frequently than men (see, for example, Holmes 1984, 1995; Preisler 1986; Coates 1987, 1989; Cameron, McAlinden and O'Leary 1989). In this chapter, I want to look at the range of functions carried out by hedges in women's friendly talk, and to assess their role in such talk. The chapter is based on a corpus of spontaneous conversation between women friends collected in the last two decades of the twentieth century. These women were recorded in pairs or in groups; their ages ranged from 12 years old to mid-forties.

To clarify what I mean by a hedge, let's look at an example where many of them appear (transcription conventions are given on pp. xiii–xv). This example comes from a conversation involving four women friends in their late thirties. This excerpt is a rare example of a failed story, 'failed' in the sense that it is greeted with discomfort and disbelief by those listening, and in the sense that the narrator, Meg, eventually falls silent and doesn't get to finish the story. She is telling her friends about meeting an old friend she hasn't seen for a while. After explaining who

Jean is, she starts to describe her reaction to Jean's appearance. (The example is slightly edited and hedges are underlined.)

(1) **Meeting an old friend**

MEG: anyway ((xx)) I think Jean's got a a a a a body hair problem/ <LAUGHTER>
BEA well I have quite a lot of body hair/
MEG: no-
BEA: how much has she got?
MEG: well-
BEA: you mean like it was coming out- . like it was coming out-
MEG: yeah/ . no I saw it on her=
BEA: oh/
MEG: =chest honestly/ and um o- on- I- I do look at this from a- with an objective clinical eye/ er but I did see what- what amounted to sort of chest hair/ . black/ she's a very dark- sort of dark skinned and sallow complexion and a lo- I mean I- I mean I hope I'm just reporting this without any edge to it/ . you know so I mean I probably-
BEA: you mean you really feel that she's turning into a gorilla? <LAUGHTER>

Meg's account of her friend up to the point where this extract begins is uncontroversial for the most part. It comes to a climax with the statement *I think Jean's got a a a a a body hair problem*. Body hair on women is a controversial topic in our culture. Meg's use of the hedge *I think*, combined with her stammering, suggests that she is anxious about how her remark will be received by her friends. As it turns out, she is right to be anxious: Bea immediately challenges her: *well I have quite a lot of body hair* and asks *how much has she got?* Meg starts to justify her statement, but becomes more and more inarticulate as she senses that her story is not going down well with her audience. The more she becomes embarrassed, the more frequently she uses hedges. By line 14 she is reduced to almost continuous hedging: *you know so I mean I probably-* and she then stops talking altogether. The situation is saved by Bea, whose outrageous comment *you mean you really feel that she's turning into a gorilla?* is greeted by laughter, laughter which releases the tension.

It is unusual to find as many hedges one after the other as we find in Meg's last, incomplete utterance, but this is a rare example of a woman realising that what she is saying is not acceptable to her friends. Most of the time in conversation with friends, what we say *is* accepted. But we still need to use hedges. The rest of the chapter will illustrate the various different ways hedges are used in talk between friends, and will explore the reasons for women's use of these forms.

The multiple functions of hedges

Hedges have many functions. This means not only that they can have different functions in different contexts, but also that, in any one instance, a hedge can be doing several things simultaneously. In this section I shall look at four of these functions: the expression of doubt and of confidence; sensitivity to others' feelings; searching for the right word; and avoidance of expert status.

The expression of doubt and confidence

The basic function of hedges is to signal that the speaker is not committed to what s/he is saying. In other words, when we hedge an utterance, we are saying that we lack confidence in the truth of the proposition expressed in that utterance. This is as true for hedges such as *really* or *I'm sure* as for forms such as *maybe* or *I think*. When Meg says *I think she's got a body hair problem*, she signals by the use of the hedge *I think* that she is not totally confident about the truth of the proposition *she's got a body hair problem*.

Examples (2), (3) and (4) illustrate this basic function. In example (2), Hannah and her friends are talking about Australian soap operas on television, and start to discuss Australian accents. Claire mentions a girl at their school, Julie, who comes from Australia but doesn't sound Australian.

(2)

CLAIRE: but you know Julie right/ she's Australian/ she- [...] she hasn't got an Australian accent/ [...]
BECKY: maybe she had elocution lessons/
CLAIRE: I doubt it/

Becky's utterance *maybe she had elocution lessons* is an attempt to explain Julie's accent, but the inclusion of the hedge *maybe* in this utterance signals her lack of commitment to the proposition *she had elocution lessons*. In effect, she says 'Here's a possible explanation, but I'm rather doubtful about it.' Her doubt is mirrored by Claire, who responds *I doubt it*.

Besides forms like *I think* and *maybe*, the auxiliary verbs *may* and *might* are important hedges which we regularly use to hint at doubt. In the following example, Helen expresses her doubt about the number of people likely to attend an adult education course she is running.

(3) [*talking about course for school governors*]
HELEN: but what it means about next week is we may not have enough for two groups 'cos I had two apologies in advance/ [...] and you know some other people may have commitments/ so I don't think we're going to run two groups/

She uses the auxiliary *may* twice in this extract; both times it signals her lack of commitment to the proposition expressed in the utterance. Her final statement, *so I don't think we're going to run two groups*, reiterates her doubt about there being two groups. Notice the way different hedges – *may, you know, I don't think* – combine in this chunk of talk to communicate the speaker's uncertainty.

The third example is taken from a point in conversation between Sue, Liz and Anna where Anna has just finished telling a story about her eccentric mother, who begged a lift on a milk float after being stranded at the station in the early morning on her way to a funeral. The hedge *probably* is used by all three speakers to hedge the proposition 'Anna's mother told the milkman (that she was going to a funeral)'.

(4)
ANNA: I bet the milkman couldn't believe it/
LIZ: [yeah
SUE: [did he know she was going to the funeral?
LIZ: probably told [him=
SUE: [probably/ yeah/
ANNA: =well she probably told them/ you know what she's like/ <CHUCKLES>

In this example, the three friends mirror each other's relative confidence about what Anna's mother did through their choice of the adverb *probably*, which is closer to confidence than to doubt.

The final example shows how hedges such as *I'm sure* and *actually* are also used by speakers to mitigate the force of what is said. In example (5), five friends are discussing whether it would be taboo to miss a parent's funeral. Meg, whose mother is getting old, says that she has been thinking about her mother's funeral.

(5)
MEG: and I imagine that my two far-flung sibs will actually make the journey/
MEG: [I'm just- I'm ((almost))- yes I'm sure they will/ but it'll be because i-
MARY: [what? to your parents? to your mother's?
MEG: it'll become a s- public statement about=
MARY: =the family/

This is an interesting example because the language here reveals the tension in Meg between her confidence that her siblings will attend their mother's funeral (expressed by *actually, will, I'm sure*) and her anxiety that they may find it difficult (expressed by *just* and by incomplete utterances and stammering). This example demonstrates the complexity and subtlety of modal usage in everyday talk.

Sensitivity to others' feelings

One of the strengths of hedges is that they can be used not just to modify the force of the propositional content of an utterance, but also to take account of the feelings of the addressee. When we talk, we communicate not just propositions and attitudes to propositions, but also attitudes to addressees (cf. Halliday 1973).

Example (6) below comes just before the extract given in example (1), where Meg talks about bumping into an old friend she had not seen for some time.

(6)
MEG: she looks very sort of um- kind of matronly really/

The hedges *sort of, kind of, really* in this utterance signal that Meg is not firmly committed to the proposition *she looks matronly*. This is not because Meg herself doubts the truth of the proposition, but because she is unsure how her friends will respond to this unflattering description of another woman. Meg does not want to offend her addressees by assuming their agreement. By using the hedges, she protects them from the full force of the controversial claim.

Of course, she also protects herself: Meg's use of hedges here allows her to wriggle out of the accusation that she has said something mean if she needs to. For example, given the negative connotations of the adjective *matronly*, if Meg is later accused of describing Jean as old or overweight, she can deny it. What she said was *kind of matronly* not *matronly*. This use of hedges to protect the speaker as well as the addressee is one of their major functions.

The idea that we need to protect ourselves and those we are speaking to can be explained in terms of Brown and Levinson's (1987) notion of face and the related concept of face needs.[2] We all have face needs, that is, the need to have our personal space respected (known as *negative face*) and the equally important need to be acknowledged and liked (*positive face*). In English, hedges are extremely useful in terms of satisfying face needs.

To clarify the way hedges protect the face needs of all participants in talk, let's look at an example where Sue complains about her husband's music. Her complaint is framed in terms of her daughter, who is asleep upstairs. The hedges in this extract allow Sue an acceptable way of complaining about her husband, and allow Liz to join in this discussion without committing herself to the dangerous line of unmitigated agreement with Sue. (It is permissible for a wife to criticise a husband, but extremely risky for others to do so.)

(7) [*Sue's husband's music gets louder in background*]
SUE: I mean how can you live with this/
LIZ: well I know its difficult when you've got a man around
[but-
SUE: [oh it drives you insane/ I mean Emma's sleeping next door to this/
LIZ: she'll probably get used to it . real[ly quickly/
SUE: [well I don't know I mean-

Sue protects her positive face (her need to have her friend's affection and respect) by not taking too strong a line: the hedges mean she can retreat from this critical position if necessary. At the same time, by using hedges she is able to voice her irritation at John's thoughtlessness, and to receive support from Liz. Liz is also tentative, since she wants to support Sue but doesn't want to be seen to be taking too critical a position. She uses hedges to protect her own face and Sue's as well. Sue's rhetorical question *how can you live with this?* also functions as a kind of hedge.

In the following example, Karen obviously feels the need to hedge the assertion that she's never been worried about whether her doctor was male or female in case Pat doesn't agree. (In this way, she protects her own face – she could retreat from her statement – and she also protects Pat's.)

(8)
KAREN: well I suppose it is I've never really had any worries like that/
PAT: no/ it wouldn't bother me/ but perhaps-
KAREN: mind you as they're getting younger . I might feel differently/
PAT: yes/

In fact, as we can see, Pat mirrors Karen's assertion with the utterance *it wouldn't bother me*, that is, it wouldn't bother her to have a male doctor. But she then starts an utterance which she doesn't complete: *but perhaps-*, which suggests that she thinks there might be circumstances where people would be bothered. Karen then gives an example of such circumstances – where (male) doctors are getting younger – and Pat agrees with her. Note the use of the modal auxiliary *might* in Karen's utterance, which hedges her statement of her feelings.

Searching for the right word

Hedges are also useful devices for signalling that we are searching for a word, or having trouble finding the right words to say what we mean. This can be reasonably trivial, as in the following example, where Becky tries to describe a sensation she gets in her nose when she is premenstrual.

(9)
BECKY: it feels like your nose is just sort of . expanding/

The hedge *sort of* alerts her friends to the fact she is trying to find the right word; it also signals that the word she eventually uses may not be the perfect choice. Note the pause after *sort of*, which is commonly found when hedges function in this way. The hedge indicates that the speaker is still active even though a pause might follow: other speakers can then give the speaker time to hunt for the mot juste.

While *sort of* and *kind of* are the two hedges most frequently used to stall for time while the speaker searches for a word, other hedges such as *really* and *you know* occur here too. The following is an example with *you know*.

(10) [*talking about a TV programme about apes*]
BEA: he [orang-utan] had you know- he had five very adequate . manip- whatever you would call hands and things/

In this example, the speaker gives up on the search for the right word: after trying with *five very adequate manip-*, she makes do with the periphrasis *whatever you would call hands and things*. As speakers, we prefer to find the right word, but sometimes we lack the relevant vocabulary – or sometimes the language itself does not have a word for the referent we are trying to name.

In the following example, Helen is talking about her younger daughter. She is trying to describe the bad situation that had existed at her daughter's primary school, and contrasts this with how well she's settled down at her new secondary school.

(11)

HELEN: she really loves it/ and she's somebody that was really being . sort of labelled as somebody that wasn't really- was anti-school almost at Riversdale Road [*primary school*]/

Helen searches for a word to describe what was happening to her daughter at Riversdale Road school, and settles on *labelled*. Notice that in this example, the pause precedes the hedge *sort of*, but Helen's struggle for words has already been signalled by the hedge *really*. As she continues to describe this situation, she begins an utterance *somebody that wasn't really-*. Her search for words leads her to the term *anti-school*, which expresses what she is trying to say, but which means she has to rephrase her utterance, changing *wasn't* to *was*. The hedges here also arise from the sensitivity of the topic, and from Helen's need to protect her own face. It is characteristic of hedges that they perform several functions simultaneously: they are extremely versatile linguistic forms.

In the next example, *sort of* is again used multi-functionally, as Gwen hypothesises about what Emily's mother was like as a teenager.

(12) [*four friends talk about what Emily's mother was like as a teenager*]

EMILY: you know what? my Mum thinks I'm much more sensible than SHE was at our age [...]

GWEN: what did she do at your age? [...] was she all- all sort of a bit of a raver?

EMILY: I think she was/

Not only is Gwen searching for an appropriate word to describe the sort of wild teenager she is imagining, she is also being careful to protect herself in case her remark turns out to be unacceptable to Emily. (As it turns out, Emily accepts the term *raver* as a description of her mother as a teenager.) Note how Gwen's utterance is full of signs of struggle: she hesitates on the word *all*, continues with *sort of* then hedges even further by premodifying *raver* with the phrase *a bit of a*.

The search for the right words is often part of women's struggle to think about things in new ways, and to come to new forms of understanding. One of the women I interviewed about women's talk commented explicitly on this aspect of talk: 'I think talking with women I'm- I'm much happier about struggling around how to say things 'cos [...] sometimes we don't have the words so er and also women give you time to struggle with it'. By contrast, there is evidence that men in all-male conversation often do not give each other time to 'struggle with it'. The following quotation comes from a man talking about his experience of a men's group; the quotation suggests that 'having enough time' was a new experience for the speaker: 'One of the most striking things about the first few sessions of the men's group was the sense of "you had enough time". You could have difficulty with your words, you could try a sentence seventeen different ways round, and nobody minded or jumped down your throat or told you how to say it' (Seidler 1991: 53). The search for the right words is an important aspect of the talk women friends do, and hedges play an important part in facilitating such talk.

Avoiding playing the expert

The use of hedges before a key word is sometimes used deliberately by speakers. Rather than meaning that the speaker is searching for the right word, hedging can be a strategy to avoid the appearance of playing the expert. By 'playing the expert', I mean that conversational game where participants take it in turns to hold the floor and to talk about a subject which they are an expert on. This is a game which seems to be played most commonly by male speakers.[3] Women, by contrast, avoid the role of expert in conversation: for women, it is very important to minimise social distance between conversational participants, and hedges appear to be a useful strategy to achieve this goal.

In the example below, Jo is telling Katy about a friend and her boyfriend who have decided to live together. Jo seems to be anxious about this.

(13)

JO:	but yeah it is a bit soon to be saying we're gonna move in |together/
KATY:	|yeah exactly <u>I mean</u> that's the thing ||<u>I mean I'm sure-</u>
JO:	||<u>I mean</u> I'm not saying it's not going to last but- (0.5)
KATY:	yeah very soon/
JO:	yeah/

Katy uses hedges such as *I mean* and *I'm sure* to avoid sounding like an expert on relationships, and she also fails to complete her utterance, as does Jo in the subsequent turn: *I mean I'm not saying it's not going to last but-*. These incomplete utterances also display their doubt about the situation and their unwillingness to take on the role of expert. Through this exchange, they arrive at a consensus, with Katy's words *very soon* echoing Jo's earlier *a bit soon*. Jo signals her acceptance of this conclusion with her *yeah*.

In the next example, the speaker (Meg) is a psychologist who is familiar with the process being described in the discussion on child abuse. Her use of *sort of* makes her appear less fluent, and thus avoids opening up distance between participants.

(14)
MEG: they can sort of um test that out by . showing people sort of video tapes

The final example comes from a conversation I recorded when my friends came round to my house one evening. The topic – a discussion of apes and language – was triggered by a science programme shown on TV the previous night.

(15) [*discussion about whether or not apes can use language*]
JEN: but I still think- well basically what my thinking is/ is that the people like Terrace [*a psycholinguist*] represent the group that on the whole does not want to admit that other species have the language whatever it is ability/ and that's- and I think I'm always opposed to that group/ 'cos I think it's the- the whole dangerous thing of saying 'We're a superior species'/

The hedges in this example, combined with vague language (i.e. the vague phrase *whatever it is* in *the language whatever it is ability* and the word *thing* in *the whole dangerous thing*) mean that I avoid sounding like an expert. There is also disfluency: both false starts and repetition of words. All these aspects of the way I talk about the topic combine to make me sound less authoritative. (The fact that this succeeded was demonstrated by the lively collaborative discussion on the topic 'Apes and language' that followed.) The preservation of equal status and the maintenance of social closeness are both important principles in friendly talk between women.

Women and hedging

Why are hedges a significant feature of the talk of women friends? I want to argue that their use is crucially related to three aspects of women's talk: women often discuss sensitive topics; women practise mutual self-disclosure; and finally women establish, and therefore need to maintain, a collaborative floor. I'll look at each of these factors in turn.

Negotiating sensitive topics

Women friends talk about a huge range of things, but this range includes a significant proportion of topics that can be labelled 'sensitive'. By 'sensitive' I mean that they are topics which are controversial in some way and which arouse strong feelings in people. These topics are usually about people and feelings. In the conversations I've analysed, the following are topics I would describe as sensitive: relationships; menstruation; illness; boys and the male body. By contrast, the conversations also involve topics which are less likely to arouse strong feelings, such as gymnastics; antiques; the school rabbit; buying a christmas tree. Sometimes, sensitive topics occur in sequence; the following sequence comes from a conversation involving five women friends: 'Taboo and funerals'; 'Child abuse'; 'Loyalty to men'; 'Fear of men'.

Here are just three brief examples of utterances containing hedges from one of these sensitive topics, 'Child abuse'.

(16) [*trying to work out why girl victims of sexual abuse are often treated unsympathetically*]

BEA: what happens to women sexwise is their fault/ and <u>I mean</u> <u>I think</u> it's <u>just</u> that taken down . extending it to little girls/

(17) [*talking about incest*]

MARY: <u>I mean</u> <u>I think</u> it was your theory <u>wasn't it</u> that- that it runs in families/

(18) [*talking about incest*]

MARY: <u>I mean</u> is it- is it to do with the mother?

Here, even though the five women involved in talking about child abuse do not bring any direct personal experience into the discussion, at the same time all have been little girls, all have children, and the subject provokes powerful feelings. The hedges in this talk of child abuse function chiefly as an interpersonal resource: the speakers use them to protect each other and themselves. Bea tries out an explanation of attitudes to girl victims in terms of attitudes to adult women and argues that this (unsympathetic, patriarchal) view of women is applied (inappropriately) to female children. Her hedges signal doubt (she is not totally committed to this position), sensitivity to her addressees (who might find the position controversial) and sensitivity to her own need to protect her face. In example (17), Mary is very careful not to pin a (possibly controversial) theory on one of her friends, and allows room for the friend

(Meg) to reject the claim. In example (18), Mary's *I mean* softens the force of the highly controversial suggestion that mothers are in some way implicated in child abuse. Mary doesn't just hedge this claim, she also phrases it as a question, which effectively hedges it further.

While each of these examples is unique, with hedges being used for a subtly different combination of reasons, in all three cases one fundamental reason for the use of hedges is that the topic itself is highly sensitive, and anything said needs to be mitigated. The discussion of sensitive topics is a regularly occurring feature in the talk of women friends. These topics trigger the use of hedges, because without hedges it would be difficult – if not impossible – to talk about sensitive matters.

Self-disclosure

Disclosing personal information is always risky, but is an important element in close relationships, because self-disclosure normally produces matching self-disclosure from others, which promotes close bonds. Self-disclosure is a key component of the talk of women friends: the ability to be ourselves, warts and all, with our friends is something we value very highly. But because self-disclosure involves highly personal material, utterances need to be softened, and hedges are a vital resource in making disclosure possible.

A very clear example of self-disclosure is given in the next example, where Becky confesses to her friends that for some time she 'fancied' Damien. Becky initiates the topic by saying 'I stopped sort of fancying him quite recently'. The hedge *sort of* is doing a lot of work here: it signals that Becky feels vulnerable about the topic 'fancying'; it also signals that 'fancy' may not be the best word for what she is talking about. She seems to want to self-disclose to her friends, yet at the same time she distances herself from her subject matter – her 'fancying' of Damien – by hedging. This utterance also presupposes that Becky 'fancying' Damien is shared knowledge. Once Becky realises that not all her friends know about this, she has to fill in the gaps in their knowledge with the following bit of self-disclosure (hedges underlined).

(19) [*talking about Damien*]

BECKY: well, when I started fancying him in the second year, I fancied him ever since then/

LORNA: yeah/ I s- I knew that sort of/

BECKY: yeah you sort of guessed/ well suddenly when I stopped fancying him/ which was over the summer holidays/

LORNA: yeah/

BECKY: and then when we came back I sort of fell in love with him again/ and then the real sort of clincher was ((xx))
JESS: <QUIET LAUGH>
BECKY: and I suddenly- because I've suddenly sort of fancying- you know people say love's blind/ I think I thought he was perfect/ apart from the ((obvious things))/
JESS: mhm/
LORNA: yeah/
BECKY: and I just suddenly have seen how awful he is and horrible=
LORNA: =yeah/
JESS: =yeah/
HANNAH: yeah/
BECKY: <SUDDEN PEAL OF LAUGHTER RELEASING TENSION>
OTHERS: <LAUGHTER>

Becky's self-disclosure makes her very vulnerable: it is embarrassing enough at the age of 14 to admit to feelings like 'love' and 'fancying'; it is worse when the object of your affections is a boy in your year at school, someone who you now think is 'awful' and 'horrible'. She hedges what she says, to protect her own face and that of her friends. Even so, this is such a sensitive topic that the hedges are not enough: Becky's embarrassment erupts in laughter at the end of her self-disclosure and triggers sympathetic laughter from her friends.

There are some topics which are so sensitive that self-disclosure would be unthinkable without some means of damping down the force of what is said. The next example comes from a discussion of the Yorkshire Ripper case. Meg discloses that after police appeals for help she forced herself to consider whether her partner might be the murderer. This leads to reciprocal self-disclosure from Sally, who admits to having gone through the same process. This is obviously a difficult fact to admit for both women: by saying something potentially disloyal to their partners, they make themselves very vulnerable. They need to protect their own face as well as that of their addressees. The strength of hedges is that they facilitate the expression of highly charged material; Meg and Sally unburden themselves to their friends, and are reassured to discover that they are not alone in having gone through this process.

(20)
MEG: I remember at the time thi- you know really thinking "now could this be M-" I think it was Mike/ [...] and I actually made a special point of thinking "could it be him"/ and I wondered if other women at the time . thought-

SALLY: oh god yes/ well I mean we were living in Yorkshire at the time/ and I . I mean I . I mean I did/ I sort of thought well "could it be John?"/

This extract includes a large number of hedges, precisely because the subject matter is so sensitive and because self-disclosure makes the speaker vulnerable. It is inconceivable that this kind of self-disclosure could take place without the use of hedges.

The collaborative floor and the need for open discussion

Another reason for the relatively frequent occurrence of hedging in the talk of women friends is that women organise their talk in terms of a collaborative floor (see Edelsky 1981; Coates 1996a, 1997b; Chapters 11 and 12 this volume). Edelsky suggested that speakers might draw on two models of turn-taking in their everyday interactions: a one-at-a-time model (like the one widely recognised by linguists – see Sacks, Schegloff and Jefferson 1974), and an alternative all-in-together model. She calls these two models the 'single', or 'singly developed', floor, and the 'collaborative', or 'collaboratively developed', floor. The main characteristic of the single floor is that one speaker speaks at a time: in other words, in a single floor speakers take turns to speak. By contrast, the defining characteristic of the collaborative floor is that the floor is potentially open to all participants simultaneously. When conversational participants adopt a collaborative floor, speakers share in the construction of talk. This means that to a large extent it is the group voice that counts rather than the voice of the individual. Consequently it is important for speakers to avoid expressing themselves in a hard-and-fast way.

Hedges play an important role in facilitating open discussion, that is, in promoting discussion where speakers avoid absolutes and where utterances are mitigated. The example given earlier of Pat and Karen discussing their doctors illustrates very clearly what I mean by the phrase 'open discussion'.

(21)
KAREN: well I suppose it is I've never really had any worries like that/
PAT: no/ it wouldn't bother me/ but perhaps-
KAREN: mind you as they're getting younger . I might feel differently/
PAT: yes/

Karen's initial statement is hedged, which means that she is not seen as taking a firm line, but would be prepared to moderate her views if necessary. Pat is free to agree with her or to nudge the discussion on with a 'yes but ...' response. She begins by agreeing, but then starts a second utterance which does the work of suggesting alternative points of view without actually stating them. The inclusion of the hedge *perhaps* here means that Karen is free to take up this new line or to stick with her original position: both are possible because Pat is tentative about proposing a new point of view. Karen responds to Pat's tentative fragmentary utterance by making a suggestion of a possible world where she might 'have worries', and Pat agrees with this step. So between them the two friends move through the following series of moves:

Position One: we have no worries about the sex of doctors: male doctors are OK.
Position Two: there are circumstances where a male doctor might be a problem.
Position Three: as we get older and doctors are younger than us, a male doctor might be problematic.

On the face of it there is nothing very remarkable about this sequence of moves. But in fact it takes great skill for such a sequence to come about. If speakers didn't hedge their assertions, it would be difficult for other speakers to bring in different points of view without sounding antagonistic.

This is precisely what happens when speakers use bald statements. In the following example (which was recorded by chance because Anna's brother, Mark, put his head round the door to say hello to his sister and her friends), Mark and Anna start arguing about the merits of wild rice.

(22)
ANNA: wild rice is nice/ you've never tasted it so-
MARK: well the Indians don't eat it so why the bloody hell should you?
ANNA: they probably do/
MARK: they don't/

This exchange is adversarial rather than collaborative (and follows earlier provocative comments by Mark). Anna makes an unhedged statement about wild rice – *wild rice is nice* – and challenges Mark on the grounds that he has no right to judge since he hasn't ever tasted it. Mark, far from building on what has gone before, interrupts her in order to introduce a totally new claim: 'Indians don't eat wild rice'. Anna disagrees with this position, but hedges her counter-claim with *probably*. Mark responds with the unhedged, bald refutation *they don't*, which just restates his original claim. It is problematic to call the sort of talk illustrated in this dialogue between Anna and Mark 'discussion' as there is no possibility of speakers shifting their ground. Without hedging, speakers take up uncompromising positions and this produces conflict. Speakers are not able to adapt or moderate their views in order to develop a more subtle, jointly agreed position.

In contrast with this, let's look at another example of the way women friends use hedges to promote open discussion. The topic 'Funerals' involves five women in the discussion of sensitive issues. Through the judicious use of hedges, they manage to express different points of view without coming into conflict. For example, Bea discloses that she did not attend her father's funeral because going to America at that point in her life was too difficult, and Sally agrees with her that it is madness to travel a long way for a funeral. Meg and Mary, however, both assert that there are no circumstances which would make them consider missing their mother's funeral. When the bare bones of the friends' positions are stated like this, it sounds as though they must involve conflict. In fact, the presence of hedges means that these women avoid taking up inflexible positions; here are a few examples taken from key points in the development of this topic (in the sequence in which they were uttered). Note how much of this discussion is carried out in hypothetical terms: I have underlined *would*, the auxiliary expressing hypothetical meaning in these utterances, since the use of hypothetical forms also functions as a hedge.

(23)

(i) SALLY: I said "Well I wouldn't go, Steve"/ and [...] as you say it was just taboo/

(ii) BEA: she [mother] said no/ I mean no point in coming/

(iii) SALLY: I mean it's not as if I'm particularly religious/

(iv) MARY: if there's a spouse then perhaps they would want you to go/

(v) MEG: but I think I would be hurt and angry if they [brothers and sister] hadn't [come to the funeral]/

(vi) JEN: I think going half way round the world is a different kettle of fish/

(vii) BEA: well it really depends on the- I mean I think it really depends on the attitude of the survivors who are there/

(viii) BEA: I think I would go now because probably- because I would want to go/

Because no one takes up a hard-and-fast position, the discussion moves along gradually, with different points of view being assimilated and accepted, so that eventually the group as a whole arrives at a consensus. This is expressed as follows.

(24) [*end of funeral discussion*]
JEN: there's two things aren't there/ there's the- the other people like your mother or father who's left/ and- or- or siblings/ and there's also how- how you feel at that time about . the easiness of going/
MARY: mhm/
BEA: mhm/
MEG: mhm/
SALLY: yeah/

Note how this summary is explicitly accepted by all members of the group, and that the summary takes account of both the main positions. Hedges are vital to the maintenance of a collaborative floor. They help to preserve openness, and they also help to avoid closure and conflict. In singly developed floors, where speakers talk one at a time, and where turns and ideas are seen to 'belong' to individual speakers, discussion will develop in a less coherent way, or will not develop but will get stuck when speakers take up diametrically opposite positions. In a collaborative floor, the group voice takes precedence, which means that speakers need to avail themselves of linguistic forms like hedges which enable them to make personal statements without blocking others from making their own personal statements.

Hedging: a misunderstood activity

In 1975, Robin Lakoff included hedges in her account of women's language and claimed that they were an important aspect of female speakers' style, a style she described as tentative and unassertive. Ever since the publication of Lakoff's essay, there has been a tendency to see hedges as unassertive and as stereotypically feminine. This view has arisen from the assumption that the only legitimate use of hedges is to indicate doubt or uncertainty. Lakoff claimed that female speakers used hedges in this way 'because [women] are socialized to believe that asserting themselves strongly isn't nice or lady-like, or even feminine' (1975: 54).

The assumption that women are unassertive is an over-generalisation, and the linking of hedges with unassertiveness is just incorrect. As I have demonstrated in this chapter, hedges are multi-functional and have a wide variety of uses. Ironically, however, the assumption that women use hedges more frequently than men seems to have some basis in fact to judge by empirical research carried out by linguists such as Janet Holmes (1984, 1995), Bent Preisler (1986) and Deborah Cameron et al. (1989). Table 2.1 gives the results of a small-scale comparison carried out by me on two conversations in my corpus, each lasting 45 minutes.

As Table 2.1 shows, the use of hedges in my conversational data supports the findings of other linguists, with female speakers using roughly twice as many of the forms listed as male speakers.

Table 2.1 Gender differences in the use of hedges

	Women	Men
I mean	79	20
well	68	45
just	59	48
I think	37	12
sort of	36	10
actually	22	8
really	15	23
TOTAL	316	166

As I've argued in this chapter, there are good reasons why women exploit the multi-functional potential of hedges in their talk. Women's greater use of hedges can be explained in part by topic choice, in part by women's tendency to self-disclose and in part by women's preference for open discussion and a collaborative floor. But recognising that women use hedges more than men does not entail recognising that women are unassertive. There is nothing intrinsically unassertive about choosing to talk about sensitive subjects or about sharing feelings and experience. On the contrary, women's ability to exploit the multi-functional potential of hedges can be seen as a strength not a weakness, and arises from women's sensitivity to interpersonal aspects of talk. Talk is never just the exchange of bits of information. Talk always involves at least two human beings, and thus involves interpersonal interaction. Hedges are a key means to modulate what is said to take account of the complex needs of speakers as social beings. In friendly talk, where *how* we talk is at least as important as *what* is talked about, hedges are a resource for doing friendship.

I don't want to restrict what I'm saying to talk between friends. While one aim of this chapter is to celebrate women and women's use of modal forms, more generally what I want to do is to celebrate the mitigating potential of hedges and to assert their importance in our everyday talk.

In all kinds of contexts, where we need to be sensitive to the face needs of others, where we need to qualify assertions to avoid total commitment to a particular point of view which we might want to withdraw from, where we engage in the struggle to find the right words, where we want to avoid taking up hard-and-fast positions and want to facilitate open discussion, hedges are a valuable resource for speakers, a resource we should never underestimate.

Notes

1. I am grateful to Roberta Facchinetti and all the other organisers of the Verona conference on Modality in Contemporary English for giving me the opportunity to revisit this paper, which appeared originally as chapter 7 of *Women Talk: Conversation between Women Friends* (1996), and I am grateful to conference participants – and the editors of the resulting book – for their helpful comments and questions (see Facchinetti, Krug and Palmer 2003).
2. The notion of 'face' and 'facework' originates in the work of Ervin Goffman (1972).
3. For example, in my 1987 paper 'Epistemic Modality and Spoken Discourse', I compare two 45-minute stretches of conversation, one involving three men, the other five women. The men discuss three main topics (home-made beer making, hi-fi systems, showing a film in class) which correspond to their own areas of expertise, whereas the women talk about a wide range of topics, from child abuse and fear of men to trains and ships in the docks, which draw on the personal experience of everyone present. (See also Coates 2004: 134.)

3
Competing Discourses of Femininity [1997]

The two most important things being accomplished in the talk of women friends are friendship and femininity. In this chapter[1] I want to focus on femininity and on the role of talk in constructing us as gendered beings, as women. ('Femininity' is a problematic word, because of the everyday connotations of the adjective 'feminine'. By 'femininity' I mean the abstract quality of being feminine, just as masculinity is the abstract quality associated with being masculine. 'Doing femininity' can be paraphrased as 'doing being a woman'. The latter is a much clearer and less ambiguous way of saying what I mean, but far too clumsy to use repeatedly.)

Most of us spend very little, if any, time thinking about gender, and we are rarely aware of 'doing' (or 'performing') gender. (By 'doing'/'performing' gender, I mean presenting ourselves to others as a gendered being.) We just take for granted that we are women. But we assume that 'being a woman' is a unitary and unified experience – in other words, we think of ourselves as 'I'/'me', that is, as singular. However, the woman we perform is not the same woman in all circumstances: we have all had the experience of feeling like a different person when we are in a different situation. For example, the 'me' that mashes a banana for a toddler is a different 'me' from the one who participates in a committee meeting or who poses as a life model at the local art school. Even in the same context we can change if something alters in that context. Liz's anecdote about her friend changing when her husband joined them for a drink is a good illustration of this:[2]

(1)

LIZ: when I was at the Health Club the other night/ and this girl I went with her husband turned up to have a drink with us in the bar/ . and like the

> whole atmosphere changed when he arrived/ <LAUGHS> [...] and she changed/ she changed/ she- she- she suddenly went tense/ you know/

We change because different audiences require different performances – and also because we sometimes feel like playing a different role. All kinds of different 'self' are possible, because our culture offers us a wide range of ways of being – but all these ways of being are *gendered*. These possible selves are not different kinds of person, but different kinds of *woman*. Moreover, the alternative versions of femininity available to the women in my recordings are specific to the so-called developed world at the end of the twentieth century.

A range of femininities

In this section I shall look at a few examples from the conversations to show what I mean by 'doing' or 'performing' femininity, and to give a sense of the range of femininities available to girls and women in Britain today.

The first example comes from a conversation where three 16-year-old girls are commenting on the appearance of the fourth, Sarah, who is trying on Gwen's make-up.

(2) [*Sarah tries on some of Gwen's make-up*]

GWEN: doesn't she look really nice?
KATE: yes/
EMILY: she DOES look nice/

GWEN: [I think with the lipstick
KATE: you should wear make-up [more often . Sarah/

GWEN: it looks good/ [Sarah your lips . s- suit lipstick/
EMILY: yeah looks [nice/

GWEN: ((I'm saying)) what you said- big lips suit [lipstick/
KATE: oohh yes/ [share it/
EMILY: [you should be [a model/

GWEN: yeah/ looks good to me/ Sarah you look really nice/
KATE: yeah/
EMILY: models have big lips/

In this talk, the girls are overtly complimenting Sarah. This is part of the routine support work that girls and women do with each other as friends. At the same time they are co-constructing a world in which the putting on and wearing of make-up is a normal part of doing femininity, and *looking nice/looking good* is an important goal. In this world, the size of your features – your eyes, your lips – is highly salient, and the fashion model is a significant figure, with high status.

The next example also comes from the talk of younger speakers, girls of 15. But they are performing a different sort of femininity. Jessica, Becky, and Hannah are talking about a crisis which occurred on the school trip (a trip which Ruth and Claire didn't go on).

(3) [*talking about disastrous time on school trip*]

Stave	Speaker	Utterance
1		
	JESS:	I can't believe that night/ I mean I can't believe ((xx))-
2		
	BECKY:	I can't- no I can't believe it either/ we were all crying/ <AMAZED>
3		
	BECKY:	I couldn't be[lieve it/ everybody [was/
	RUTH:	[who was crying?
	HANNAH:	[everybody/
	JESS:	apart from me/
4		
	BECKY:	yeah/ <LAUGHING>
	JESS:	I was in bed/ <LAUGHTER>
	RUTH:	((no but)) what were you crying about?
5		
	BECKY:	because- ((well)) I was crying because Hannah was crying/ Hannah
	HANNAH:	<GIGGLES>
6		
	BECKY:	was crying because Ben was um a sexist bastard/ <LAUGHS>
7		
	BECKY:	[and Vicky was crying because Susan was going to be sent home/
	HANNAH:	[%oh he was REALly horrible to me%/
8		
	BECKY:	and I was crying because [she never cries/
	CLAIRE:	[did she get sent home?
9		
	BECKY:	no/
	HANNAH:	and I was crying because Vicky [was crying/ no/
	CLAIRE:	[did she get sent home?

The three friends who are describing what happened agree on the significance of crying. They recount this episode in a tone of amusement, even pride: they seem to be saying 'We're real girls'. The phrase *was/were crying* occurs 10 times in all (12 times if we include those utterances with an ellipted verb, such as *everybody was*, stave 3). The repetition of this phrase functions to emphasize that crying was the key feature of this particular night, and to underline the fact that everyone was involved. Both Becky and Hannah say that they were crying, and they both claim that Vicky was crying. (Jessica, the only one who was not crying, explains *I was in bed*). Their reasons for their crying focus on friendship: Becky cried because Hannah was upset; Vicky cried because she thought her friend was being sent home. The only boy mentioned – Ben – was *not* crying: he is one of the reasons that Hannah was crying. Crying is constructed here as a gendered behaviour, something girls do at times of emotional crisis.

Crying is a stereotypical way of performing femininity. This version of femininity continues into adulthood, though, as the next example shows, adult women have some reservations about expressing their feelings in this way.

(4) [*Anna arrives from work late and explains why she is upset*]

ANNA: I just had such a bad week/ and then my boss just stood in the office

---

ANNA: tonight and told me and his deputy that we're both crap managers

---

ANNA: basically/
SUE: oh/
LIZ: oh god/

[...]

ANNA: I get so angry at myself for crying/ but . I wish I could just . ooh!

ANNA: punch him on the nose or something/
SUE: you shouldn't let it get to you/

ANNA: [I know/ but-
LIZ: [at least you CAN cry/ because I think you should let it out/

ANNA: [but it's bad/ because it makes [them think
SUE: [I know/ <GROANS>
LIZ: it's when you don't [cry/

ANNA: you're a wimp/
SUE: yeah/
LIZ: yeah/

Anna, like Becky and Hannah, talks about an episode that is characterised by strong emotion, which she responded to by crying. Her use of the powerful phrase *crap manager* to describe herself reveals how negatively she has interpreted what her boss said to her. (Later she says glumly *maybe he's right, maybe I am a crap manager.*) The three friends demonstrate that they share the assumption that if someone significant, such as your boss, is displeased with you, then crying is a 'normal' reaction. But they talk about this reaction with more ambivalence than Becky and her friends. Anna wonders whether crying was the appropriate response to her boss. She wonders whether she should have punched him on the nose (thus revealing an awareness that anger rather than sadness might have been her chief emotion). Liz supports her in her account of herself, taking the position that it's better to *let it out*, but Sue's advice is to stay calm (*you shouldn't let it get to you*). Liz implicitly alludes to the gendered nature of crying when she says *at least you CAN cry*, implying that there are those who can't: men. Anna herself worries that crying is a weak move: it may perform femininity but it also performs powerlessness (*it makes them think you're a wimp*), which is not the impression Anna wants to give to her male boss.

In the next example these same three friends talk about assertiveness training.

(5) [*topic = assertiveness courses*]

ANNA: Linda's going on an assertiveness training course at work/

ANNA: [I ought to go with her/
SUE: [J o h n' s M u m went on one/
LIZ: I'd love to go on one/

ANNA: assertiveness?=
SUE: =assertiveness/ and she said "I only- I'm only doing it
LIZ: I really would/

SUE: so that I can be like you Susan"/ I said "But I'm not assertive"/

SUE: I mean she's more assertive than anyone I know/

There seems to be an underlying assumption here that assertiveness training is for women: both the people mentioned in association with it are female – Linda from Anna's office and John's mum (Sue's mother-in-law). (However, Sue's claim that her mother-in-law is *more assertive than anyone I know* is ambiguous: does *anyone* refer to all Sue's acquaintances, or just to women she knows?) Both Anna and Liz express positive attitudes to the idea of assertiveness training: they both say they would like to go on a course. Sue is more sceptical. Her statement *John's Mum went on one* communicates 'everyone's doing it these days', and her brief story about what John's mother said to her reveals a profound gap between John's mother's reading of Sue as assertive and her own sense of herself as unassertive, with a parallel discrepancy in her sense of her mother-in-law as very assertive and not in need of any training. As women move into more prominent positions in the workplace, we have to juggle with our self-presentation to find ways to perform ourselves as both competent and at the same time feminine (see Chapter 10 for further discussion of this point). Whether assertiveness is the answer is unclear; certainly the rhetoric that women need some kind of training perpetuates the idea that it is women who don't fit in the public sphere and therefore women who have to change.

The final example is an instance of a woman sharing her sense of achievement with her friends. Janet has been for an interview; the following extract shows her responding to her friend's request to 'tell us about it'.

(6) [*Janet's job interview*]

MEG: did you get your job?
MARY: oh did you go for a job? <HIGH, SURPRISED>

MEG: ((xxxx))
JANET: ((xxxx))
JEN: what job?
MARY: tell us about it/

[...]

JANET: [somebody got mugged on the day
MARY: [what job is it?

JANET: of the inter[view/ and so they said they were interviewing
HELEN: [oh hell/

JANET: her at the end of last week/ 'cos they couldn't not interview

---

JANET: her just 'cos she'd got mugged=
MEG: [so anyway they
BEA: =no that would be [((very unfair/))

JANET: =they told me that there was only
MEG: told you that apart from that=

JANET: me and her= =it's external affairs officer for the
MARY: =what job is it?=

JANET: Regional Health Authority=
MARY: =oh I remember/ I remember you were- yes/

JANET: it's quite a good job= =I was really good in this interview
MARY: =yes/
HELEN: yes=

JANET: because I was so unbothered about whether I got the job/ I think

---

JANET: that's the actual [crunch of [the thing= =it takes the pressure
HELEN: [mhm/ =mhm= mhm/
JEN: [Meg's told me that/

JANET: off you enTIREly if you- if you know it's not all or nothing/
HELEN: yes/

Although the five other women present all contribute in various ways to this stretch of talk, Janet's story is the focus of attention. It's important to note that women friends allow each other space not just to complain or talk about problems, but also to talk about successes and feelings of achievement. In this example, Janet asserts that the job is *quite a good job* and that she was *really good* in the interview. This is a much more forceful version of femininity, and the interest that Janet's friends display in the details of her story shows that this story has resonance for them all as potential job-seekers, women who want to succeed in the public world outside the home. At the same time, Janet explains her good self-presentation in terms of not caring about the outcome (because she already has a job). The modesty of this claim balances her description of herself as *really good.* (Compare this with Sue's denial of herself as being assertive.) The balancing act that Janet carries out here shows that even with close friends, presenting oneself as competent rather than weak or vulnerable has to be done with care; women have to avoid the accusation of showing off.

All these examples, as well as showing female speakers talking *about* issues connected with femininity and self-presentation, show girls and women *doing* femininity. They present themselves as different kinds of woman, concerned both about their external appearance and about social performance, sometimes more emotional, sometimes more hard-nosed. The talk we do in our daily lives gives us access to these different modes of being, these different versions of femininity. This is because language plays a crucial part in structuring our experience.

Language and the construction of different 'selves'

It would be more accurate to say that discourse,[3] rather than language, plays a crucial part in structuring our experience. The whole idea of 'language' is something of a fiction: what we normally refer to as 'language' can more realistically be seen as a heterogeneous collection of discourses (see Gavey 1989; Lee 1992). Each of us has access to a range of discourses, and it is these different discourses which give us access to, or enable us to perform, different 'selves'. A discourse can be conceptualised as a 'system of statements which cohere around common meanings and values' (Hollway 1983: 131). So, for example, in contemporary Britain there are discourses which can be labelled 'conservative' – that is, discourses which emphasise values and meanings where the status quo is cherished – and there are discourses which could be labelled 'patriarchal' that is, discourses which emphasise meanings and values which assume the superiority of males. Dominant discourses such as these appear 'natural': they are powerful precisely because they are able to make invisible the fact that they are just one among many different discourses.[4]

One of the advantages of talking about 'discourses' rather than about 'language' is that the concept 'discourse' acknowledges the value-laden nature of language. There is no neutral discourse: whenever we speak we have to choose between different systems of meaning, different sets of values. This approach allows me to show how language is implicated in our construction of different 'selves': different discourses position us in different ways in relation to the world.

Using the phrase 'discourses position us' gives the impression that speakers are passive, are at the mercy of different discourses. But language use is *dynamic*: we make choices when we speak; we can resist and subvert. Social and cultural change are possible precisely because we do not use the discourses available to us uncritically, but participate actively in the construction of meaning. Talk is particularly significant in our construction and re-construction of ourselves as women, as gendered subjects. As Simone de Beauvoir said, 'One is not born a woman, one becomes one' (de Beauvoir 1988), and we go on 'becoming' all through life. This is done in many different ways, through all aspects of behaviour, through the way we dress, the way we move, but particularly through the way we talk. Each time we speak, we are saying

"This is (a version of) me", and, as I've argued, we are also saying "I am a woman", because the 'I'/'me' is always gendered. How this is done has been illustrated briefly in the opening section of this chapter. In the rest of the chapter I propose to re-examine the conversations of these women friends to explore some of the tensions arising from *competing* versions of what it is to be a woman, and to pinpoint the resistant discourses available to women today.

Competing discourses

To clarify what I mean by 'discourse', and to demonstrate how discourses can position us differently in relation to the world, I'll begin by looking at a few brief examples. The first two both come from conversations about mothers. In the first, Meg is talking about the function of funerals.

(7)
MEG: I would see it [*funeral*] as honouring her memory in some way/

The second comes at a point in conversation when Sue has stated that she phones her mother but her mother never phones her.

(8)
SUE: [((xx)) I'm not very close to my mother really/
LIZ: ['cos most mothers are a pain in the bum/

In the first example, Meg positions herself as a loving and dutiful daughter. She and her friends discuss whether it would be taboo to miss your mother's funeral. They draw on a dominant discourse where the family is revered and parents are to be honoured, a discourse which upholds the taboo against missing your mother's funeral. The second example represents mothers in a very different way. Here Sue and Liz resist dominant discourses of the family and express feelings which reveal a different picture of mother–daughter relations. This discourse challenges the hegemonic idea that all families are happy and all parents benevolent. We have all probably experienced both positions, and may even hold both views simultaneously. This is possible because of the existence of alternative discourses, alternative ways of thinking about the world.

The next two examples also draw on discourses relating to the family; they both come from conversations about children. In the first, Pat tells Karen about the end-of-term plays at her children's primary school.

(9) [*topic = end-of-term school plays*]

KAREN:	did Peter do his song?		was he good?	
PAT:		yes/		he was marvellous/

KAREN:		oh the-
PAT:	he was marvellous/ every kid in it was marvellous/	

KAREN:	I think they always are/
PAT:	

The second example comes at a moment in a conversation between Anna, Liz and Sue where they have been talking about a family they all know with difficult children. Their expression of negative feelings about these particular children (*they were ghastly children*) leads them to consider their attitude to children in general.

(10)

ANNA:	
SUE:	
LIZ:	I think it's a- . a fallacy as well that you like every child/

ANNA:		no/ . that's right/	
SUE:	mhm/		I still quite often don't like
LIZ:	'cos you don't/		

ANNA:		<LAUGHS>	
SUE:	children/	<LAUGHS>	
LIZ:			actually I think you particularly dislike your own/

Again, we can see the clash between the dominant discourse, which says that children are 'marvellous', and where all mothers take pride in their child's achievements, and an alternative discourse which asserts that not all children are likeable (in fact, some are *ghastly*) and that it is not compulsory for adults to like all children. For women speakers, particularly women who are themselves mothers (Sue and Liz), this is a very subversive discourse. Dominant ideas of femininity (and of motherhood) do not allow for the expression of negative feelings about children. Anna, Sue and Liz support each other in sustaining a radically different view, one which starts with the proposition 'you don't like every child' (Liz, supported by Anna), which moves on to 'I quite often don't like children' (Sue),[5] and then to 'I think you particularly dislike your own' (Liz), a very strong position which directly challenges the idea of women as loving, caring, nurturing beings for whom having children is the ultimate experience of their lives.

Finally, here are two examples drawn from talk about the body and appearance. The first arises in a conversation where Pat shows Karen her new sundress and they discuss the new style and whether it makes you look fat.

(11) [*topic = new sundress*]
KARAEN: you'll look at yourself in the mirror and you'll think "God I look fat"/

The second example comes in a conversation where Hannah has called Jessica's thighs fat, Jessica has protested at this and Becky (in the role of peace-maker) has insisted that hers are unpleasantly thin (*mine are skinny as a pencil – ugh!*). Hannah then suggests that they would both be happier if Jessica gave some of her fat to Becky.

(12) [*topic = size of Jessica's and Becky's thighs*]
HANNAH: well if you think your thighs are fat and you think your thighs are thin/ you just scrape off a bit of fat and plaster it on/

Both these examples draw on an ideology which insists that women should maintain their bodies at a size which accords with current fashion (these days, this means slim). Hannah takes up a resistant position in relation to that view, by making fun of Jessica and Becky. Karen and Pat, by contrast, adopt a discourse which positions them as accepting the dominant ideology. Their conversation is full of references to size and appearance – Karen says later in the same conversation (with reference to some dresses she's seen in the market) *the thing is with them you've got to be ever so skinny I think to wear them*. Moreover, where the ideology imposed by this dominant discourse clashes with reality, in other words, when the perfect body constructed by the dominant discourse doesn't match our actual bodies, we tend to assume that it is we who are at fault. Note how Pat and Karen use laughter to help them deal with the tension produced by the clash between the ideal and the real:

(13)

KAREN:	I've only got about four inches between my bust and my waist/
PAT:	yeah/

KAREN:	<LAUGHS>
PAT:	<LAUGHS> you sound quite deformed <LAUGHS>

These examples give some idea of the conflicts surrounding contemporary ideas of femininity. The dominant discourse constitutes women as loving, dutiful (in relation to parents), uncritical (in relation to children) and caring about our appearance, in particular by trying to stay slim. But as some of the examples illustrate, women are not passive in the face of this dominant ideology: we can resist by drawing on alternative discourses where we assert the right to say that sometimes we can't stand our mothers or sometimes our kids drive us mad, or where we mock the dominant view of ideal thigh size.

Competing views of men

The dominant discourses in our society teach us to see ourselves in relation to men. Insofar as dominant discourses place men at the centre of the universe, then women are always marginal and only have meaning when fulfilling roles that are significant for men, as mother, as partner, as daughter. In this section I shall look at some of the ways in which women (and girls) talk about men. Our talk about men does powerful work in our construction of ourselves as (certain kinds of) feminine subject.[6] It is certainly noticeable that girls in their early teens start talking compulsively about boys, as part of the negotiation of identity involved in the transition from girlhood to womanhood. I'll begin with two examples from girls in my sample (Emily is 16 years old, Becky 14).

(14) [*talking about poster of pop star*]
EMILY: what a hunk!

(15) [*talking about boy at school*]

BECKY:	did you really know?		that I still fancied Damien?	
CLAIRE:		what?		
JESS:				yeah/

BECKY:	I was too embarrassed to admit it though/

Adolescent girls relate both to male fantasy figures, such as singers and film stars, and to real boys (boys, such as Damien, whom they go to school with). Emily, in the first of these examples, is more outspoken in her admiration for the man pictured in the poster on Gwen's wall than Becky is about Damien in the second. Where the male in question is known, then there is embarrassment as well as more positive feelings. But both examples draw on vocabulary – *hunk*, *fancy* – that was not present in the girls' talk a few years earlier,[7] vocabulary which constitutes them as heterosexual feminine subjects.

When the adult women in my sample talk about men in their lives, we find the whole gamut of emotions from love through amused tolerance to anger and contempt. The first two examples both come from the interviews.[8]

(16) [*talking about husband*]
JILL: in a funny way I suppose Roger's my best friend/

(17) [*talking about husband*]
MARY: well my partner's my friend you see/ [...] if you like Dave's my best friend/ so- so I feel totally relaxed with him/ and [...] I look forward to doing more things together/

While Jill and Mary express very positive feelings about their partners, Pat's story about her partner in the next example is more critical. But despite her evaluation of his characteristic behaviour as *dreadful*, her feelings are clearly affectionate rather than hostile.

(18) [*talking about husband*]

PAT: he gives me these little um . notes when he sends me shopping/ you ought to see the notes I get with anything that I don't actually . deal with myself/ like framing bits or anything like that/ you get this long sort of paragraph/ which more or less starts with "Go out

---

PAT: of the house/ proceed down the road" <LAUGHS> you know/
KAREN: I know/

PAT: sometimes there's a map of where the shop is/ and sometimes there's a little drawing of what the thing ought to look like/ and I always play to the gallery by going into the shop and showing them the

---

PAT: note/ <LAUGHS> [and they fall [about/
KAREN: absolutely/ [why not/ [about/ that's right/

PAT: dreadful/

Sue's criticism of her husband in the next example cannot be described as affectionate. But her complaints about the noisiness of his music-making (which are a recurrent feature of her conversations with Anna and Liz) occur against a background where John is seen by all three women as a good bloke, in comparison with men in Anna's and Liz's lives. (For example, Anna comments at one point in the discussion of coupledom and relationships: *there's always a voice of reason I think with John, he's- he's very mature like that.*)

(19) [*Sue's husband's music gets louder*]

SUE: I mean how can you live with this/
LIZ: well I know its difficult when

SUE: [oh it drives you insane/
LIZ: you've got a man around [but-

The four examples I've given so far are all from speakers who are married. But among the women I've recorded are several who are divorced or separated. The next two examples come from moments in conversation where an estranged or ex-husband is the subject of conversation. (The first of these I'm including deliberately as a warning of the penalties which can be incurred by anyone unwise or unethical enough to record their friends surreptitiously.[9])

(20) [*discussing Jen's arrangements to get her ex-husband to help with her move to London*]

MEG: I mean I wouldn't um rely on him for something as vital as that/

[*Jen leaves room to answer phone*] [...]

SALLY: your faces when Jennifer said that- that Paul was going to do
MEG: <LAUGHS——

SALLY: the move/ .hh I wish I'd got a camera/ <LAUGHING>((it)) was
MEG: ———> <LAUGHS——

SALLY: sort of - ((xx)) in total disbelief/ I think the most difficult
MEG: ———> mhm/

SALLY: is- is that when you've loved someone/ you- you half the time you
MEG:

SALLY: forget their faults [don't you? and still maybe love them/ ...
MEG: [yeah/

Note the way Meg hedges her critical comments at the beginning of this example, prefacing what she says with *I mean* and then phrasing her utterance in a hypothetical way with *would*. Hedges are necessary as this is a very face-threatening subject. It's also noticeable how protective this group of friends are of one of their number: they clearly think that I (Jen) am acting foolishly in trusting my ex-husband. But Sally avoids outright criticism of me by positioning herself in a discourse where women are viewed as making bad decisions or acting stupidly because their judgement is clouded by emotion. While this discourse provides women with an excuse for bad decisions or stupid behaviour, it positions us as emotional, as non-rational (in contrast with men, who are positioned as rational).

The second of these examples focuses more explicitly on the male: Liz and Sue together describe Liz's husband's behaviour after he left Liz and the two children.

(21) [*vindictiveness of estranged husbands*]

LIZ:	I was like terrified/ I thought I was

LIZ:	going to ((be)) on the [streets/
SUE:	[I think he was so horrible as well/

LIZ:	[he was not supportive at all/
SUE:	[I mean he was really nasty/ but he wasn't even not supportive/

LIZ:	[oh he was vindictive/ he really wanted me to suffer/
SUE:	he was . vindic[tive/ yeah/

LIZ:	[he really wanted- yeah/
SUE:	[and his children/ that was the thing/ his children to go with

SUE:	it/ oh . horrible/

Here, Sue and Liz explicitly label the man as bad, using words like *horrible, nasty, vindictive*. But at the same time, the man is portrayed as active, the women as more passive: *I was like terrified, he really wanted me to suffer*. And it is only because of Sue's intervention that Liz amends the weaker *not supportive* to the stronger *vindictive*. (Similarly, Becky's words in the example we looked at earlier, *Hannah was crying because Ben was a sexist bastard*, label the boy Ben as bad, drawing on a feminist anti-sexist discourse, but present Hannah's response as weak.)

The final example comes from a discussion of coupledom which took place between Sue, Liz and Anna. During the course of this talk, the women ponder whether it is better to be in a couple or independent. Anna comes down on the side of independence:

(22) [*discussing the relative merits of coupledom and independence*]
ANNA: I just sometimes think I probably never will get married again/ or never be with anybody again/ 'cos I just love my life on my own/

While the women in these examples are positioned in a variety of ways – as women who love men, as women who are critical of men, as women who prefer to live alone – they all share the dominant worldview in which heterosocial relations are seen as the norm. In other words, for all these women (and for the girls in my sample) the construction of themselves as feminine involves simultaneously the construction of themselves as heterosocial. As is typical of dominant discourses, this process is virtually invisible: this means that criticism or resistance becomes very difficult. And because my sample contains no women who are lesbian, a non-heterosocial discourse is not voiced.

Resistant discourses

However, resistance to the androcentric norms of the dominant culture does occur. There is evidence in the conversations that the women in my sample have access not only to dominant (androcentric) discourses but also to resistant discourses, particularly feminist discourses, which offer alternative positions, alternative ways of being a woman. In the final example above, we heard Anna resisting the normative pressures to live as part of a (heterosexual) couple. Here are four more examples of women using resistant discourses.

The first draws on a psychotherapeutic discourse which challenges the construct 'the happy family'.

(23) [*topic = Anna's mother and her sister Diana*]

ANNA:	but now looking back on it she [A's mother] was really bad to her/
SUE:	mhm/
LIZ:	why?

ANNA:	and [Diana says that-
SUE:	[it's funny because your mum holds up the thing
LIZ:	I wonder why/

ANNA:	yeah/ [that's right/ well that's-
SUE:	of the happy family quite a lot doesn't [she?

ANNA:	you have to don't you? that's the [conspiracy/
SUE:	yeah/ [that's it/

Anna resists the normative pressures to speak of her family and of relationships between her mother and her siblings in glowing terms. In the talk preceding this extract she self-discloses to her friends about some of the problems in her family, then, with Sue's support, goes on to challenge the idea of the happy family and names the discourse that promotes it a 'conspiracy'.

The next example shows how women friends help each other to struggle against prevailing discourses. Helen challenges me – and the discourse I adopt – by refusing to accept my description of recent events in my life.

(24) [*talking about jobs*]

HELEN:	you haven't been applying for jobs as well have you? oh have you?
JEN:	yes/

HELEN:	that's right/ so-
JEN:	there's one at Cambridge/ <LAUGHS> Cambridge! <LAUGHING>

HELEN:	so have you applied [for it? [oh no but that's TERRIBLE
JEN:	[oh what hubris/ [%honestly%

HELEN:	though isn't it? <HIGH, APPALLED> I mean [you can't imagine any men
JEN:	[oh you mean I'm being((xx))-

HELEN:	sitting round/ . saying about their applications that it's hubris/
JEN:	

HELEN:	you're conditioned to think that/
JEN:	oh all right/ <MOCK GRUMPY>

Helen draws on a liberal feminist discourse which resists the idea that women and men do things differently or have different abilities. She also draws on the feminist idea that socialisation rather than biology determines our sense of ourselves as inferior, arguing that we are socialised to internalise such views – *you're conditioned to think that*. In this brief dialogue we see how friends can challenge each other's views and resist each other's discourses at the same time as supporting each other, since in effect Helen is saying 'You have as good a right as any man to apply for a job at Cambridge University.' We can accept each other's challenges – and can therefore adopt more radical positions – because we feel supported and validated by each other.

The next example comes from a discussion of child abuse. This discussion, like the one between Anna, Sue and Liz above, focuses on the family, but this time the emphasis is on the tendency to blame the mother when families malfunction.

(25) [*discussion of child abuse*]

MEG: one of the things often said about the incestuous family is that um it's really the mother's fault one way or another/ [...] I mean I'm so terrified of joining in the blaming of mothers/ [...]

MARY: but I mean so much research is male-dominated/ I mean it's just- it's staggering isn't it?

Here we find a group of women discussing a topic which forces them to consider the nature of patriarchy. They struggle to avoid adopting a more conventional discourse on the family and on sexuality, and draw on a feminist discourse to challenge conventional views, explicitly naming *the blaming of mothers* as the construction of a more patriarchal discourse, and using the phrase *male-dominated,* which allies them all with a feminist position which sees male–female relations in terms of dominance and oppression. (But it's interesting to note the presence of the phrase *the incestuous family,* a phrase which does the work of concealing *who* in the family abuses other members of that family, and thus a phrase which clearly serves patriarchal, not feminist, interests.[10])

The last example comes in a stretch of conversation where Liz and Anna have been telling anecdotes about men in their lives (brothers, ex-husbands) who have let them down or behaved badly.

(26) [*talking about the inadequacy of some men*]

ANNA:	women are just vastly superior/		[thank god I'm a
LIZ:		they ARE/ VASTly	[superior/
SUE:		<LAUGHS———	———————

ANNA:	woman/ and not like that/	
LIZ:		yeah/
SUE:	———————————>	

Anna's statement draws on a radical feminist discourse which claims that, far from being inferior, women are in fact superior. This is a very powerful discourse, since it positions women as being positive about themselves, it allows us to like ourselves and to say things like *thank god I'm a woman.* But Sue's laughter indicates that these three friends make these remarks fully aware of the discrepancy between what they are saying and dominant ideas about women and men. The laughter signals that they can amuse themselves by expressing this view to each other, but suggests that they may have doubts about its relevance to their lives in the outside world.

Tensions and contradictions

Given the range of discursive positions available to us, it is not surprising that we present ourselves in talk as different kinds of woman, sometimes more forceful and assertive, sometimes more passive and ineffectual. The clash between different positions produces tensions and contradictions in our talk, where competing discourses come into contact with each other. Earlier brief examples have illustrated that we draw on a range of discourses, but in this section I want to look at a few longer examples to show how different discourses co-exist in a single conversation.

First, here's an extract from a conversation between Hannah, Becky, Claire and Jessica when they are 14 years old. The topic is periods, and at this point they are talking about mood swings.

(27)

HANNAH:	everything seemed to be going wrong and everything/
HANNAH:	it was horrible/ [...] it was really horrible
HANNAH:	[that day/
JESS:	[but you know when I [had that really bad . um
CLAIRE:	[do you get PMT ((xxx))
HANNAH:	<LAUGHS>
BECKY:	yeah/ I'm a bitch/ <LAUGHS> I'm
JESS:	pre-menstrual tension/
HANNAH:	so I've noticed/ no- no but [some-
BECKY:	REally HORrible/ no but- [so whenever
HANNAH:	="Right I might be horrible
BECKY:	I'm on my period I say to Hannah um=
HANNAH:	to you but=
BECKY:	="Don't take any notice"/

This passage is part of a more lengthy chain of mutual self-disclosure on the subject of mood swings. The girls in turn tell anecdotes to illustrate how pre-menstrual tension affects them. Throughout this section of the conversation at least three discourses are simultaneously present: a medical discourse, a repressive discourse and a more resistant feminist discourse. The friends choose terms such as *pre-menstrual tension* in their talk about their periods; these words are part of a medical discourse. A feminist discourse expressing solidarity and sisterhood is realised through overlapping turns, expressions of agreement and the joint construction of text (Becky and Hannah share in constructing the utterance *so whenever I'm on my period I say to Hannah um 'Right I might be horrible to you but don't take any notice'*). The sequence of self-disclosing anecdotes (here we have the end of Hannah's and the beginning of Becky's) involving mirroring and exchange is another feature of this discourse. The third discourse present is a discourse of repression: the girls jointly represent themselves as beings who are *affected*, at the mercy of larger forces, rather than as *agents*, in control of their lives. This is realised through their choice of stative verbs: *was, had, got,* and through the use of negative words such as *horrible* and *bitch*. Through the use of these discourses the girls are simultaneously positioned as having solidarity with each other and as oppressed.

Contradictions are also apparent if we look at a longer extract from the conversation where Anna says *women are just vastly superior.* The subject of men's inadequacy is part of the larger topic 'Relationships', and follows on from a discussion of husbands and obedience, and of coupledom. Anna tells a story about the break-up of her last relationship, and complains that men seem to find it hard to understand when a relationship is over. Liz responds with a story about her ex-husband, who had come round the previous weekend to help her clear out her loft. She describes wryly how she had *made a point of it being my loft and my rubbish*, so she ends up doing most of the work, and as she leaves for her last trip to the dump she recounts how her ex-husband, now sitting watching football on television, got out a five pound note and asked her to buy him some fish and chips. Her point is that she considers such behaviour appalling (though she does in fact buy his fish and chips). Anna then tells a matching story about her brother (Mark) who had recently come and leaned against the kitchen door, complaining of depression, while she was 'humping twenty-five kilos of cement across the kitchen'. It is at this point that Anna says that women are superior.

(28)

ANNA: I mean in a way it doesn't upset me things like that any more/

ANNA: ['cos I just laugh/ 'cos I think well . women are just
LIZ: [no they don't upset you/ you laugh about it/ yes/

ANNA: vastly superior/ [thank god I'm a woman/ and
LIZ: they ARE/ VASTly [superior/
SUE: <LAUGHS———————————

ANNA: not like that/
LIZ: yeah/
SUE: —————————>

This leads into a long discussion between the three friends about men and the reasons for some of them being so inadequate. It is this last section that I want to examine in some detail. The three friends move from a radical discourse which is self-affirming, which asserts the value of women, to an oppressive, woman-blaming discourse.

(29)

ANNA: why though why are boys like that? why are they?
SUE: it must be ((about having the
LIZ: boys ARE

ANNA: I mean my mother- my mother and my youngest sister both ring Mark up
SUE: xxx too far apart))
LIZ: like that/

ANNA: regularly/ and my- my younger sister Felicity writes to him/ and she

---

ANNA: says . um "We- Mummy and I are really worried about you 'cos you're

---

ANNA: so depressed/ and you know if there's anything we can do just give us

---

ANNA: a ring"/ and I said to her "But it makes him worse"=
LIZ: =yeah/
SUE: =yeah/

ANNA: [he's been like it since my father died/ and that's over a year
LIZ: [it feeds it/ yeah/ yeah/

ANNA: now/ and it all affected us very badly/ but you know life is
LIZ: yeah/ yeah/

ANNA: to get on with= =and the more you pander to him being depressed/
LIZ: =yeah=

ANNA: and telling him "Oh poor thing never mind"= [he's
LIZ: =[the more he'll [revel
SUE: =[no he loves it/

ANNA: going to get worse/ it makes me so cross/
LIZ: in it/ yes/ that's right/

ANNA: and I think in a- in a w- in a way it's women who perpetuate that/

ANNA: it's women who . despise weak men and then just produce more of
SUE: oh yeah/

ANNA: them/ and say to them you know "Don't worry darling/ it'll all be all
ANNA: right/ and you don't have to-
SUE: "I'll look after you"/ <LAUGHS>

Anna, focusing on the particular case of her brother, argues that it is her mother who is to blame, and generalises from this that women are to blame for producing weak men. Liz and Sue go along with this argument. They add minimal responses as well as more substantive forms of agreement; they also jointly construct utterances with Anna: Anna's *the more you pander to him ...* is completed by Liz with *the more he'll revel in it*, and Anna's *it's women who ... say to them ... 'Don't worry darling it'll be all right'* is completed by Sue with *'I'll look after you'*. Liz then develops this woman-blaming theme as follows, introducing the notion of the 'strong' woman.

(30)

LIZ: it's probably because everybody's- if he's had strong women in the

---

ANNA: it probably is/ [it probably-
SUE: oh god/ yes/ that's right/
LIZ: house/ and other people- and other people have made [decisions

---

ANNA: [yes/ it's awful I know/ I do appreciate that/ I mean I'm
SUE:
LIZ: FOR him [you see/

ANNA: quite bombastic/ [SUE EXITS TO GO TO LOO]

At this point, Anna starts to blame herself rather than her mother for her brother's weakness. She includes herself in the category 'strong women' with her apologetic statement *I'm quite bombastic*. This switch from mothers to themselves is continued by Liz, who starts to talk about her worries about her own son, who is away at boarding school.

(31)

LIZ:	I worry that I'm too strong/ that's the rea- one of the reasons I
ANNA:	[yes/
LIZ:	sent Dean away/ [...] because um I'm strong/ and he [leans on me
ANNA:	Mark does it/ I mean [I- I pay all the bills/
LIZ:	for decisions/ [yeah/
ANNA:	I [do the mortgage/ I do the insurance/ [I- .hh I ring up the bank
LIZ:	[yeah/ [yeah/
ANNA:	when they won't give us an overdraft/ I negotiate the building
LIZ:	
ANNA:	society when they won't [lend us m- the amount-
LIZ:	[well that starts from being
ANNA:	=it does/ it does/ yeah/ but at the same time . I just
LIZ:	very young=
ANNA:	think if I don't do it/ HE's not going to do it/ and then that's
ANNA:	[more worry back on me because it's not being done/
LIZ:	[but you- yeah/ and you- you- you'd have to do it
ANNA:	yeah/ it's easier to do it for
LIZ:	for yourself anyway/ so you do it/
ANNA:	both of you/

In the above passage, Anna and Liz collude in a view of themselves as strong and therefore potentially dangerous to males who live with them. They then collaborate in arguing that they are forced to be active and competent because if they weren't, things wouldn't get done and they would be the ones to suffer. Having worked themselves into a position where they feel they have a good reason for taking responsibility for the bills and the mortgage, Liz initiates a more positive move by asserting that women are normally prevented from realising how easy it is to run your own life – to deal with the *bills and mortgages and everything else.*

(32)

LIZ:	but it's a myth you know/ I wish a lot of women would
LIZ:	realize that it's a complete and utter myth/ . this- this being on
LIZ:	your ow- I mean . when I was first- when I was first thrown out
LIZ:	there on my own if you like/ I was bloody terrified/ bills and
ANNA: LIZ:	yeah/ but how much have you learnt since you mortgages and everything else/ but- but yeah
ANNA: LIZ:	first ((xx)) but once you get on with it there's nothing- there's- .
ANNA: LIZ:	there's nothing [to it really/ [there's nothing to it/

This last section of their talk about women's competence and men's incompetence represents a dramatic shift of position. Here, rather than bewailing her competence, Liz is celebrating it. And rather than claiming that women as a group are powerful and dangerous and produce weak and damaged men, she argues that women are prevented from understanding how easy it is to be independent (though she doesn't name *who* is responsible for preventing this). She feels strongly that women should be given the information they need – and thus, she implies, should have the right to be competent autonomous people in their own right. This bit of talk ends with the triumphant repetition of the phrase *there's nothing to it* by both Liz and Anna. So, we see Liz and Anna (with Sue in the earlier part) holding the contradictory positions that (i) boys and men are inadequate; (ii) women are superior to men; (iii) it's good to be a woman; (iv) women are too strong; (v) women are to blame for men's inadequacy; (vi) women have to be strong/competent because otherwise nothing would get done; (vii) running a house is easy; (viii) women are misled into thinking it's difficult.

At the heart of these contradictions is ambivalence about being 'strong'. These women friends are positioned by a patriarchal discourse to see strength as incompatible with femininity and somehow bad, even dangerous. Simultaneously, their exposure to resistant feminist discourses means they also have a sense of strength as good, as part of a different type of femininity, a femininity which is distinct from masculinity but not inferior to it. The problem seems to be that they find it hard to sustain the latter, feminist position: their assertions that they are strong trigger anxiety about weakness in men. In other words, they fall back onto a worldview that sees all relationships in hierarchical terms, so if one group is strong, the other group must be weak (or less strong), and if men are weak, that is somehow women's responsibility.

Women's anxiety about our strength is closely related to our ambivalence about power. I've chosen the final extract to show a woman using a more powerful discourse. Meg, in the next example, starts to talk about her experience on an interview panel. This follows on from Janet's story about her recent interview for a job. But where Janet is telling a story where she, the protagonist, was an interviewee, Meg chooses to tell a story where she is in the powerful position of being one of the interviewers. There are several discourses present in the extract, but I want to focus on two: a powerful professional discourse, and a sexist patriarchal discourse.

(33) [*topic = interviews*]

MEG: we did the interviews for the- [...] you know I'd been shortlisting/ and there were twenty-four/ and um inCREDibly well-qualified/ and the twenty-four that applied for er nine places . all had um good degrees in psychology/ I mean and some of them had . M- M Phils and D Phils and um .hh PhDs/ you know they were very well qualified/ and . all- virtually all of them had done some . proper ongoing research into child abuse or-

---

MEG: the M- it's called the M Clin Psychol/
MARY: what's the course?

MEG: it's the qualification I did/ masters in clinical [psychology/
MARY: yes/ [mhm/

MEG: um . anyway we interviewed them on two days running/ Thursday and Friday/ and ((something)) really funny thing happened/ . one was an extremely pretty girl that's doing . um er er- what's the diploma? a- a- a Master's in Child Development at Newcastle with Professor Newton/ and she got a SPLENdid

---

MEG: reference from Professor Newton/
JEN: you used to have Professor

MEG: [yeah/ yeah/ but s- and saying things
JEN: Newton [didn't you?
HELEN: did you? mhm/

MEG:	like- can't remember the girl's name/ Nicola I think/ saying um you know "She's academically u- u- unimpeachable/ she's absolutely superb/ she's also an extremely nice girl/ and she's . the sort that joins in well at the party/ and is always- has al- always there- er also there for the washing up"/ <LAUGHTER>

MEG:	that was a nice little domestic note/ anyway um-
HELEN:	they wouldn't

MEG:		[well there WAS
HELEN:	have said that about a bloke [((xx))/	
SALLY:	[I was going to	[say/

MEG:	that/ um . anyway during the interview um . it went okay/ . um she's- she's the sort of- she has a very pleasant manner/ and she answered quite competently/ and at the end/ um David Blair said to her . um "You've been working with autistic children"/ she's done two special projects with autistic children/ [...] he said to her . um "Do you believe um there's any relationship between dyslexia and autism?"/ <u>and she</u>

MEG:	<u>absolutely panicked</u>/ <AGHAST> and it was TERRible for us
BEA:	heavens/
HELEN:	mhm/

MEG:	to watch/

Meg presents herself here as a competent professional. This is done in part through the use of specialised vocabulary, such as *shortlisting, clinical psychology, reference, dyslexia, autism,* and the abbreviated terms *MPhil, D Phil* and *M Clin Psychol,* which assume in-group knowledge. It's also done prosodically, with the rhythm and stress patterns of phrases like *she got a SPLENdid reference from Professor Newton* carrying powerful signals about social class and educational level which are readily understood by British English speakers. Meg also accomplishes professionalism through her presentation of herself as someone with agency, a doer, not a person who is done to: *I'd been shortlisting*; *it's the qualification I did*; *we interviewed them ...*, which is implicitly contrasted with the young woman interviewee who is presented as *an extremely pretty girl* who has a *very pleasant manner* and who *answered quite competently.* The presentation of the young interviewee is derogatory: Meg's description of her doesn't just accomplish power; it also accomplishes the oppression of women. Not only is the young woman called a 'girl' (thus reducing her to non-adult status), but she is described in terms of her appearance, which is clearly irrelevant to the situation. Later, Meg repeats Professor Newton's reference with approval, though its allusion to the young woman's willingness to wash up after parties is blatantly sexist. Meg initially describes this as *a nice little domestic note,* and it is only when Helen challenges this position with the comment *they wouldn't have said that about a bloke* that she concedes there might be a problem with this aspect of the reference.

It seems as though women like Meg – women who were among the first to take on more senior positions in professions like law and medicine and psychology – can only adopt a powerful role if they also take on the patriarchal values that normally accompany such power. So, Meg's self-presentation here illustrates the tensions associated with doing femininity and power at the same time: Meg succeeds in doing power, but at the same time she presents herself as colluding in an ideology that denigrates and trivialises women. The crux of her story to her friends is that a very talented young woman panicked in her interview – in other words, the younger woman lost all claim to competence by contrast with the calm professionals on the panel. Meg's self-presentation works in part because of the contrast between herself – calm, competent, professional – and the young woman who panics.

On the other hand, there are features of her talk which undermine the discourse of power. She hesitates or says *um* and *er* frequently, as well as stammering and repeating her words. She has brief lapses of memory when she appeals for help to her friends – *what's the diploma?* She also includes hedges in her account – *you know, I mean, sort of.* In part, these 'lapses' are designed to reduce the distance between herself and her addressees: as I've said in earlier chapters, women friends avoid playing the expert where possible. But these features of Meg's talk also accomplish a femininity that is not powerful, that needs help and support. This latter aspect of her talk demonstrates how problematic it is for us as women to claim power for ourselves.

Conclusion

As the examples in this chapter have illustrated, there is no single unified way of doing femininity, of being a woman. In the contemporary developed world, many different versions of femininity are available to us. Different discourses give us access to different femininities. More mainstream discourses position us in more conventional ways, while more radical or subversive discourses offer us alternative ways of being, alternative ways of doing femininity. We are unwittingly involved in the ceaseless struggle to define gender: as Chris Weedon (1987: 98) puts it 'The nature of femininity and masculinity is one of the key sites of discursive struggle for the individual'.

The meaning of 'woman' has changed through time, and at any given time will vary – between, for example, meanings associated with more madonna-like images of femininity and meanings associated with more whore-like images. There is no such thing as a 'woman'; the meaning of 'woman' will depend on which discourse the word occurs in. 'Discourses do not just reflect or represent social entities and relations, they construct or "constitute" them; different discourses constitute key entities [such as "woman"] ... in different ways' (Fairclough 1992: 3–4). What 'being a woman' means at this moment in late twentieth-century Britain is a site of struggle, with dominant ideologies being challenged by more feminist ones.

It seems to me that the talk we do with our women friends is particularly important in terms of our sense of ourselves as women, because in our talk we collaborate in constructing a shared view of what constitutes womanhood. We also support each other in resisting particular versions of femininity and in preferring others, and we help each other (consciously or unconsciously) to reconcile conflicting or contradictory femininities. We do this as part of the ongoing work of doing friendship.

Notes

1. I am grateful to Mike Baynham, Jenny Cheshire, Norma Grieve, Janet Holmes, Alson Lee, David Lee, Jean Mulder, Mary Porter, Cate Poynton and Amanda Sinclair, who read earlier versions of the chapter: their comments have been invaluable.
2. For transcription conventions, see pp. xiii–xv.
3. The term 'discourse' is particularly associated with the work of Michel Foucault. For further discussion of Foucault's theories of discourse, see Fairclough 1992; Weedon 1987.
4. The analysis of linguistic texts in terms of discourse is associated with the branch of linguistics known as Critical Discourse Analysis and with the work of Norman Fairclough – see in particular Fairclough 1992.
5. At the time this conversation was recorded, Sue had gone back to college as a mature student to train as a primary school teacher.
6. The term 'subject' as used here pulls together three different strands of thought, one more political (we are not free but *subject to* the power of others), one more philosophical (we are thinking *subjects*, sites of consciousness) and one more grammatical (sentences have *subjects* – they are what the sentence is about). (See O'Sullivan 1983.) The word also gains meaning from its opposition to *object*, even though, ironically, the two words are often very close in meaning. Here, for example, it would be equally true to say 'our talk

about men does powerful work in our construction of ourselves as feminine *objects*'. Showing how women are *objectified* in patriarchal discourses has been one of the goals of feminist discourse analysis.

7. I can say this with confidence about Hannah and her friends, since I have recordings of them since they were 12. But although I knew Emily when she was 12, I only recorded her with her friends when they were 16, so I have no definite proof that her language changed.
8. There are few good examples of positive talk about significant males in the conversational data. This could be because one of the chief functions of women's friendly talk is to allow us to talk about our anxieties and problems, and about our triumphs in the outside world. Ongoing good relationships do not seem to be a salient topic of conversation.
9. It had not crossed my mind that I might have to leave the room during recording. On this particular occasion I had to go and answer the phone, and my friends started to talk about me after I had left the room. I have only listened to the first few seconds of this talk, as it seems to me that I have absolutely no right to know what they said in my absence.
10. I am grateful to David Lee (personal correspondence) for alerting me to the slipperiness of this phrase.

4

Changing Femininities: The Talk of Teenage Girls [1999]

In this chapter,[1] I shall ask the question: When do girls start to talk like women? There is little research which focuses on developmental aspects of language use in relation to gender, and we therefore know very little about the ways in which children become gendered speakers. I shall make the assumption that 'talking like a woman' is something that speakers learn to do, not something we are born with. I shall also assume that we now have a reasonably clear idea of the speaking practices of women (see, in particular, Coates 1996a; Holmes 1995) and that girls do not share these practices. Girls' talk has been studied in a variety of cultures and from a variety of perspectives (see Eckert 1993; Eder 1993; Goodwin 1990), but these studies are synchronic. They present us with a snapshot of girls' speaking practices but do not help us to answer the question of how – and when – these practices are modified in the direction of the adult norm.[2]

My aim in this chapter is to analyse girls' talk to explore the ways in which teenage girls negotiate their identity during adolescence as they move from girlhood to womanhood. I shall take the position that discourses are 'practices that systematically form the objects of which they speak' (Foucault 1972: 49). I will argue that one of the chief things that is being done in the talk of teenage girls is the construction of gendered subjectivity: in the girls' case, the construction of femininity. In contemporary Western society, performing femininity entails performing heterosexuality, the 'compulsory heterosexuality' discussed by Adrienne Rich (1980). I will show how girls' sense of their femininity is at times contradictory and precarious; they experiment with a range of discourse styles and subject positions.[3] I will also attempt to show how 'doing femininity' changes as the girls get older, as they move from a more childlike identity to a more womanlike identity.

The data

The data drawn on come from transcriptions of the talk of four girls: Harriet, Jenny, Laura and Vanessa. They are white middle-class girls who live in North London and have known each other since they were very young: Harriet and Jenny met at play school when they were four; Jenny and Laura knew each other through their families throughout their childhood; Vanessa, Jenny and Harriet were at primary school together. But they only became a group when at age 11, when they were all placed in the same tutor group at a North London coeducational comprehensive school. This is when I first met them, and I recorded them from when they were 12 until they were 15. They agreed to turn on a tape-recorder when they were together, and they were free to delete any portions of their talk that they did not want me to hear. They contacted me each time they filled a 90-minute audiotape.[4]

Postfeminism?

This chapter challenges the notion that we live in a postfeminist era, that women's struggles are over. On the contrary, the talk of these teenage girls shows them moving from a more carefree to a more problematic phase, in which they struggle, more or less consciously, with dominant norms of femininity. Their apparent conformity to adult norms of feminine behaviour is facilitated in part by their adoption of others' voices. At the age of 12, they play with a wide range of voices; the intertextuality that is characteristic of their talk seems to offer them freedom to explore different identities. As they get older, however, the continuing intertextuality found in their talk seems to constrain rather than liberate them.

Whether these girls are typical of their generation is a question this chapter cannot answer, given the limitations of the database. Certainly, they represent a particular class (middle) and a particular ethnicity (white) in a particular country (England). It is likely that the talk of girls from working-class backgrounds and from other ethnic groups will differ in a variety of ways (see, for example, recent work by Bucholtz 2011; Goodwin 2003; Mendoza-Denton 2007; Pichler 2009). But given that these girls come from a relatively privileged background, it is surely striking that they appear to have difficulty maintaining more agentive identities and to be internalising patriarchal values that undermine them as developing women.[5] We must explain how and why girls in relatively powerful positions, materially speaking, at times acquiesce to their own discursive powerlessness.

Discoursal range

The girls' talk often occurs against the background of some activity: flipping through old copies of *Just 17* (a teenage magazine), looking at a Body Shop catalogue, eating pizza, lying on the floor doing gymnastics, making friendship bracelets. One interesting finding is that at the beginning (when they were only 12) it took them months to fill a 90-minute audiotape: the tape would contain several separate conversations, recorded on different occasions. By the time they are 14 and 15, they fill a 90-minute tape at one session and the tape runs out while they are still talking. These later tapes are, in this respect, like those made for me by adult participants in my research on all-female talk (see Coates 1989, 1991, 1994b, 1996a).

The girls talk about a huge range of topics in the conversations I have on tape, the inevitable topics of female adolescence in the late twentieth century in Britain: pop stars, *Neighbours* (a TV soap opera), cosmetics, blackheads, school, boys, shopping, clothes, pets, to mention just a few. On the earlier tapes they also have ridiculous quasi-philosophical debates on subjects such as 'Would you rather be a rabbit or a goldfish?' or 'Would you prefer a big face with tiny features or a skinny face with big features?' Such debates do not appear on the later tapes: by the time the girls are 14 and 15 their talk has become much more focused on the personal.

I want to start by looking at the range of discourses which appear in the girls' talk. Examples (1–7) come from the early tapes, that is, from tapes made when the girls are 12 and 13.

(1) Factual/scientific
J: did you know that the testicles produce thirty billion sperm in each month?

(2) Pseudo-scientific

L: my skin/ instead of having normal oily skin like any ord- ordinary teenager/ <LAUGHTER>

L: er my skin in so dry/ [yesterday I I I-
J: [% I've got % [well look at me . I've got oil-
H: [maybe you wash it too much/

L: [it's combination/
J: I've got oil here/ [oily here/ combination/ I've got combination skin/

---

(3) Maternal
H: I know somebody who's just had a baby/ it's about two days old/ really sweet/

(4) Repressive

L: Harriet don't stand over me with your skirt on/ %bloody hell% [...] Harriet <SHRIEKS>
H: I can't help it <WHINEY VOICE>
J: ((it's only some)) knickers Laura/ don't be so prudish/

(5) Romantic love

(i) V: who do you think's the most good looking out of Bros? [...].
J: sometimes I reckon one of the twins/
V: I don't/ I think Craig's the best looking/

(ii) [sings] "I may not be perfect but I'm all yours"
[sings] "Love changes everything"

(6) Liberal

J: and the sound you can- kind of buzzing sound- it's this vibrator thing of Mum of um

J: Harriet's Mum and if you put it round your chin-
L: you're vibrating Harriet's Mum/God/

J: if you put it on your chin- oh god/ . oh come here Vaness/
L: <LAUGHTER> it's a massager/

J: [on your bone it feels really funny/ well what would happen on
V: no/ <WAILS> [...] [it makes my teeth crunch/

J: on on your elbow?/ . not much/ <LAUGHS>

(7) Resistant/feminist

J: [*reading from old copy of* Just 17] have you got a boy friend? what's wrong with you? this looks quite interesting/ [...]
H: I haven't got a boyfriend/ nothing's wrong with me I don't think/

This wide range of discourses is still apparent in the later tapes, made when the girls were 14 and 15. The main difference is that a new discourse has been added to their repertoire, a discourse I shall call Consciousness Raising (CR) or self-disclosure. This is a discourse characterised by the expression of information of a highly personal nature. It is a subjective discourse, in contrast with others in the girls' repertoire. In other words, although other discourses may touch on topics such as bodies or boyfriends, they do not involve intimate self-disclosure. The new discourse makes the girls vulnerable in a way the others do not. Not surprisingly, then, it is also characterised by reciprocity: sections of conversation where this discourse appears normally involve two or more girls in mirroring self-disclosure.[6] I use the label 'Consciousness Raising' with the deliberate aim of calling attention to the similarity between this mode of talk and its antecedents in the consciousness raising of the Women's Liberation Movement, particularly in the 1950s and 1960s, when women would meet in groups for the express purpose of talking about our personal experience, to become empowered through an understanding that our experience was not unique but was shared by other women under patriarchy. It is noteworthy that the girls have mothers who were themselves teenagers in the 1950s and 1960s, and although I am not saying that mothers have explicitly taught their daughters a particular way of talking, it is certainly the case that these girls, like many others of their generation, are growing up in households in which feminism is as routinely accepted as wholemeal bread.

Table 4.1 represents in tabular form the contrast between the discoursal ranges of the girls at two different ages.

Table 4.1 Discoursal range of friendship group, by age

Age 12–13	Age 14–15
Factual/scientific	Factual/scientific
Pseudo-scientific	Pseudo-scientific
Maternal	Maternal
Repressive	Repressive
Romantic love	Romantic love
Liberal	Liberal
Resistant/feminist	Resistant/feminist
.	
.	.
	.
	Consciousness Raising/self-disclosure

The discursive range found in the girls' talk at 14 and 15 years of age is illustrated in examples (8–12) below.

(8) Factual/scientific

(i) V: Laura, what's a jock strap?
L: it's a jo- it's what men use- it's their like their equivalent to a bra/ and they hold their dick up with it/

(ii) J: [talking about periods] I feel bloated . round "the abdominal regions" or whatever you say/

(9) Repressive/patriarchal

(i)

L: why's he always teasing Polly?
H: 'cos [she's got big tits/
V: [((xx)) she's got big tits/

(ii)

H: ((x)) fat thighs/ they are/
J: oh Harriet/ [they're not fat/ .
V: [don't be so horrible/ ah!

J: mine are skinny as a pencil/ . ugh!

(iii) L: I don't want to bitch about this but I I just sort of think she's a bit of a um a little bit of a flirt/

(10) Liberal

V: [*talking about her mother and brother*] oh ((xx)) walking about/ pinning up his trousers/ and he was going "Don't ((xx)) my dick"/ <LAUGHS> and then he said "Don't prick my dick" or something/ and Mum said "Don't you mean your willy?"/ <H LAUGHS> and he went- and he went "My prick"/ and your Mum went- my Mum said "Don't prick your prick"/ <LAUGH> "((xx)) your prick"/ and they were going on and on/ I was going "Mum" <LAUGHTER>

H: oh no how embarrassing/

(11) Resistant/feminist

J: [*talking about boys harassing them by twanging bra straps*] remember in the first year/ [...] and I- and I just turned round and said "I don't wear a bra"/ and they went – <LAUGHS> "So – er er er" like this/ and he got really flustered/

(12) CR/self-disclosure

(i) why is it always that in school that your knickers start going up your bum?

(ii) [*J talks about a boy in their year that she used to fancy*]

J: well when I started fancying him in the SEcond year/ I fancied him ever since then/

L: yeah/ I [s]- I knew that/ sort of/
J: yeah you sort of guessed/ [...]

J: and then/ the real sort of clincher was ((still xx)) and I suddenly-
V: <%LAUGHS%>

J: because I suddenly sort of fancying- you know people say love's [blind/ I think I
V: [oh but d'you

J: thought he was perfect apart from the [((obvious things))/ and I just suddenly have
L: [yeah/
V: think- [mhm/

J: seen how awful he is and horrible/ <PEAL OF LOUD LAUGHTER = release of tension>
L: [yeah/
V: [yeah/ <MATCHING LAUGH>
H: yeah/ <LOW CHUCKLE>

The range of discourses occurring in the girls' talk positions them in a variety of different ways, not all consistent with each other. Even in these short extracts, we can see instances where the discourses come into conflict. For example, in (4), Jenny challenges Laura's repressive discourse, accusing her of being *prudish*; in example (7), Harriet resists the heterosocial pressures of the magazine article; and in example (11), Jenny recounts an incident where she challenges the boys who were sexually harassing her. These examples are not surprising: after all, there is no single unified way of doing femininity, of being a woman. Different discourses give these girls access to different femininities. More mainstream discourses position them in more conventional ways, whereas more radical or subversive discourses offer them alternative ways of being, alternative ways of doing femininity. They are unwittingly involved in the ceaseless struggle to define gender (Weedon 1987).

Intertextuality

As the examples given above demonstrate, this kind of talk between friends is immensely complex: it is far more heterogeneous than, for example, language occurring in the public domain in such contexts as the law courts or Parliament or even the school classroom. And what makes it even more complex and heterogeneous is the intertextuality we find here. These texts are a very clear example of what Bakhtin is talking about when he says 'our speech ... is filled with others' words, varying degrees of otherness and varying degrees of "our-own-ness", varying degrees of awareness and detachment. These words of others carry with them their own expression, their own evaluative tone, which we assimilate, rework and reaccentuate' (1986: 89). The intertextuality in these texts is often 'manifest'; that is, other texts are explicitly marked by being introduced by words like *he says* or *she goes* or by being performed in a noticeably different voice.

Voices

Intertextuality has already been illustrated in example (5), in which the girls sing pop songs; (7), where Jenny reads from a copy of *Just 17*; and (10), where we hear the voices of Vanessa's mother and brother. Further examples are given in (13–16) below.

(13)

H: <LAUGHS> with grandpa it's so funny/ you know when you see sport on television

H: like you're- you're supporting a team/
L: [oorghhh] <SHOUTS IN PSEUDO-MALE VOICE>
Others: <LAUGHTER>

H: if one team is losing you know/ if his team is losing it's "Oh you silly asses/

H: excuse my language/ oh you silly asses"/

(14)
L: he thinks he's god's gift, man, god's gift to women/ . as Kylie says in Neighbours/ she goes "god's sake, you think you're god's gift to women"/

(15)
V: Monica's so weird/ .
J: pardon? <LAUGHTER>
V: Monica sometimes kind of hyper hyper/
J: and sometimes kind of lowper lowper/
V: no and <LAUGHTER> sometimes kind of "We should care for the animals of this world" you know/

(16)
J: [sings] Safeway- everything you want from a store but it costs- it's going to cost a lot more

In example (13), Harriet 'does' her grandfather's voice, adopting a markedly old-fashioned 'posh' accent. In (14), Laura adopts the voice of a character in the soap opera *Neighbours*. In (15), Vanessa uses a different voice to represent the weirdness of their school friend Monica. And example (16), like the examples given in (5), is sung rather than spoken; this one is a (corrupted) advertising jingle for a supermarket chain.

We have already seen how discourses can conflict with one another. The girls frequently subvert the voices they use, particularly where they have marked these as 'other' by adopting another voice. Jenny subverts the advertising jingle given in (16) by altering the words to give a message that is certainly not what the supermarket wants the public to think. And it's Jenny again whose word play (*hyper hyper/lowper lowper*) in example (15) undermines what Vanessa is saying.

Maternal voice

The maternal voice is omnipresent in these texts: the girls refer to and compare their mothers a phenomenal number of times, particularly in the earlier tapes. (As the next section suggests, the maternal voice is to some extent displaced by boys' voices as the girls reach their midteens.) Fathers are referred to infrequently. When the girls compare their mothers, they cannot be said to be competing in the normally accepted sense of the word. There is a sense of amused rivalry at times, but it is essentially playful. The girls' references to their mothers seem to do a great deal of work: they allow them the solidarity of confirming that their mothers are of the same type, and they permit the girls to express a kind of proud affection for these odd, non-teenage beings. There is a tension between a perception of their mothers as women, and a strong sense of them as occupants of a particular role, the mother, to whom they relate as daughters.

Examples (17–19) give some idea of the ways in which mothers' voices are represented in the girls' talk. Example (17) is from a conversation recorded when the girls were 12; examples (18) and (19) are from recordings at age 13.

(17)
V: here's Mum: "oh all the fashions are f- are for short hair and clean bodies aren't they?"/
J: <LAUGHS> who said that?/
V: Mum/
J: clean bodies/ you wouldn't like a dirty body would you?/

(18)
H: you said like seven times in that sentence/
J: <LAUGHS>
L: sorry/ I say like all the time/
V: my mum alway- my mum's always saying "Don't say that"/

(19)

L: my Mum gets . sss- SO angry when people sniff/ <LAUGHTER>

J: it's ((so)). the same with . erm- [no . your Mum it's the hiccups/
H: [MY Mum . my Mum goes neurotic ((xx)) if

H: you sniff/
V: my Mum doesn't mind so much/ but she says "blow your nose/ blow your nose/

V: %blow your [nose%/ <LAUGHS>
L: [oh my Mum goes "for God's sake blow your nose" <SHOUTS> <LAUGHTER>

The girls quote their mothers explicitly, and then defend their opinions, or they say things in their own voices that show how they have internalised the maternal voice. So, in (17) Jenny says *you wouldn't like a dirty body would you?* in support of the position voiced by Vanessa's mother. They are also eager to match each other's claims about their mothers, so after Laura has stated her mother's aversion to sniffing, Harriet makes a matching statement, Vanessa brings in her mother's voice: *Blow your nose!* and, using the same phrase, Laura contrasts her impatient, outraged mother with Vanessa's more quiet, resigned one. Where the mothers' voices appear, they are nearly always presented in a positive light.

Example (20) is an exception. Here Jenny tells a story about her mother's lack of sympathy for her menstrual cramps.

(20)

J: she was saying "You're pathetic/ you're- there's nothing wrong with you/ you don't want to go into school"/ and I just got out of the bath/ and I put my shirt on when I was still wet/ and I said "I don't care/ I'm just going to go into school"/ ... "Oh Jenny don't go"/

In this example, Jenny self-discloses about a painful episode at home. The support she expects (and receives) from her friends is implicitly contrasted with the mother's failure to support her at this particular time. The fact that such examples are rare would suggest that the girls' view of their mothers is positive; only on occasions when their mothers fail to support them – and when they therefore need to gain support from each other – do they seem to be prepared to voice criticism or report events that undercut the positive image of the mother.

Boys' voices

The mothers' voices are present throughout the conversations I've recorded, from when the girls are 12 to when they are 15. But what is striking about the later conversations is the growing prominence of boys' voices. When the girls were younger, the male voices were those of fathers, brothers or grandfathers, or pop stars and characters from soap operas. At age 14 and older, it is real boys they talk about and whose voices we hear in the texts. Examples of boys' voices in the girls' talk are given in examples (21–23).

(21) she jumped out/ and she couldn't get back in/ <LAUGHS> and all the boys were standing and going "What are you doing out there, man?"/

(22) and Keith's sort of going "oh you're too fucking proud to talk to, you're too fucking proud to talk to me"/ ((what do you expect?))/ if they're bloody- ((if)) they bloody swear at us/

(23) I was in the library/ and we were- we were just sitting down and ... [Gerald] just went jumping round the book table and going "HEY"/

<LAUGHTER> ((xx)) like really strange thing going "You like me now?"/ <FAKE VOICE>

The use of words like *fucking* is restricted to contexts like (22), where Laura has adopted a male voice; there is virtually no swearing otherwise. And in example (23), the use of a mock Anglo-Indian accent only occurs in a context like this, where one of the girls is mimicking a boy. In other words, the girls demonstrate an awareness of some of the features which accomplish youthful masculinity, but do not adopt them for their own use (by contrast with aspects of their mothers' voices, which they do make use of themselves).

Three examples in detail

I turn now to three more extended extracts, to give some idea of how these discourses interact, how the different voices are done, how the talk varies in terms of specific linguistic features and how it changes as the girls get older.

The first extract comes from a tape-recording made when the girls were 12 years old; they are in Harriet's bedroom, looking at old photographs.

Text A: Aunts, babies and testicles

[*Harriet shows photos of her two aunts*]

1
H: Mary= ((xx))
V: so that's aunt- =Mary and that's aunt Jane/ ((xAnn)) aunt Ann/

2
H:
J: I've got a great aunt Mary/
V: trum trum <TRUMPETING NOISE> everyone seems to have a

3
H: I have/
J: well I've got a great great
L: haven't even got a great aunt/
V: great aunt Mary/

4
H:
J: aunt Mary/ <LAUGHS> no she's a [step great great aunt Mary/
V: [do you know anyone who's pregnant? everyone seems

5
H: [yeah I [do
J: [no [no I'm not <LAUGHING>
L: [no
V: to be pregnant at the moment/

6

H: I know somebody who's just had a baby/ it's about two days old/

7

H: really sweet/

?: oh! <MOCK MATERNAL>

V: Harriet you always know people who've just had babies

8

H: [babies are dropping out everywhere/

J: did you know that- [did you know that the testicles produce

V: and things/ ((Harriet said))

9

H: yeah [you know- you know that ((xxxx))

J: thirty billion sperm in each month?

L: [did you know <LOUD> ((xxxxxxxxxxxxxxx))

10

L: did you know that the testicles – produce erm oh a thousand every second and six

11

L: million every hour?

V: what- what do they do all their life? <LAUGHTER>

In this extract several different discourses are present, among which we can mention the following: a familial discourse which positions the girls as feminine subjects, 'doing' family concerns (staves 1–4); a maternal discourse, already discussed as example (3) (staves 4–8); and a factual/scientific discourse (which starts at line 8). Note how Vanessa subverts Harriet's maternal discourse in staves 7–8, and how she also subverts Laura's factual/scientific discourse in stave 11.

Linguistically, there are several features of this passage which are worthy of comment:

1. topic change is rapid;
2. speech is tied to ongoing activity: (a) looking at photos; (b) the *did you know* questions arise from reading *Just 17* and a Fact Book;
3. turn-taking patterns are anarchic: the girls are all eager to talk, and they interrupt each other in order to grab the floor (see interruptions in staves 4, 8, 9);
4. information-seeking questions are used to move the conversation along or switch topic;
5. back-channel support is absent: forms like *yes* and *yeah* occur only after direct questions;
6. utterances are unmitigated (in other words, there is a total absence of hedging devices), and disagreement is openly expressed.

The second extract comes from a conversation recorded when the girls are 13 years old. They are all at Harriet's house and are just finishing a meal.

Text B: South African grapefruit juice

1

H: [*reading blurb on Safeways juice carton*] "Del Monte"/ <DELIBERATE VOICE>

2

H: "man from-" oh yeah . I'll go and ask my Mum then/ <LEAVES ROOM>

3

J: what's Mum gonna . ((I mean)) what's Harriet gonna do?
V: ask her if it comes from

4

J: [Del Monte <DELIBERATELY>
V: South Africa probably= [it probably does/
L: =what does? what?

5

H: Laura – Laura . Del Monte is South African/
V: "Del Monte he say Yes" <SING-SONG>
L: it is?

6

H: ((xxx get)) no it is South African/
V: you've got South African grapefruit juice/ <SHOUTS>

7

H: Mum said [it was/
J: [well . she might not be wrong- might
L: [let's hope you never have [it again/

8

J: be wrong/ . ((xx say))
V: my Mum says she doesn't feel strongly about that/

9

H: she should feel strongly/
V: she doesn't/
L: she doesn't or she does? huh/ <TUTTING NOISE>

10

H: 'cos the white people exploit the black people/ to work in factories/

11

H: so they can produce that/
J: erm-
V: well she doesn't/ I asked her if she's going

12

H: what?
J: |my Mum says . that Safeways is a lot more expensive/ my Mum says
V: |to go- ((xx))

13

H: I know/ . so?/
J: that Safeways is a lot more expensive/ you always used to say

14		
H:		[not THAT much
J:	that it wasn't when I said . "it's much more expensive"/ and you	[said-
15		
H:	more expensive/ like . three p more expensive or something/	%no%
V:		not ten p/
16		
H:		[yeah/
J:	even if it's three p "the three ps mount up"/	
V:	<LAUGHS>	[((so to speak))/

At the discursive level, we can observe an a-political discourse, voiced by Vanessa and Vanessa's mother; this discourse is opposed by an anti-racist discourse, voiced by Harriet (staves 1–11). In the second half of the passage, Jenny's 'good housekeeping' discourse is contested by Harriet.

A great deal is going on intertextually in this extract. In staves 1, 2 and 5 we hear snatches of jingles advertising Del Monte products. In staves 8 and 9, we hear Vanessa's mother's views on buying South African produce. In lines 12 and 13, Jenny's mother's voice is heard, while in line 18 Jenny performs herself, reproducing her mother's words. Finally, in stave 16, Jenny defuses the conflict between herself and Harriet by adopting a mock-serious voice which makes a joke of her statement: *the 3 ps mount up*.

At the linguistic level, the following patterns can be observed:

1. topic change is less frenetic;
2. speech is tied in with activity again (the talk here arises from Harriet's reading of the grapefruit juice carton);
3. turn-taking is adversarial: there are examples of interruption in staves 7, 12 and 14, and in both staves 12 and 14 next speaker seizes the turn and stops current speaker from finishing;
4. back-channel support is absent;
5. hedges are absent and conflict is unmitigated: (a) Vanessa and Harriet argue about the ethics of buying South African produce; (b) Jenny and Harriet argue about whether or not Safeways is an expensive place to shop – note Harriet's extremely confrontational challenge in line13: *I know – so?*;

The third extract, Text C, from a conversation recorded when the girls were 14, is longer: one topic (about periods) is sustained over several minutes of talk. The full text is given in the appendix to this chapter (see pp. 98–100).

We can pick out three dominant discourses in Text C: first, a medical/factual discourse which is characterised by lexis related to back aches, headaches, hysteria and PMT (pre-menstrual tension); second, a discourse of Consciousness Raising and self-disclosure; and third, a repressive (or patriarchal) discourse. At the intertextual level, we can observe Jenny 'doing' her Mum in stave 8 (*Is that you coming up to your periods then?*); Jenny and Harriet re-enacting themselves in staves 27 and 28; Jenny adopting Justin's voice in staves 35–36 (*Jenny looks like she's about to burst into tears*); and finally Vanessa saying *oh dear* in a baby voice which signals mock concern.

The linguistic strategies used by the girls have changed dramatically from the earlier conversations. The main characteristics of their talk in this extract are as follows:

1. one topic is sustained over several minutes (and begins before the start of this extract);
2. speech is *not* tied to activity; talk is the sole focus;
3. turn-taking patterns have changed noticeably: there is considerable overlap but overlap is nearly always supportive rather than interruptive (e.g. staves 4,12, 21, 27, 29);
4. there is frequent use of minimal responses (e.g. staves 2, 4, 5, 12, 16, 19, 20, 29, 30, 31, 33);
5. hedges are used, especially *really, just, sort of* (e.g. staves 2, 4, 12, 13, 22, 25, 28, 32).

Finally, I want to return to the discursive patterns manifest in the talk of the 14-year-old girls. The three dominant discourses in this extract – a medical discourse, a discourse of Consciousness Raising and self-disclosure, and a repressive (or patriarchal) discourse – are intertwined. In order to illustrate this intertwining. I shall examine in detail two brief extracts from the text 'Periods'.

The first extract focuses on backache (see Text C, staves 1–5). This passage shows very clearly the way the three discourses are intertwined. The CR discourse manifests itself through patterns of agreement. First, there is a chain of agreement in relation to backache: Jenny initiates this (*my back is connected with my periods*), and the theme is taken up by Vanessa (*I get really bad back ... ache*) and then by Laura (*so do I/ back aches/*). A second chain of agreement revolves around the subject of hot water bottles: Vanessa initiates this (*hot water bottles help*), and her statement is echoed by Harriet and Jenny (*hot water bottles help*) and then by Laura (*help so much*). This pattern of agreement can be termed 'reciprocal self-disclosure'. Other key features of the CR discourse here are lexical repetition, collaborative overlap, and the frequent use of well-placed minimal responses.

At the same time, the girls' choice of lexis such as *bad back* and *back ache* positions them within a medical discourse where periods are understood in a frame of ailments or ill health, with *back rest* and *hot water bottles* coming from a lexical set pertaining to possible cures. A third, repressive discourse is realised in part through syntax. The girls represent themselves as affected rather than as agent (*hot water bottles help me*): the proposition *x helps me* presupposes *I need help.* Verbs are stative: *is, get.* The only agentive verb in this short excerpt occurs in conjunction with the negated modal *can't,* where *can't* means *not able/ not possible*: *I can't go ...* is thus a statement of powerlessness.

Another short extract from later in the same text shows again how the three discourses interact. This passage focuses on premenstrual tension (Text C, staves 23–37). It is part of a lengthier chain of mutual self-disclosure on the subject of mood swings. The three discourses are again simultaneously present. The lexis associated with PMT is part of a medical discourse. The CR discourse expressing solidarity and sisterhood is realised through overlapping turns, expressions of agreement and the joint construction of text (Jenny and Harriet share in constructing the utterance *so whenever I'm on my period I say to Harriet um 'Right I might be horrible to you but don't take any notice'*). Again they jointly represent themselves as affected rather than as agents through their choice of stative verbs – *was, had, got* – and through the use of negative lexis such as *horrible* and *bitch.* Thus the girls are simultaneously positioned as sisters, in a feminist sense, and as oppressed.

Friendship and femininity

Now that we have looked at a few extracts in greater detail, we can try to summarise what is going on in the girls' talk. The two main things that are being 'done' in this talk are friendship and femininity, and these are interlinked in complex ways.

Doing friendship changes as the girls get older. When they are 12 years old, one of the key ways they accomplish friendship is by playing with language. They flip in and out of subject positions, singing snatches of pop songs, chanting advertising slogans, mimicking the voices of mothers, friends and teachers. They also subvert the discourses they use in a variety of ways. They treat topics like coloured balls to be tossed around and then discarded. And, as their laughter testifies, they are having fun doing this. The ludic aspect of the girls' talk is constitutive of friendship: flipping from subject position to subject position constitutes doing friendship for these girls at this age.

But clearly they are also accomplishing femininity. As we have seen, the variety of discourses that appear in these conversations position the girls as different kinds of feminine subject, some of them in direct conflict with each other. This is possible because what has been recorded is backstage talk, to use Erving Goffman's (1971) term. It is one of the functions of backstage that 'the performer can relax' and that 'the team can run through its performance' (Goffman 1971: 115). This allows a degree of experimentation which would be too risky in other contexts.

But as the girls get older, their talk changes. They experiment less, and certain discourses become more prominent: doing friendship now means supporting new ways of doing femininity. It is not that they shift to a completely new set of discourses: as examples (8)–(12) show, there is much that is consistent with the earlier talk. But as they reach ages 14 and 15, the new discourse that I have called CR/self-disclosure emerges as significant, and the ludic aspect of their talk decreases. Life is much more serious: they are struggling with changes in their world and look to each other for support, support that is expressed in the form of matching self-disclosure rather than in more playful ways.

When I first started work on this material, I focused on linguistic features such as minimal responses, turn-taking patterns, hedging. I was amazed at how much the 12-year-olds' talk differed from the talk of adult women friends in my corpus. I was equally amazed at the way they changed over the years, beginning to talk more like adult female speakers. I have to confess that in my excitement about what was going on at the micro-linguistic level I imagined that any paper I gave on the girls' talk would be a sort of triumphalist narrative, showing the girls' development from being relatively anarchic, egocentric conversationalists to being more cooperative, sisterly co-participants in talk.

As I have worked on this chapter, I have realised that such a claim would misrepresent my data. While I want to argue that the girls have become more sophisticated as language users, I also want to assert that this is much less important than what is going on at the discursive level. There seems to me to be a significant difference between the girls' talk when they are young and when they are older. The conversations I've recorded when the girls were 12 and 13 demonstrate convincingly that they are social agents 'capable of resistance and innovations produced out of the clash between contradictory subject positions and practices'

(Weedon 1987: 125). At this age they are not only shaped by the discourses but they also resist and subvert them.

By contrast, there is less evidence of the girls' agency in the later conversations. I was initially fooled by their growing use of the discourse of Consciousness Raising, with its origins in the Women's Liberation Movement, into thinking they were part of a brave new feminist world. But if we look again at Text C ('Periods') we can see how they are positioned here as oppressed, as suffering, as at the mercy of their bodies. They talk about their bodies in a medicalised way which is overwhelmingly negative. Worse, they name themselves as 'bad' (e.g. *I'm a bitch – I'm really horrible*). This later talk shows how well they have internalised the values of patriarchy, and I think we have to ask whether these young white middle-class girls – a privileged group, who will be the professional women of the next generation – are in fact liberated. Or is it more accurate to say that, although they think they are speaking, they are in fact being spoken?

Conclusion

This chapter has looked at a particular group of girls at a particular, transitional, moment in their adolescence. The conversations recorded when they were younger (12 and 13 years old) are snapshots of them at the end of childhood, beginning to identify as teenagers but exploring their world and the discourses available to them in a playful and carefree way. The mood has changed in the conversations recorded in their mid-teens (ages 14 and 15): the girls seem less playful and, as I have demonstrated, are positioned by dominant discourses so that they present themselves as relatively powerless. This is an age which Brown and Gilligan (1992: 4) have described as 'a time of disconnection' for girls.

But it would be wrong to end the chapter on this gloomy note. I interviewed Harriet and Jenny in their late teens (Harriet was 18, Jenny nearly 18), when they were about to leave home and go to university. What struck me in this long (90-minute), loosely structured interview was their positive attitude to life, their confidence and their reflexivity. They were able to reflect on their teenage years in a very clear way. When I suggested to them that their talk had changed and that they had been very different when they were 12, they agreed: for them the significant difference was their new awareness of their feelings. As Jenny says *when you're 12 [...] you don't think about feeling,* and Harriet adds *you experience diff- really differently things between the age of twelve and eighteen.* Now on the brink of leaving home and going to university, they seem comfortable with their sense of themselves as emotional beings. Perhaps girls aged 14/15 struggle with the loss of childhood and with the strong feelings that accompany the changes in their lives (including changes in their bodies). The evidence of this later tape is that 14/15 is a transitional phase between childhood and womanhood, and between egocentric playfulness and emotional maturity. They were for a time relatively impotent in the face of dominant discourses, but by 18 they seem much better equipped to deal with the world; it is noticeable that they now present themselves as agents in their lives rather than as powerless.

To give an example, their talk about boys has changed considerably. There is no giggling and screaming about 'fancying' boys; instead they talk in a matter-of-fact way about 'real' boys. Boys have mutated into people you can have friendships with as well as go out with. Jenny talks about a boy who is one of her 'really good friends': *I can phone him up and sort of be really rude to him and he just goes "oh shut up" like that and whereas if I did that to a girl they might sort of go "ooh what's wrong?" and stuff [...] I don't know, it's completely different and I really like it.* Harriet, who has spent two years at an International School, now has as many friends who are boys as are girls. She also talks about boyfriends – the most recent boyfriend lasted a year, though she comments that they argued a lot (*we were always arguing*) whereas she and Jenny never argue. Jenny, by contrast, says she doesn't have a boyfriend, and voices a subversive discourse which questions the inevitability of the heterosocial order. After describing her older sister's pattern of being in love with one boy after another, she says *from a young age I just sort of saw it as a bit of a dodgy thing I think . and that's part of the reason why [...] it doesn't figure as a very important point in my life/ I've got really- I think I've got some really really good friends.* This new ability to question and subvert the dominant discourses, in particular patriarchal and heteronormative discourses, is linked to the girls' new stronger awareness of the importance of female friendship.

This awareness is one of the most prominent features of the informal interview: the girls assert the value of their friendships (both within the group and their particular best-friendship) and the significance of these friendships in their passage through their teens. As Jenny puts it, friendship is important because it means *just having someone that you can just be yourself with ... with Harriet and my older friends I feel completely I can be myself entirely.* Jenny's emphasis on *being myself entirely* brings us back to the question of identity. This chapter has explored the changing identities of girls through close analysis of conversational data. I have argued that the girls' sense of their femininity is at times contradictory and precarious, and I have attempted to show how 'doing femininity' changes as the girls get older. But the construction of identity does not stoop at the age of 15 or 18. It is an ongoing and constantly contested process. Like all of us, these girls are involved in the struggle to define gender: 'The nature of femininity and masculinity is one of the key sites of discursive struggle for the individual' (Weedon 1987: 98). But the evidence of the interview data suggests that the outlook for young women like Harriet, Jenny, Laura and Vanessa is not as bleak as might be suggested by their talk in their mid-teens. By the time they reach 18 they are much clearer about who they are and what they want and about the value of female friendship. In the long term, it is friendships like these that help us to resist particular versions of femininity and to prefer others, as well as to reconcile contradictory femininities. Although the evidence from adult women speakers is far from unilaterally positive (see Coates 1996a, 1997c), it would seem that girls in their mid-teens have a particularly difficult time. Yet during this stage they learn new ways of talking and become aware of the importance of friendship as they struggle to 'be themselves'.

Appendix

Text C: Periods

1
J: my back- my back is connected with my periods and I

2
J: ((xx)) yeah/
L: [so do I/ I get
V: so's mine/ I get really bad back [ei]- [back ache down there/

3
J: ((xxx))
L: ((get)) back aches- I can't go like that/ and I can't go like

4
J: <QUIET LAUGH> [yeah/
L: that and I just ((xx)) a back rest/
V: [but . [ho] hot water bottles help/

5
H: [hot water bottles help me [as well/
J: [hot water bottles help/
L: [help so much/ yeah it's lovely/

.
.
.

6
J: well whenever there's anything wrong with me/ whenever I'm feeling at all

7
J: upset/ or I've got a headache or something/ my Mum always thinks it's my

8
J: period/ she says "Is that you coming up to your periods then?"/

9
H: <LOW LAUGH> <LAUGH>
J: and I say "No – it's ((xx)) weeks away actually"

10
H: [well
L: ((sometimes I'm just sitting there)) [like- I suddenly feel as if I'm

11
H: [I was lying in the bath-
L: going to cry right/ [((xx)) suddenly- it just suddenly your eyes
?: [yes

12
J: [your
L: like this/ if your face goes hot/ and you- then it just goes [((xx))
?: oh right/ mhm/

13
J: eyes sting/ your nose is-
L they sudden- they just like comes ((like a heat wave))/

14
H: [well what-
J: it feels like your nose is just sort of . expanding/ [or something/
L: [it sometimes

15
L: happens in a lesson/ you're just sort of sitting there going-

16
H: [well what happened
J: I get that- [I got that last time [((xxxxxxxxxxxxxxx))
L: it goes "hwoom"/ [yeah/
V: [((xxxx))

17
H: to me was . it was one day this week/ and I was just SO hysterical/

18
H: and I was lying in the bath/ and I was sobbing/ I sobbed s- constantly

19
H: for half an hour/ and I was just getting so- and every time I
J: mhm/

20
H: I dropped the soap or something [in the bath water/ I'd go "aaah"/
J: [yes I know I get so-

21
H: I'd scream/ and I'd go like this/ and every time I dropped the top or

22
H: something- and like everything seemed to be going wrong and

23
H: everything/ it was horrible [...] it was really horrible [that day/
V: [but you know

24
L: [do you get PMT? ((xx))
V: when I had [that really bad . um pre-menstrual tension?

25
H: <LAUGHS> <LAUGHS> so I've
J: yeah I'm a bitch/ <LAUGHS> I'm REally HORrible/

26
H: noticed/ [no/ no but [some-
J: [no but- [so whenever I'm on my period/ I say to Harriet

27
H: ="Right I might be horrible to you but- [can you-
J: um= "Don't take [any notice"/

28
H: some of you move up ((xx))
J: [no but remember that time I had really
L: [which ((xx)) which ((xx))

29
J: really bad back pain/ . it was on a Friday/
L: yeah I know/

30
H: yeah
J: and remember I cried after school/ I cried IN school as well and

31
H: really?
J: nobody noticed/ yeah/ [yeah it was in SPACE*/ and I was just
V: [when was this?

32
J: crying/ and I was sitting really upright/ . and I sort of just buried

33
J: my head/ and I cried/ not for very long/ just sort of .
V: mhm/

34
J: [a few tears/ I know/ and Jus- and I just looked up
V: [I hate it when no-one notices/

35
J: like this/ and and Justin said "Jenny looks like she's about to burst

36
J: into tears" <LAUGHS> like this/ and ((xxx)) he's the only person that

37
J: noticed/
V oh dear/ <BABY VOICE>

[* SPACE = Social, Personal and Careers Education]

Notes

1. Earlier versions of this chapter were given to the Roehampton Institute Language Research Group, Sociolinguistics Symposium 10 (Lancaster University, England) and the 3rd Berkeley Women and Language Conference. I am grateful to all those who gave me helpful comments and criticism; in particular, I'd like to thank Joanna Thornborrow for her insightful contributions to my thinking about discourses.
2. An exception in the specific area of grammatical variation is Edina Eisikovits' (1988) study which compared the talk of 13-year-olds and 16-year-olds in Sydney, Australia, and which showed how girls' speech moved closer to standard norms as they got older, whereas boys increased their use of non-standard forms.
3. I use the term 'discourse' both in the more linguistic sense of 'a way of speaking associated with a particular worldview' and in the broader sense of 'social practice' (Fairclough 1989; Lee 1992).
4. I cannot express too warmly my gratitude to Harriet, Jenny, Laura and Vanessa for participating in this research and for allowing me to use transcripts of their conversations. (Note: their real names are used throughout as this is what they wanted.) Transcription conventions are given on pp. xiii–xv.
5. The question of whether the issue is one of loss of self-esteem (see Brown and Gilligan 1992; Pipher 1994) or more of power and ideology (see Fairclough 1992; Weedon 1987) is one that deserves further exploration. Whereas these white middle-class girls become more interactionally constrained as they move into adolescence, for many African American and Latina girls, language in interaction continues to be an important resource for personal agency (see Goodwin 1999; Mendoza-Denton 1999).
6. Mirroring is a key structural principle of the talk of adult women (Coates 1996a).

5

Women Behaving Badly: Female Speakers Backstage [2000]

In this chapter,[1] I want to explore women's (and girls') self-presentation in contexts where they seem most relaxed, most off-record. I shall draw on the work of Erving Goffman in this analysis, in particular on his notions of 'frontstage' and 'backstage' (Goffman 1971). Like Goffman, I define myself as 'an anthropological fieldworker whose "tribe" [is] the unnoticed world of everyday interaction under our own noses' (Collins 1988: 44). I shall focus on those aspects of women's backstage performance of self which do not fit prevailing norms of femininity, in other words, women's performance of 'not-nice' selves, as well as reports of – and fantasies about – behaving 'badly'. I shall argue that the backstage talk possible only with close friends provides women with an arena where norms can be subverted and challenged and alternative selves explored.

Women and 'being nice'

In 1996, Jenny Joseph's poem 'Warning' was voted Britain's favourite post-war poem in a BBC poll. This is how it begins:

When I am an old woman I shall wear purple
With a red hat which doesn't go, and doesn't suit me.
And I shall spend my pension on brandy and summer gloves
And satin sandals, and say we've no money for butter.
I shall sit down on the pavement when I'm tired
And gobble up samples in shops and press alarm bells
And run my stick along the public railings
And make up for the sobriety of my youth.
I shall go out in my slippers in the rain

And pick flowers in other people's gardens
And learn to spit ...

The poem's popularity suggests that its message – a woman threatening that in her old age she will overthrow the constraints of conventional femininity – has struck a chord with many women. The poem celebrates a woman who dares to challenge conventional norms, a woman who declares that she will refuse to conform. Conformity here involves appearance, domestic duties and behaving 'nicely'; challenging these norms means behaving 'badly' and having fun.

I do not want to suggest that women never have fun and never behave 'badly', except backstage. In recent times there have been many examples of young high-profile media women doing 'behaving badly' frontstage (examples are Amy Winehouse, Charlotte Church, Britney Spears, Paris Hilton)[2]. The popularity of the British television comedy series *Absolutely Fabulous*, where the two main characters behave outrageously, also suggests a growing fascination with, and tolerance of, women leading independent lives. But the reaction of the tabloid press to an incident when Melanie Blatt of AllSaints exposed her abdomen on stage at a concert – she was five months pregnant at the time – indicates that while women may now feel able to challenge the norms in public, such behaviour is still perceived as unladylike and shocking. In other words, the norms of conventional – hegemonic – femininity are still in place.

Doing femininity according to these norms crucially involves being 'nice'. The ideal of femininity, established in the nineteenth century, is the 'perfect wife and mother', the epitome of niceness (Purvis 1987: 255). Brown and Gilligan (1992) have explored in moving detail the struggles that girls have with the social pressure to be nice. Their study involved nearly 100 girls between the ages of 7 and 18, students at the Laurel School for Girls (a private day school in Cleveland, Ohio). They suggest that adolescence is, for girls, 'a time of disconnection' when they struggle 'over speaking and not speaking, knowing and not knowing, feeling and not feeling' (Brown and Gilligan 1992: 4). They show how a girl feels that 'people will not be nice to her if she is not nice to them' (1992: 60). But the girls interviewed by Brown and Gilligan are aware that being nice to others often involves them in hiding what they really feel, in not saying what they really feel. This dilemma continues into adulthood. Adult women feel under pressure to be nice, but also need to express the whole range of feelings, nice and less nice.

The same is not true for men. In the extract from the poem given above, for example, the woman's threat that she will learn to spit violates a norm about adult *female* behaviour in Britain today, not adult male behaviour: no one is shocked by the sight of a man spitting in the street or on the football pitch. Moreover, it seems that in the late twentieth century, while women feel obliged to try to behave nicely, male speakers will overtly deny niceness. A good example of this is Pilkington's (1998) study of the backstage talk of four groups of same-sex speakers. Her analysis of their talk revealed striking gender differences: 'The men ... frequently abuse one another. ... [They] often made comments that indicated that they looked upon this abusive behaviour as a positive thing and polite behaviour as something negative. Jim says to Ray at one point, "Don't try to make out that I'm nice"; he then goes on to comment, "I like complete bastards"' (Pilkington 1998: 267). The contrast between Jim's insistence that he is *not* nice and the struggles of the girls interviewed by Brown and Gilligan to conform to ideals of feminine 'niceness' is striking.[3]

It seems that, in the modern world, 'behaving badly' has positive connotations when associated with men, but negative connotations when associated with women. This means that certain kinds of behaviour are taboo for women. Yet the evidence of the poem I started with is that there is a strong desire in women to challenge these constraints.

Frontstage and backstage

So where is this challenge expressed? I shall draw on Goffman's (1971) dramaturgical metaphors of 'frontstage' and 'backstage' to explore the way women deal with aspects of the self which do not accord with conventional norms of femininity. For all of us, frontstage performance is much more carefully controlled, and much more susceptible to prevailing norms of politeness and decorum. Informal personal conversations are widely acknowledged to be backstage activity. This does not mean that in interaction with friends we are not performing, but the distinction between performer and audience is blurred: there is a sense of 'all-in-together', and failures in performance cease to be a worry. 'There can be plenty of performance failures here [i.e. backstage]: in fact the sharing of such failures as they actually transpire is what makes up the "informality" of the talk, and the sense of ease and intimacy of selves that goes with it' (Collins 1988: 56). This means that burping or sneezing in the middle of an utterance to a friend will actually underline the friendliness of the encounter.

Given the constraints on appropriate behaviour for women in public spaces, even today, it is not surprising that women have always had a particular relish for the 'sense of ease and intimacy of selves' that goes with informal backstage talk. Goffman himself noticed that women's interaction with other women provides a particularly good example of backstage. In *The Presentation of Self in Everyday Life* he quotes a long extract from Simon de Beauvoir's *The Second Sex* which ends as follows:

> With other women, a woman is behind the scenes; she is polishing her equipment, but not in battle; she is getting her costume together, preparing her make-up, laying out her tactics; she is lingering in dressing gown and slippers in the wings before making her entrance on the stage; she likes this warm, easy, relaxed atmosphere. ... For some women this warm and frivolous intimacy is dearer than the serious pomp of relations with men. (de Beauvoir quoted in Goffman 1971: 115)

In this chapter I shall draw on a corpus[4] of both mixed and same-sex conversation gathered over 15 years with the aim of exploring the speaking practices of (white, middle- and working-class) women and men with their friends, in pairs and in larger groups. Speakers ranged in age from 12 to 50 years old. The corpus consists of spontaneously occurring conversations, recorded with the agreement of the participants in settings chosen by the participants themselves: in the case of the women this was invariably the home, apart from one group of adolescent girls who recorded themselves in a room in their local youth club. (This contrasts with male participants, who chose a wide range of settings: in their homes, in pubs, in a university office after hours, in a youth club, even in a garden shed in the case of one group of (dope-smoking) adolescent boys.)

Women's backstage talk

Backstage talk can be described as 'performers' shop talk' (Collins 1988: 56). One of the things women friends do with each other is talk over their performance frontstage, describing the feelings that accompanied the performance. During such talk, women will often say things which contradict the polite front maintained during the performance. Such contradictions are an intrinsic part of backstage talk: 'A back region or backstage may be defined as a place, relative to a given performance, where the impression fostered by the performance is knowingly contradicted as a matter of course' (Goffman 1971: 114).

The following extract[5] from a conversation between two young women friends illustrates this nicely. One of the friends (Ann) has complained of having a bad day at work.

(1)

1
JUDE: why did you have a bad day?
ANN: got into work this morning

2
JUDE: oh dear/ [how did you break them?
ANN: and broke two mugs/ then [er-

3
JUDE: [what did they say?
ANN: dropped 'em/ <LAUGHS> [then er I got all the bloody

4
ANN: snotty customers/ stupid people/ . had one lady who er

5
ANN: bought twelve glasses/ and I was wrapping them all up/

6
ANN: and she'd told me after I'd wrapped six of them up/

7
ANN: "Can you take the price off the bottom of them"/

8
ANN: stupid cow/ "Yes certainly Madam"/ so I unwrapped

9
ANN: them all and rewrapped them/

Ann's story of her 'bad day' makes very clear distinctions between frontstage and backstage. In her frontstage persona, she describes herself as answering the customer politely and doing what she is asked to do without question. The two speakers also implicitly acknowledge that breaking things at work is a failure of performance. At the same time, Ann intersperses her narrative with comments which tell Jude what she really felt at work. She refers to the customers she'd served as *bloody snotty customers* and *stupid people* (staves 3–4), and her comment *stupid cow* (stave 8) about one particular customer is juxtaposed with her acting out of her own super-polite persona saying to this customer *Yes certainly Madam.*

So in this example, Ann tells the story of her day to a friend and presents herself in a way which directly contradicts the impression she had carried off at work. At work, the exigencies of her role as a (female) shop worker require her to perform herself as 'nice'; at home, talking to a close friend, she performs a very different self, one who is not nice, who is rude about the customers and who resents doing what they ask. We have to infer that 'behaving badly' like this backstage – that is, owning our less nice, our more impolite and unsociable feelings – is accepted and even welcomed between friends, precisely because backstage is the appropriate arena for dropping your front, and because reciprocal admissions of 'not-niceness' reinforce solidarity.

I want to look now at the backstage talk of some very young speakers, three four-year-old girls. This example provides a very striking case of female speakers performing 'not-nice' selves, in the context of fantasy play. The three speakers here (G1, G2 and G3) are playing with dolls in the 'Wendy Corner' of their British nursery kindergarten class. The girls decide in their personae as Mothers that they need to bath the babies. They move through a sequence of utterances: 'G3 suggests the water is hot; G2 says "Let's boil the babies"; G1: "Yes let's boil them and boil them"; G2: "We'll boil them till their skins fall off"' (Cook-Gumperz 2001: 43).

This example comes from data collected by Jenny Cook-Gumperz in research exploring the role of play – specifically the role of talk in play – in the formation of gender identity. Girls' pretend play often involves games where girls enact domestic scenarios (see also Goodwin 1988, 1990). In modern Western societies, learning to be a woman involves learning how to be a 'good mother', to the extent that 'An idealised figure of the Good Mother casts a long shadow' over the lives of girls and women (Ruddick 1989: 31; see also Weedon 1987: 33–34). Play has a key role in this learning. Cook-Gumperz argues that 'one important function of the game [of Mummies and Babies] is to allow the ... girls, in their game talk, to explore their gender role as women' (Cook-Gumperz 1995: 416). But clearly, the game *is* a game and the girls are aware of this: they exploit the backstage nature of their play together away from adults (though in this case not away from the concealed tape-recorder) to explore the role of women as mother by pushing at the limits, and by acting out being *bad* mothers.

The expression of such violent and blatantly un-maternal feelings by four-year-old girls is simultaneously amusing and shocking. The expression of similar un-maternal feelings in relation to real children by adult women is much more shocking. The next example (example 2) comes from a conversation between three women in their 30s who have been friends for many years.

(2)

1

ANNA: some people when they have children just think- just

2

ANNA: assume that everybody loves kids/ [that everybody
SUE:
LIZ: oh I know/ [they do/

3

ANNA: they know [all they have to [do-
SUE: [((xxx)) [who wants to see them))
LIZ: [especially theirs/

4

ANNA: it's like Michael's sister was like that wasn't she?=
SUE: =mhm/
LIZ:

5

ANNA: "you must love [((2 sylls))/ they're so wonderful"/
SUE: [they were HORrible/
LIZ:

6

ANNA: and they were GHASTly children/
SUE:
LIZ: nobody ever says

7

LIZ: that do they/ <LAUGHING>

In this example, we see the three friends exploring the clash between the assumption that *everybody loves kids* (stave 2) and that all children are *wonderful* (stave 5) and the reality that some children are *not* wonderful – *they were horrible* (stave 5); *they were ghastly children* (stave 6). There is explicit acknowledgement that to call children 'horrible' or 'ghastly' is taboo – Liz says *nobody ever says that do they* (staves 6–7). This is an interesting comment, since the three women are in fact saying precisely that. Liz's remark can be understood to mean 'nobody ever says that when they are frontstage'. The frontstage performance of Woman/Mother entails certain sorts of behaviour and precludes others. Saying 'children are wonderful' is expected, but saying 'children are horrible' is taboo. The fact that these women feel able to express subversive views with each other demonstrates the backstage nature of women's friendly talk. These women exemplify very clearly Goffman's description of backstage as a place where 'the performer can relax; he [*sic*] can drop his front, forgo speaking his lines, and step out of character' (1971: 115). These women are relaxed: they have dropped their front, and stepped out of character.

Having agreed that they have negative feelings about some children, the three friends go on to consider their attitude to children in general.

This next extract from their conversation is initiated by Anna, the only one of the three who does not have children.

(3)

1

ANNA: can I just ask you two as mothers/ did you used

2

ANNA: to feel particularly fond of children before you

3

ANNA: had them?=
SUE: =no/= how can I say that? I used to
LIZ: =no/

4

ANNA: [you did didn't you/
SUE: work with them/<LAUGHS> [but no/
LIZ:

5

ANNA:
SUE: no/
LIZ: I didn't/ I wasn't very maternal at all/ - no/

6

ANNA: 'cos Janet and I without [children .
SUE:
LIZ: [you just get used to them/

7

ANNA: you know you feel- you DO feel a bit mean sometimes/

8

ANNA: but I just can't understand that assumption that people

9

ANNA: have that everybody loves-
SUE: you can't go round-
LIZ:

10

ANNA: [((xx)) certain children . I
SUE: I wouldn't expect [anybody to((xxx)) my child/
LIZ: [no I wouldn't/

11

ANNA: really like/ but parents [like that ((just))-
SUE:
LIZ: [I think it's- I think

12

ANNA:
SUE:
LIZ: it's a- . a fallacy as well that you like every

13

ANNA: no/ . that's right/
SUE: [mhm/ I still
LIZ: child/ ['cos you don't/

14
ANNA: <LAUGHS>
SUE: quite often don't like children/ <LAUGHS>
LIZ: actually

15
LIZ: I think you particularly dislike your own/

Here we see a subtle shift from the proposition 'some children are horrible' to the proposition 'I don't like every child' (*I think it's a fallacy as well that you like every child*, Liz, staves 11–13), and from here to the even more taboo proposition 'I don't like children' (Sue and Liz both say *no* in stave 2 in response to Anna's question *did you used to feel particularly fond of children before you had them?*, and Sue says *I still quite often don't like children* in staves 13–14). This shift is marked syntactically by a change in grammatical subject. The earlier propositions involved sentences where the subject of the sentence is 'children', for example, *they were horrible* or *they were ghastly children* (note that the women's involvement is not marked syntactically in these sentences). By contrast, the later propositions position the women as the (pronominal) subjects, through the use of 'I' or the impersonal pronoun 'you'. Liz's final utterance (*actually I think you particularly dislike your own*, staves 14–15) marks a further step in bringing the propositions close to home: here Liz not only has women as the pronominal subject (*you*) but transforms the children from some generalised group to specific children – 'your own' – in other words, precisely that sub-set of children who, in your frontstage performance, you are not allowed to be un-maternal towards.

The backstage talk we see here is highly subversive. Dominant discourses of femininity (and of motherhood) do not allow for the expression of negative feelings about children. Anna, Sue and Liz support each other in sustaining a radically different discourse, one which challenges the idea of women as loving, caring, nurturing beings for whom having children is the ultimate experience of their lives.

The next two examples come from conversation between a different group of women friends, women who are about ten years older than Anna, Sue and Liz, and who live in the north of England rather than the south. One of the women – Meg – talks about meeting an old friend, Jean, whom she has felt estranged from since her divorce. She then goes on to tell a story about the rivalry between her son and Jean's son, where she openly expresses her negative feelings towards Jean's husband, Stan, and her unconcealed pleasure at their son's failure to get a brilliant degree, despite his early promise.[6]

(4)

[Stan's] one of those few- one of the few people in the world that I feel deeply spiteful towards,
and it's all to do with his son and my son.
My son's a little bit older than his son,
but when they were both young lads about fourteen or something,
he said to me, "Well you know Jacob isn't of the same calibre as Max,
and <u>Max is a genius</u> <SLOW AND PRECISE>
and er you know thi- not many people are blessed with having a genius as a child".
[Sally: *oh god.*]
[Bea: *was he still wetting the bed at this stage?]*
but it was true that Max's incredibly creative child,
he could do absolutely everything,
he w- he made fantastic Meccano models,
and he was the brightest boy they'd ever had in his- in the previous school,
and he went to Birkenhead School ((on a)) scholarship.
[...]
Well he became a religious maniac
which I thought was a lovely come-uppance because they're socialists and Marxists
and it was very difficult for them to cope with.
Anyway Max got a 2.2!
[Jen: *oh fantastic! I always thought he was dull as ditchwater.*]

The talk that follows this story shows Meg working hard to contextualise it; in other words, she feels the need to make clear that she would only behave in the way the story portrays in particular circumstances.

(5)

1
MEG: you know how er to some people you kind of e- exaggerate

2
MEG: about your children/ most people you play them down

3
MEG: and say what absolute rogues and rotters they are/

4
MEG: but one- one- the the the she- they represent the few

5
MEG: people that I f- feel I have to boast about my [children/
BEA: [mhm/

6
MEG: so I gave this .hh SPLENdid account of my kids you see/

7
MEG: and I er I went on about this ex- extraordinary job that

8 ———
MEG: Jacob's got or GOing to have/ and of course he's

9 ———
MEG: nowhere near this job working [in a Trade Union/
BEA: [this Trade Union/

10 ———
MEG: 'cos I just think it sounds nice you see/ <LAUGHING>
BEA: yes/

11 ———
MEG: and I could see that Jean also thought it sounded nice/

12 ———
MEG: because they are very political people/ [((xxxx))
BEA: [mhm/
JEN: yes it would

13 ———
MEG: yes/ [absolutely/
JEN: absolutely fit their idea of what their [son should-

14 ———
MEG: and then I said "oh what did you say Max was doing?"/

15 ———
MEG: and she said "oh he's working at Harwell"/

16 ———
MEG: I thought "oooh god" you know/ ((it's something with
BEA: ((2 sylls))

17 ———
MEG: [nuclear-)) yes/ a [tomic/ . I mean he may be
SALLY: [oh yes/ nuclear/ [gosh/

18 ———
MEG: on the side of n- antinuc [but-
BEA: ((doesn't sound
JEN: [oh I doubt it/ I very much
SALLY: ((xxxxxxxxxxxxx

19 ———
MEG:
BEA: like it))
JEN: doubt it/ it's part of the Establishment=
SALLY: xxxxxx)) =yes it is/

20 ———
MEG: mhm/
BEA: [i- isn't it awful the way
SALLY: oh [gosh/

21 ———
BEA: you DO get set up with some people though/

22 ———
BEA: where you- you- you'd actually take pleasure-

23 ———
BEA: instead of taking pleasure in the triumphs

24 ———
BEA: of their children= and thinking oh isn't it-
MEG: =yeah/

25
BEA: it- . you know isn't it wonderful that's Emma's got

26
BEA: distinction in her . violin exam or something/ [...]

27
BEA: you think "yeah - she fails! innit great!" <GROWLY VOICE>
MEG: yeah/

28
BEA: you know/i- i- i- [it's horrid/ but I've got people
SALLY: yeah/ [it's horrid/ yes/

29
BEA: that I feel like that/

This discussion is followed by a story from Bea, which continues the theme of delighting in the failure of a friend's – or ex-friend's – child. Serial story-telling, where speakers in turn tell anecdotes on a common theme, is a common feature of friendly talk (see Galloway Young 1987; Shepherd 1997; Norrick 2005). In women's talk, serial story-telling often takes the form of reciprocal self-disclosure (Coates 1996a, 1996b).

(6)

I feel like that about a friend of mine who lives in New York
who's- well she refers to her son as her little star,
and that doesn't help.
and when I arrived at the- at the- at her apartment to stay,
and she and her husband were both out at their exciting jobs in publishing,
and this lad of s- of seven or eight let me in,
and asked if he could make me some coffee.
[Sally: *oh he is a little star then.*]
You know he IS a little star,
and he's so perfect that you just want to jump up and down 'im
and see if he'd squish you know,
[...]
and I'm so hoping that something marvellous will happen
and he'll run away from home
and – or you know something will squelch this ...

These two stories and the discussion which accompanies them are again classic backstage talk: the women friends feel able to let down their fronts, to drop their normal 'nice' scripts. Both stories tell of ex-friends who offended or irritated the narrators in one way or another, and both stories declare the narrator's pleasure in the failure (real or imagined) of the ex-friend's offspring. Meg's presentation of Stan through reported speech portrays him negatively – as a parent who is insensitive to others (through his comparison of his son and Meg's) and who has ridiculously inflated ideas about his son (the reality being that he only got a lower second-class degree). Speakers exploit reported speech to adopt a variety of voices, and to animate characters in their stories in ways which fit the bias of their story. Reported speech has an important evaluative function in story-telling (Maybin 1996) and women talking backstage explore alternative femininities through playing with different voices.

One thing that stands out about these two stories is that both Meg and Bea describe their feelings with relish: they make no attempt to hedge what they are saying. Meg says *[Stan's] one of the few people in the world that I feel deeply spiteful towards.* Admitting to feeling 'deeply spiteful' about someone is not part of women's normal frontstage performance. Bea's story reveals her irritation with (and possibly envy of) her New York friend, in particular her exciting job in publishing and her son who she calls a 'little star'. (This phrase irritates her since it contravenes the norm that mothers should be modest about their children's talents and should refrain from eulogising them in public.) Bea's remark *and he's so perfect that you just want to jump up and down 'im and see if he'd squish you know* (lines 9–10) is not only not maternal and not-nice, it also betrays feelings of violence which are outside the range of 'normal' femininity. But Bea's words express a fantasy, and so are more comparable to the little girls' *let's boil the babies* than to Meg's gloating over Stan's son's mediocre degree.

Celebrating deviant women

The evidence I've looked at so far involves women exposing their not-nice selves to each other either through discussion of not-nice, un-feminine feelings, or through recounting past actions which show them behaving 'badly', or through sharing fantasies about behaving 'badly'. I now want to look at another strategy common in women's talk which has an important role to play in the expression of 'not-niceness'. It has been widely observed that women monitor and attempt to control community norms through discussing *other* women's behaviour (Goodwin 1990; Eckert 1993, 1998; Coates 1996a). These observations have often focused on the way groups position themselves in opposition to the values or attitudes betrayed by third parties, that is, by querying or criticising or even condemning the behaviour of others. But this same strategy – the discussion of others' actions – can be used as an opportunity to celebrate 'bad' behaviour, and has the great advantage of simultaneously keeping the speakers at one remove from such overtly 'bad' behaviour. The next example (example 7) is an extract from a conversation about Anna's mother, who, Anna claims, is *such a character* (stave 6).

(7)

1 ———
SUE: it's not kind of your normal family when you go up to

2 ———
ANNA: [.hh she used to be-
SUE: Anna's Mum's/ she's- she's [quite an exciting lady/

3 ———
ANNA: she used to be [so- she used to be so
LIZ: [are they Liverpool born and bred?

4 ———
ANNA: beautiful when she was [young my mother/
SUE: [yes/

5 ———
ANNA: so beautiful/ %no [no%/
SUE: [but she I mean she's a great laugh/

6 ———
ANNA: oh she's such a character/
SUE: she's great fun/

7 ———
ANNA: mhm/ -
SUE: yeah/ she really is/ . she was the one

8 ———
SUE: who went out and said to those people

9 ———
ANNA:
SUE: "Did you know Susan's a vegetarian?" <WHISPERS>
LIZ: <SHRIEK OF LAUGHTER>

10 ———
ANNA: she's a [really-
SUE: ((xxxxxxxxxxxxxxxxxx laughing))
LIZ: [as if this was a crime/

11 ———
ANNA: she's a major embarrassment/
SUE: yeah/ <LAUGHING>

12 ———
ANNA: do you know what she did recently?

This question leads into a series of stories, all told by Anna, which demonstrate Anna's mother's eccentricity: in the first, the mother pulls a jogger's tracksuit bottoms down after he claims that her dog has bitten him;[7] in the second she puts up tents in the garden, complete with electricity and TV, because a visitor is allergic to her cats; in the third Anna herself meets a boy on the beach who announces that Anna's mother is adopting him. At this point Liz comments *It must really be fun to have a mother like that* and Anna tells the fourth story, which recounts how her mother arrived a her ex-husband's funeral:

(8)

when my father died last year
she came down to the funeral
and she got a train <LAUGHING> . she got a train that got into Euston at about-
she got the sleeper
and it got into Euston about six thirty in the morning,
and she said to Charles and I "I'll get the train to Esher,
just make sure that the answering machine's not on and that you're up,
so that somebody can come and get me from Esher station",
and I was staying with my stepmother to keep her company,
so it was all in Charles's hands,
and of course he forgot,
he was fast asleep in bed,
so my mother gets to Esher station at seven thirty in the morning.
and there's no Charles
and its pouring with rain
so . what does she do?
she walks round the corner,
sees that there's a milk depot, a Unigate milk depot,
and she walked in,
and she asked one of the milkmen to give her a lift to the house, <LAUGHING>
and she arrived on a milk float <LAUGHING> for my dad's funeral. <CHUCKLING>

As the fuller transcript below shows, Anna's friends respond to this story with a great deal of laughter, some of it almost uncontrollable:

(9)

1 ---

ANNA: so what does she do? she walks round the corner/

2 ---

ANNA: sees that there's a milk depot- a Unigate Milk depot/
SUE: <LAUGHS>

3 ---

ANNA:
SUE: <LAUGHS> oh yeah/ <LAUGHS>
LIZ: <SHRIEKS WITH LAUGHTER> "I've been on a milk fl-

---

4 ———————————————————
ANNA: and she walked in and she asked one of the
LIZ: milk lorry"/
5 ———————————————————
ANNA: milkmen to give her a lift to my house/ <LAUGHING>
6 ———————————————————
ANNA: and she arrived on a milk float
SUE: I bet she did/ <LAUGHING> <LAUGHS>
LIZ: <LAUGHS>
7 ———————————————————
ANNA: for my dad's funeral/ <LAUGHING> oh my god <LAUGHING>
SUE: <LAUGHS>
LIZ: <LAUGHS>
8 ———————————————————
ANNA:
SUE: . oh I love it/ it's so funny/ <LAUGHING>
LIZ: <LAUGHS>

Sue's comment *oh I love it/ it's so funny/* (in stave 8) is an explicit recognition of the positive pleasure such a story provides. Anna's mother, who features in many stories told by Anna to her friends, is an unconventional character who allows for the discussion of unusual, un-feminine behaviour – and for the celebration of such behaviour. Note that the three friends position Anna's mother as out of the ordinary (*it's not kind of your normal family when you go up to Anna's Mum's* – example 7, stave 1), yet speak of her in positive terms (*she's quite an exciting lady* – example 7, stave 2; *she's a great laugh/ she's great fun/* – example 7, staves 5–6; *oh she's such a character* – example 7, stave 6).

The story concerns an everyday event – a family funeral – but the ingredients are unconventional from the start, since the dead man will be mourned by both his ex-wife (Anna's mother) and his second wife (Anna's step-mother). What makes the story so funny is the incongruity of an older woman dressed for a funeral travelling in a milk float. The fact that this is a third-person narrative, not a personal account, is potentially liberating, as the friends themselves are not implicated in the behaviour described.

Backstage constraints

Although backstage behaviour is much more relaxed than frontstage, there are still constraints. Being backstage 'does not mean that friendly talkers are exempt from problems of framing and staging' (Collins 1988:

56). Moreover, even as the blurring of performer and audience typical of backstage talk produces solidarity among talkers, so it is still important that speakers present themselves as 'good persons', to protect both their own face and that of fellow-speakers. In any context, whether formal or informal, a speaker will select the 'least self-threatening position in the circumstances' (Goffman 1981: 326).

This means that, even in talk between close women friends, where self-disclosure is reciprocal and taboo feelings can be acknowledged, speakers have to pay attention to their performance, to the extent that speakers confirm in themselves and each other a sense of being a 'good person'. This is obviously a tricky task where the topic under discussion involves speakers presenting themselves as 'not nice'.

It is noticeable that in many conversations where we find women performing selves that could be seen as un-feminine and not-nice, the participants themselves comment critically on the behaviour they have revealed. In example (5), before telling her story of the boy who is *a little star* that she would like to *squish* (example 6), Bea describes as *awful* the feeling which she and her friends are all admitting to: *isn't it awful* [author's emphasis] *the way you DO get set up with some people though where you- you- you'd actually take pleasure- instead of taking pleasure in the triumphs of their children ... you think "yeah – she fails! innit great!"* *<GROWLY VOICE>* (staves 20–27). This is followed by a discussion where Mary (who arrived after Meg's and Bea's stories were told) also expresses unhappiness with the idea that we take pleasure from other people's failure, even though she agrees she has done this.

(10)

1			
MARY:	but I don't like feeling like that=		
MEG:			=no I don't like
JEN:			=oh it's horrid/

2			
MARY:		you know/	
MEG:	feeling like that/	but um	[((I think it's
BEA:			[well it seems

3		
MARY:	[but I DO do it/	[a lot/
MEG:	[xx))	[yeah/ =yeah/ oh I feel it
BEA:	[like we all do feel like	[that=
SALLY:		=yes/

4		
MARY:		yeah/
MEG:	a lot/ I feel it most- more than I don't feel/	
OTHERS:		<LAUGHTER>

5 ——————————————————————
MARY: the older I get the more of a horrible bitch I get/
6 ——————————————————————
MARY: <LAUGHS>

This discussion is a clear demonstration of the tension between the need to express not-nice feelings and the need to keep a foothold in the conventional frontstage world where women are always nice and mothers are always loving. On the not-nice side, Bea (staves 2–3) asserts that they all feel these not-nice feelings about other people's children, and simultaneously Mary admits *I DO do it a lot* (stave 3). Meg (staves 3–4) pushes this further by claiming that she is more likely to have 'bad' than 'good' feelings about other people's children, an admission which is received with supportive laughter by the others. On the other hand, Mary's claim that she doesn't like feeling *like that* (stave 1) is supported emphatically by Meg and Jen, and Mary later labels herself as a *horrible bitch* (stave 5). In other words, rather than celebrating the fact that as she gets older she feels freer to behave badly, Mary frames her behaviour as a negative, un-feminine development.

This tension between frontstage and backstage norms is a feature of all backstage talk. It is exacerbated in the case of women speakers by their position in society, in particular their relationship to symbolic capital (Bourdieu 1977; Eckert 1993, 1998). According to this perspective, women need to gain symbolic capital on the basis of their character and their relationships with others. Women's symbolic capital is evaluated in relation to community norms, so it is very important that women attempt to control these norms. Penelope Eckert claims that all-female talk is 'the major means by which they do this' (1993: 35). This means that women need to pay attention to frontstage norms of femininity even while letting their hair down backstage.

As a result, in women's backstage talk we find women relaxing and letting down the conventional, 'nice' front they normally maintain frontstage. But we also find women expressing ambivalence about these alternative, subversive aspects of their identities. This may be done by explicit self-labelling, as we saw with Mary's remark in example (10) *the older I get the more of a horrible bitch I get*. Alternatively, it may be expressed in the uneasy response of fellow-speakers. The next example comes from a conversation involving four 14-year-old girls. Clare's explanation of what a jockstrap is leads into her disclosing her fantasies about a boy in their class:

(11)

1
HANNAH: Clare/ what's a jock strap?

2
HANNAH:
CLARE: it's a jo- . it's what men use/ it's their

3
HANNAH:
CLARE: like their equivalent to a bra/ and they hold

4
HANNAH:
CLARE: their dick up with it [((and their balls))/
JESS: ['cos like when they do tie

5
HANNAH:
CLARE:
JESS: it round and they walk round/ you know/ <LAUGHS>

6
HANNAH: especially when people do things like ice hockey

7
HANNAH: [and stuff like that/ where it could get harmed
BECKY: [oh/

8
HANNAH: easily/ or like- <LAUGHS> or it could get put
CLARE: like DEAN! ((xxx))

9
HANNAH: under a lot of – [strain-
CLARE: I can imagine [Jason like

10
HANNAH:
CLARE: putting gel on his hair/ you know/ and he's
JESS: <SHRIEK>

11
HANNAH:
CLARE: sort of trimming it . and- and combing it
JESS: ugh/

12
HANNAH: [Clare!
CLARE: every day/ . so disgusting/
BECKY: <LAUGHS> ((it's [you who's

13
CLARE: I can imagine him doing
BECKY: being)) disgusting Clare/

14
CLARE: that though/ he's so s- vain/ he's such a bastard/

As this extract reveals, Clare's self-disclosure is met with negative reactions by her friends. Jess responds by shrieking in horror (stave 10) and making disgusted noises (*ugh* – stave 11); Hannah exclaims *Clare!* in a disapproving tone (stave 12); Becky says *it's you who's being disgusting Clare* (staves 12–13), though she laughs with amusement rather than disgust. We should also note that while Clare discloses these fantasies about Jason grooming his pubic hair, fantasies which position her as daring and unconventional, she simultaneously presents herself as finding this vision of Jason *disgusting* (stave 12). Moreover, after her friends react disapprovingly, she defends her position with the claims that Jason is both *vain* and *such a bastard*, claims which justify her fantasy.

The girls' talk here is clearly playful: the talk following the extract above continues to focus on Jason and boys and there is no sense that Clare has really shocked her friends. It is more that in this group of friends she is often the one who voices the more daring position. The four friends play with ideas of good and bad girl behaviour; because they are backstage they can explore bad girl behaviour but, as here, they balance such talk with comments and stories which anchor them in a more conventional femininity.

Even when the talk is of third parties behaving 'badly', as in Anna's story of her mother (example 8 above), there is some ambivalence expressed. While Sue and Liz are openly celebratory about Anna's mother (see, for example, Liz's comment *it must be really fun to have a mum like that*), Anna herself tempers her stories with remarks such as *she's lunatic* and *she's absolutely nutty.* While these comments are said affectionately, in a context where Anna overall expresses amused admiration of her mother, the choice of the words 'lunatic' and 'nutty' positions the mother at the abnormal end of some imaginary spectrum, and distances her from Anna and her friends (who therefore are positioned as more 'normal').

Our need to position ourselves as relatively 'normal' as well as nice is a constant restraining factor. Women continually monitor both their own and other women's performances in a variety of ways. None of us is ever free of the need to keep up some sort of front; as Goffman puts it, 'by and large, it seems [the speaker] selects that footing which provides him [*sic*] the least self-threatening position in the circumstances, or, differently phrased, the most defensive alignment he can muster' (1981: 325–326).

Backstage: safety-net or revolutionary cell?

In this chapter I have explored the ways in which women express not-nice aspects of themselves, despite frontstage pressures to conform to prevailing norms of femininity. I have argued, following Goffman, that backstage is a region which allows the performer to drop her front and talk openly with fellow-performers about aspects of herself which don't fit her frontstage role. Backstage interaction fulfils a vital need in women's lives to talk about behaving badly, whether this means recounting incidents where we ourselves behaved badly, or whether it means fantasising about such behaviour, or whether it means discussing and celebrating the unconventional behaviour of other women. In other words, backstage talk allows women to support each other in challenging or subverting frontstage norms, and in exploring alternative selves.

However, the data I have collected suggests that women feel obliged to balance such subversion by adopting, often simultaneously, more conventional discourses where they express ambivalence about, or label negatively, these less conventionally feminine aspects of themselves. Different discourses give us access to different femininities and we are all unwittingly involved in the ceaseless struggle to define gender. As Weedon puts it, 'The nature of femininity and masculinity is one of the key sites of discursive struggle for the individual' (1987: 98).

The evidence of the conversations I have recorded is that women take great pleasure in exploring aspects of themselves which cannot normally be expressed frontstage. The 'warm, easy, relaxed atmosphere' (de Beauvoir quoted in Goffman 1971: 115) of backstage provides women with a relatively safe space to express less conventionally feminine, less 'nice' aspects of themselves. Women, like men, need to assert their right to wholeness, to having not-nice as well as nice feelings. Jenny Joseph's poem 'Warning' is a rare frontstage assertion of such feelings. That the poem is such a favourite is testimony to women's desire to have the right to be not-nice.

It remains to be seen whether the overt expression of alternative and subversive femininities backstage only serves to perpetuate the hetero-patriarchal order, by providing women with an outlet for the frustrations of frontstage performance. Or is it possible that such backstage rehearsals may eventually lead to new frontstage performances?

Notes

1. This chapter is a revised and expanded version of a paper published in the *Journal of Sociolinguistics* (volume 3, number 1), which was itself based on

a paper presented at Sociolinguistics Symposium 12, University of London, March 1998. I'd like to thank all those who have given me feedback on the paper, particularly Jenny Cheshire and Justine Coupland.

2. I am grateful to Justine Coupland, who suggested this line of argument, and to Anita Biressi, who advised me on more recent examples.
3. Further glimpses into contemporary laddishness are afforded by Cameron (1997), Gough and Edwards (1998), Kaminer and Dixon (1995), and Kuiper (1997) and, more recently, by Coates (2003a) and Frosh et al. (2002).
4. The following table gives details of the corpus (further details and an account of the methodology employed can be found in Coates 1996a, ch. 1).

Table 5.1 Details of corpus

Number of	All-female	All-male	Mixed	Total
Conversations	20	20	10	50
Speakers	26	33	29	88
Hours of talk	19 h 45 m	11 h 40 m	6 h	37 h 25 m

5. Transcription conventions are given on pp. xiii–xv.
6. Narratives are presented in the format devised by Wallace Chafe (1980), where each line represents an 'idea-unit'.
7. This story, 'My mother and the jogger', can be found in Chapter 1 of this volume (pp. 16–17).

Part II

Language in All-Male Groups

6
One-at-a-Time: The Organisation of Men's Talk [1997]

Until the publication of Sally Johnson and Ulrike Meinhof's (1997) book *Language and Masculinity*, the talk of men and boys, and, in particular, the talk of all-male groups, had been not been the focus of much sociolinguistic research.[1] This, paradoxically, was a direct result of androcentric tendencies in sociolinguistic research. Because male practices were accepted as the norm, with women's practices being viewed as deviant (see Cameron 1992; Coates 1993: 16–37; Graddol and Swann 1989), male speaking patterns have been taken for granted, and not seen as a salient topic for investigation. It is also probably true to say that the (less noticed and therefore arguably more pernicious) heterosocial tendencies of academic research have meant that sociolinguistic work has focused on speakers in mixed groups, so it is cross-sex talk (and cross-sex miscommunication) which has been analysed and discussed.

What we do know about the informal talk of male speakers is highly skewed towards younger males and towards non-domestic contexts such as the street, the playground, the rugby changing-room. We know, for example, about the linguistic behaviour of Black male adolescents in Harlem (Labov 1972a), of young Black males in Philadelphia (Goodwin 1990), of male rugby players in New Zealand (Kuiper 1991), of 12-year-old schoolboys in Edinburgh (Reid 1978), of adolescent boys in Reading (Cheshire 1982), of college students in the USA (Cameron 1997), while experimental data from same-sex friendship pairs is discussed in the volume edited by Bruce Dorval (1990).

None of this work focuses explicitly on those patterns of talk associated with the organisation of conversation conventionally known as 'turn-taking'. This is what I want to examine in this chapter. I want to look at the ways in which a conversational floor is constructed in all-male conversation, and at the relationship between different speakers' contributions. I shall argue that, while women talking with women friends tend to adopt a collaborative floor, men talking with male friends stick to a one-at-a-time floor. I shall base this claim on an analysis of a corpus of conversations involving single-sex talk among friends.

The construction of a conversational floor

It had been assumed until recently that all conversation follows the one-at-a-time turn-taking model described in the article 'A Simplest Systematics for the Organisation of Turn Taking in Conversation' by Harvey Sacks, Emanuel Schegloff and Gail Jefferson (1974, henceforth SSJ). More recently, some analysts have suggested that this model does not account for all conversational practice, and that speakers sometimes draw on another, more collaborative, model (Falk 1980; Edelsky 1981; Coates 1989, 1991, 1994, 1997b; Chafe 1994, 1995).

The first detailed description of a more collaborative way of talking was given by Carole Edelsky in her ground-breaking paper 'Who's Got the Floor?' (1981). She suggested there that we need to distinguish between what she calls the single (or singly developed) floor and the collaborative (or collaboratively developed) floor. The main characteristic of the single floor is that one speaker speaks at a time, while the defining characteristic of the collaborative floor is that the floor is potentially open to all participants simultaneously. This means that the collaborative floor typically involves both the co-construction of utterances and overlapping speech, where several voices contribute to talk at the same time. As a result, some commentators use the term 'polyphonic' to refer to the kind of talk found in a collaborative floor, where there are 'separate voices articulating different melodies at once' (Chafe 1995: 4).

Research carried out in English-speaking communities in Australia, North America and Britain on all-female talk, where the women (or girls) involved are either friends or sisters, shows that polyphonic talk is a significant feature of such talk (Coates 1996a, 1997b; Coates and Jordan 1997; J. Davies 2003; Eppler 2009; Scheibman 1995). This more collaborative pattern of conversational organisation has also been found in mixed groups (Edelsky 1981; Bublitz 1988) and in male–female pairs (Falk 1980; Johnson 1990; Chafe 1995), so it is not the case that polyphonic talk is exclusively a feature of all-female talk. But whether or not it occurs in all-male talk is still unclear, and is the question to be addressed in this chapter.[2]

Men friends talking

Let's look at three brief (but typical) extracts from the all-male conversations.[3]

(1) [*four friends (early 40s) talk in a pub; topic = the 1960s*]

BILL: for instance they made a hell of a lot of mistakes
ALAN: %mhm%

BILL: ((by me))/ you look at these massive concrete

BILL: council estates they wouldn't dream of building now/ . but .
ALAN: mhm/ mhm/
BRIAN: mhm/

BILL: at least they tried/ you know at least there was a Labour

---

BILL: Government/ I mean I can remember a Labour Government/ but the

---

BILL: students can't/ . you know I'd- I'd just eligible to vote/
JOHN: no/ it's true/
ALAN: mhm/
BRIAN: no/

BILL: and Thatcher came to power/ and you- and you kind of think .
BRIAN: mhm/

BILL: just . does your head in really/

---

(2) [*three friends (early 20s) talk in Alex's flat about a shared creative project*]

TIM: how long have you been thinking about it then?
SEB: well I k- I thought

TIM: [((just))- =yeah=
SEB: about [it when I was living in Archway/ ((but it))= =you know

---

SEB: it's ready to be done/
ALEX: what? the Fantin-Latour portrait? sorry/

SEB: [well yeah ((I mean)) it's not a Fantin-Latour/ because
ALEX: ((what)) [((xx))

SEB: I- I think I'm- I'm better than Fantin-Latour=
ALEX: =yeah yeah I know/

ALEX: but I mean that sort of thing/

---

(3) [*three friends (mid-30s) talk at Mike's house about using a film projector*]

DICK: wh- which projector do you use? ((do they)) have one of

DICK: ((their own? xx))
TONY: two/ . we've got two projectors/
MIKE: that's important/

DICK:
TONY: from school/ you know the ((x)) school/
MIKE: mhm/

DICK: what's the advantage of two Tony? it means you can switch

DICK: reels?//
TONY: you can have two reels working/ you know/ two reels set up/
MIKE: mhm/

TONY: and switch from one to the other/

The SSJ model of turn-taking has as its central tenet that one speaker speaks at a time, and that participants in talk cooperate in the orderly transition of turns from current speaker to next speaker. The three texts above are a good illustration of the model. In all three of these extracts we observe speakers orienting implicitly to the rules articulated by SSJ. The succinct summary of these rules – 'No gap, no overlap' (see, for example, Moerman and Sacks 1971) – draws attention to the two main claims made by the model. 'No gap' refers to the claim that participants in conversation interpret syntactic, semantic and prosodic clues so accurately to predict the end of current speaker's turn that there is no perceptible gap between the end of one turn and the beginning of the next. The 'no overlap' claim complements this by asserting that participants in conversation predict the end of current speaker's turn so accurately that they start to speak just when current speaker stops and not before.

As predicted by the SSJ model, one of three things happens at points in talk where speaker-change is a possibility (that is, at Transition Relevance Places or TRPs, in SSJ's terminology; TRPs are marked with a double oblique, //, in these examples). Either current speaker nominates next speaker, as in example (3), where speaker Dick addresses Tony directly:

DICK: what's the advantage of two Tony?// it means you can switch

DICK: reels?
TONY: you can have two reels working//

or next speaker self-selects, as Alex does in the following extract from example (2):

SEB: it's ready to be done//
ALEX: what?// the Fantin-Latour portrait?//

---

or current speaker continues (the default option):

BILL: but . at least they tried you know// at least there was a Labour

---

BILL: Government// I mean I can remember a Labour Government// but the

---

BILL: students can't//

No overlap

What is striking about the all-male conversations in my corpus, to anyone who is familiar with all-female talk, is the lack of overlap. The talk of women friends is characteristically all-in-together rather than one-at-a-time, and involves frequent simultaneous speech (see Coates 1994, 1996a, 1997b for a detailed account of such talk). In this kind of talk the group takes priority over the individual, and the women's voices combine to construct a shared text. A good metaphor for talking about this is a musical one: the talk of women friends is a kind of jam session. Here are three brief examples from conversations between female friends to make the contrast clear. (In these examples, an extended square bracket indicates the start of overlap between utterances.)

In the first, Sue is telling a story about a couple she knows where the wife won't let the husband play his guitar:

(4)

SUE: she pushes him to [the abs-
ANNA: [he'll probably stab her with the

SUE: [she pushes him to the limit/ [yeah I
LIZ: =yeah grrr <VICIOUS NOISE>
ANNA: bread knife one [day= [she'll wake

SUE: think he will/ I think he'll rebel
LIZ: ="here you are Ginny" <LAUGHS———>
ANNA: up dead= <LAUGHS———>

The second comes from a conversation between two friends who have met for coffee at Pat's house. Barbara has come past Pat's old house on the bus, so Pat asks her whether she noticed that the door had been painted.

(5)

PAT: did you see they've painted our old front door green/
BARB: yes/

PAT: bright . green/ London country buses green/
BARB: we noticed that/ very bright green/

PAT: it looks ludicrous doesn't it?
BARB: we were unimpressed/

The third is taken from a conversation involving four 14-year-olds, friends for many years. Here they are discussing back-ache associated with their periods:

(6)

BECKY: ((well)) my back- my back is connected with my periods

BECKY: and I ((xx)) yeah/
JESS: so's mine/ I get really bad back a-

BECKY: ((xxx))
JESS: back ache down there/
LORNA: ((so do I)) I get- ((get)) back aches/ I can't go like

BECKY: <QUIET LAUGH> yeah/
LORNA: that/ and I can't go like that/ and I just ((xx)) a back rest/

HANNAH: hot water bottles help me
BECKY: hot water bottles help/
JESS: but . ho- hot water bottles help/

HANNAH: as well/
LORNA: help so much/ yeah it's lovely.....

All three examples demonstrate how easily speakers can speak and listen at the same time. Simultaneous talk of this kind does not threaten comprehension, but on the contrary permits a more multi-layered development of topics.

However, simultaneous talk of this kind is rare in the all-male conversations I have collected.[4] Overlap only occurs in the following circumstances:

(i) Overlap occurs where a participant gives back-channel support with minimal responses such as *mhm* and *yeah*:

(7)

BILL: you look at these massive concrete council estates

BILL: they wouldn't [dream of building now/ .
ALAN: [mhm/ mhm/

(ii) Overlap occurs where two participants add minimal responses at the same time:

(8)

BILL: students can't/ . [you know I'd- I'd just eligible to vote/
JOHN: no/ [it's true/
ALAN: [mhm/
BRIAN: no/

(iii) Overlap can occur when next speaker slightly over-anticipates a TRP:

(9)

TIM: it's really strange that you don't drink actually=
ALEX: =why?=

TIM: well [yeah/
ALEX: [((do I?))/ yeah but only like
SEB: =((he does drink a bit))/

ALEX: [((a sip of beer))/
SEB: [I know- I know a few people who don't drink nowadays/

(iv) Overlap can occur where a potential next speaker mistimes the start of a turn (note that Tim does not continue but allows Seb to keep the floor):

(10)

TIM: [((just))-
SEB: I thought about [it when I was living in Archway/

(v) Overlap can arise from misunderstanding. In the following example Bill produces a series of rhetorical questions (still on the topic of the 1960s). Alan responds as if to a 'normal' question, which results in Bill and Alan speaking at the same time until they manage to disentangle themselves:

(11)

BILL: d'you think if we were French we'd think "All right that's it"?

BILL: er do you think if we were French we'd be very different?
ALAN: yes/

BILL: d'you think [because it's sixty-eight- be different/
ALAN: [we- we- we- we- talk about- well what we've

ALAN: forgotten here.................

Although overlap is infrequent in all-male talk, where it occurs much of it is clearly supportive. The first three examples in this section, all involving back-channel support, illustrate this. We also find overlap where participants other than current speaker say something at the same time as current speaker which is clearly a form of agreement, as illustrated in the next two examples:

(12) [*topic = revolution in the 1960s*]

ALAN: and there was Prague/ the Prague [spring/ and .....
BILL: [spring/
JOHN: yeah/

---

(13) [*topic = joint creative project*]

SEB: there's some con[nection with that bit as well/
TIM: [connection/ yeah/

These overlaps occur at points which are not TRPs, but in neither of them is a participant making a bid for the floor. These contributions are rather more elaborate than simple minimal responses, but fulfil the same function. The same phenomenon is illustrated in the next, more complex, example, where John's contribution *Wenceslas Square*, echoed by Bill, both supports Alan's utterance and simultaneously adds to it. The proof that this is construed by Alan as supportive is shown by his incorporation of these words into his own turn.

(14) [*topic = Dubcek making a political speech in Prague*]

ALAN: and you can see it on the video you know/

ALAN: on the- on the ch- an- an audience that filled . in this

---

ALAN: huge squ[are every available square inch/ Wenceslas square/
JOHN: [Wenceslas squ[are/
BILL: [Wenceslas square yeah/

When male friends collaborate in the search for a word, overlap sometimes occurs, as in the following:

(15) [*topic = politics and Czechoslovakia*]

B: the man of er Pra[gue himself/ what's his name?
F: [((Dubcek)) Dub[cek/ =Alexander
E: [Dubcek=

B: =Dubcek actually there in the middle of . Czechoslovakia/
F: Dubcek=

Note that these examples of overlap all involve repetition; in other words, the speakers use words already used by, or simultaneously used by, another speaker. This must defuse the potential for such turns to be interpreted as interruptions (see next section).

Overlap and interruption

A key distinction between conversations involving a one-at-a-time floor and those involving a collaborative floor resides in the *meaning* attached to simultaneous talk. Where the floor is jointly owned by all participants, then overlapping speech is an inevitable consequence; in other words, simultaneous speech is a normal component of the conversational jam session. But where a one-at-a-time floor is operating, any overlap is potentially a violation of current speaker's turn at talk, specifically of their right to speak. In other words, in a one-at-a-time floor, overlap will be construed as interruption unless it is of the minor kind described above. This means that in friendly talk using a one-at-a-time floor, between people who want to be considered as equals, overlap will be avoided. This is precisely what we find in the all-male conversations I've collected: they are characterised not only by lack of overlap, but also by lack of interruption. This is hardly surprising: dominance moves such as interruption would be inappropriate in talk whose main goal is to maintain friendship.

The link between overlap and interruption for those who prefer a one-at-a-time floor was made explicit in the reaction of one of my participants to a description of women's collaborative talk. He said to me: 'But how do women know how to do simultaneous talk? Why don't you [i.e. women] think you're being interrupted?' Mary Talbot (1992) analyses a conversation in which a husband misinterprets his wife's attempts to contribute to the story he is telling about them coming through Customs. He labels them as 'interruption', rather than as contributions to a shared narrative. It seems that the conversational strategies which accomplish friendship among women may be construed as moves to seize the floor by speakers assuming a one-at-a-time floor.

Collaborative talk

As I have already suggested, the collaborative floor involves more than just overlap. The fact that a collaborative floor is jointly occupied simultaneously by all participants has many linguistic consequences, of which overlap is only one (probably the most striking). In particular, the collaborative floor also involves the shared construction of utterances and the frequent occurrence of minimal responses and laughter. (Minimal responses and laughter signal that participants are present in the shared floor even if they are not saying anything substantive; this contrasts with the meaning they carry in a one-at-a-time floor, where they acknowledge current speaker's right to the floor. See Coates 1997b for a detailed account of the collaborative floor.) The following brief extract from a conversation between five women friends demonstrates that, even where there is little overlap, talk involving a collaborative floor is significantly different from talk involving a one-at-a-time floor.

(16) [*topic = Apes and language*]

MARY:	I mean they can shuffle words around and	[make a different meaning/
BEA:		[draw up a conclusion/

BEA:	((xxx))-	
JEN:		they put two words together to form a compound/
MEG:		yeah/

MARY:		[that's right=
BEA:		=mhm/
JEN:	to mean something that they didn't have a	[lexical item for/

MARY:	[that's right/		for	[a brazilnut/
BEA:			a stoneberry for a-	[a brazilnut/
JEN:	[which is-			
HELEN:		right/		

The most striking feature of this passage is the ease with which the speakers operate as a single voice (the main strand of talk is underlined to show this more clearly). Mary's utterance is continued by Jen and then by Bea, with Mary joining in with Bea at the end. Meg and Helen say nothing substantive, but their minimal responses (as well as those of Bea and Mary) mark their continued presence in the shared floor. As this extract demonstrates, for women friends, who says what is not always important: the joint expression of shared ideas takes precedence over the individual voice.

There is evidence that the women who participated in my research explicitly value this kind of talk. The following is an extract from an interview I carried out with two friends, Bea and Meg, who are struggling to describe what they call the 'shape' of women's talk (italics indicate key words and phrases).

(17)

BEA: Yes, I'm trying to remember now sort of talking with Geoffrey [her partner]. I'll- I'll tell him . something, then he'll often come back with something of his own, but it's- it's not quite- it's not quite the same. It's more *separate* somehow.

MEG: mhm

BEA: I can't really describe what it is but the- the things don't sort of *blesh in together*, it's sort of one *separate* thing and another *separate* thing [...]

JEN: And do you feel more or less satisfied with any of these shapes?

BEA: I think I prefer *the feminine shape* which- which IS more

MEG: mhm

BEA: *melding in together.*

Bea's uses the verbs 'blesh' and 'meld' to describe the characteristic quality of talk with other women which differentiates it from what she calls the more 'separate' quality of talk with her male partner. Her assertion that women 'blesh in together' or 'meld in together' supports the claim that all-female talk is more like a jam session, that is, more polyphonic.

Men's friendship, men's talk

Why would polyphonic talk be a common feature of all-female talk but not of all-male talk? I would like to look more closely at some key features of all-male talk before suggesting reasons.

Topic

There is considerable evidence that women and men tend to discuss different topics in same-sex groups (see, for example, Aries 1976; Haas 1979; Aries and Johnson 1983; Seidler 1989; Pilkington 1998; Connell 1995). It seems that, with each other, men avoid self-disclosure and prefer to talk about more impersonal topics such as current affairs, travel or sport. A man interviewed about his relationship with his best friend (reported in Davidson and Duberman 1982) said 'We are pretty open with each other, I guess. Mostly we talk about sex, horses, guns, and the army.' In one of the conversations in my sample, the men friends discuss the 1960s at some length, and this topic can be divided into subtopics such as Bob Dylan, revolution and why it hasn't happened in Britain, Marxism, students today. By contrast, a conversation involving women of similar age and background has as its main topic sequence taboo and mothers' funerals, child abuse, loyalty to husbands, the Yorkshire Ripper case, fear of men. The brief examples from all-male conversation given in this chapter have been chosen to illustrate turn-taking patterns, but nearly all of them involve impersonal topics: planning a joint creative project, using a film projector, the Prague Spring. When talk does become more personal, it deals with matters such as drinking habits or personal achievements rather than feelings (see Johnson and Finlay 1997; Meinhof 1997; Pujolar 1997).

Topic is not a simple overlay category: topic choice has profound consequences for other linguistic choices. Hedging, for example, is closely correlated with particular topics, those which deal with personal and/or sensitive matters (Coates 1987, 1996a; and see Chapter 2, this volume). In terms of floor-holding patterns, non-personal topics encourage one-at-a-time floor-holding because these topics lend themselves to what I call 'expertism', which I shall describe in the next section.

Monologues and playing the expert

Monologues – that is, stretches of conversation where one speaker holds the floor for a considerable time – are characteristic of the talk of male friends. They seem to be associated with playing the expert. By 'playing the expert' I mean that conversational game where participants take it in turns to hold the floor and to talk about a subject which they are an expert on. This is a game which seems to be played most commonly by male speakers; women, by contrast, avoid the role of expert in conversation (see Coates 1996a, 2004).

In the conversation from which example (3) is taken, for example, there are three main topics: home-made beer making, hi-fi equipment, film projectors and the logistics of switching from one to the other. These three topics correlate with areas of expertise of the three friends who are spending an evening together, and this means that each of them gets a turn at being the expert, and a turn at 'doing' a monologue. In the conversation from which example (1) is taken, the four friends discussing the 1960s all have an interest in the topic, and in this case there is some vying for the floor as their expertise overlaps. But in general they organise their talk as a series of monologues, with each of them having a turn to hold the floor. Example (1) gave part of Bill's monologue; here is a longer example with John's preceding monologue:

(18)

JOHN: I've got this tremendous ambivalence about the 60s/ (('cos

---

JOHN: I've got you know kind of)) on the one hand I see it as

---

JOHN: being this- . this potentially revolutionary era you know/

JOHN: and on the other hand .hh a- a bunch of middle class -

JOHN: creeps [((xx)) [growing growing their hair long/
BRIAN: [oh I agree with [John ((xx))

JOHN: and sort of- and really nothing particularly happened/ .hh

---

BILL: well I wasn't middle class but I grew my hair long/ <LAUGHS>

BRIAN: [so did I/ <LAUGHS>
JOHN: [well I mean yes/ we [ ]- I mean I did too/ but the-

JOHN: and I wear the- wore the- you know the bell bottom pants

---

JOHN: were de rigueur and all the rest of it/ but um . I er I I I do-

---

JOHN: I do think that there was a kind of a- it was a change/

JOHN: a k- a- a change/ . not revolutionary necessarily/ but

JOHN: it was a change/ . ((and))
BILL: I think it was hopeful from what I-

JOHN: [yeah I think the change was hope/ [that's what it is/ yeah/
BILL: [I ((x))- [that that's what I ((can see

JOHN: - I'm glad you said that/
BILL: from x))- from my my view is that- is that- is that for instance
ALAN: %mhm%

BILL: they made a hell of a lot of mistakes ((by me))/

BILL: you look at these massive concrete council estates

BILL: they wouldn't dream of building now/ . but . at least they
ALAN: mhm/ mhm/
BRIAN: mhm/

BILL: tried/ you know at least there was a Labour Government/.....

Bill's monologue continues for some time: here is a brief extract, with minimal responses unattributed to save space:

(19)
BILL: and I think that though they made lots of mistakes/ and I think again it's fusing that myth and reality/ (*yeah*) is that if you actually historically . start writing about Wilson/ he was corrupt/(*mhm*) he was devious/ . corporations still ((*ran*)) you know the record companies just as much as they do now/(*yeah*) but whether or not it was the people believed (*ah*) that there was more amateurism about/ I think people genuinely believed (*mhm*) that the Beatles were amateurish/ . you know um but brilliant/ (*mhm*) . whereas now any group that's picked up is immediately run by the record company/ they're in it (*xx*) for money/ and the millions <LAUGHS> take over before that talent is squeezed out of them/ (*yeah*)

I've quoted at some length from this conversation to make the point that speakers take it in turns to hold the floor, and that their monologues can be extensive. For most of the time, the speaker who is giving the monologue holds the floor, with only occasional minimal responses from other participants. However, the preceding example demonstrates how the transition from one speaker to another may occasionally involve lengthy overlap which briefly disrupts the one-at-a-time floor.

(20)

JOHN: it was a change/ . ((and))
BILL: I think it was hopeful from what I-

JOHN: [yeah I think the change was hope/ [that's what it is/ yeah/
BILL: [I ((x))- [that that's what I ((can see

JOHN: - I'm glad you said that/
BILL: from x))- from my- my view is that- is that- is that for instance

---

BILL: they made a hell of a lot of mistakes....

Bill interprets John's *it was a change* as the final utterance of his monologue, and begins his own monologue with the claim *I think it was hopeful.* John agrees with this interpretation: his agreement (*yeah I think the change was hope*) overlaps with Bill's continuing talk, and is clearly unsettling for Bill, whose talk at this point is full of repetition and false starts (*from x- from my- my view is that- is that- is that*). But the evidence is that John intends his words to be supportive; he is not making a bid to regain the floor – having stated his agreement he relinquishes the floor to Bill, who develops his initial statement in his own monologue.

Questions

Questions occur with some regularity in conversations such as these which encourage speakers to play the expert, and they play a significant role in terms of turn-exchange. They are used primarily to seek information, as the examples given at the beginning of this chapter illustrated. For example, in example (2), Tim asks Seb *how long have you been thinking about it then?* and in example (3) Dick asks Tony *which projector do you use? do they have one of their own?* Both these examples illustrate how friends ask each other information-seeking questions which explicitly offer the floor to the addressee and, as in the second of these examples, invite them to play the expert. Here is another example of this kind of question from a discussion about speech synthesisers between two friends in college (this example shows that addressees are not always able to take up the role of expert):

(21) [*two friends (30s) discuss speech synthesisers*]
PETER: what else do they use it for apart from the deaf? or do they have other applications- I don't mean the deaf/ I mean the dumb/ do they have other applications?

ROB: well they didn't develop it for the dumb/ I can't remember why they did develop it/ um - I don't know/

At other times, questions are used as a way of introducing a new topic which the speaker can talk expertly about. In the following example, Peter's answer demonstrates that he interprets Rob's question not as a simple request for information but as having the pragmatic force of saying 'If you don't know about this, I can talk about it at some length.'

(22)
ROB: do you know of the Pennsylvania experiment?
PETER: no/ tell me about it/ [Rob proceeds to talk]

Information-seeking questions, then, are a regular feature of all-male conversation (but are rare in the talk of women friends; see Coates 2004: 130–131, 134–135).

Ownership of ideas

In a one-at-a-time floor a speaker simultaneously has a turn and holds the floor. Turns are seen as individually owned (so a speaker can protest 'It's my turn' if another speaker attempts to talk). It is characteristic of men's friendly talk (and of much talk in the public domain) that the ideas expressed by individuals in those turns are also seen as individually owned. Participants in conversation typically make comments like *oh I agree with John* or *I'm glad you said that,* or refer to what has been said as *your point* (all examples from my data). This careful attention to who owns which ideas is in complete contrast with the conversational practices of women friends, where the normal pattern is for ideas to be developed collaboratively and seen as the property of the group (see example 16, and Coates 1997b).

The goals of talk

These contrasting patterns need to be examined in relation to the goals of talk. All talk involves information-exchange, but, in the talk of women friends, exchanging information is less important as a goal of talk than establishing and maintaining good social relations. In fact, it's generally assumed that the maintenance of good social relationships is the main goal of all informal talk between equals. 'It is not appropriate behaviour in situations of informal conversation to pack your speech with information and deliver it in formally complete sentences' (Brown

1977: 117). However, it seems that the accomplishment of friendship for some men involves precisely this – the exchange of information.

This valuing of information, that is, of factual information, is clearly related to men's preference for impersonal topics, and for topics which coincide with areas of expertise. Where information-exchange has high priority, monologues will be tolerated. (In women's friendly talk, by contrast, monologues are abnormal, except where someone tells a story – but narrators have privileged access to the floor in all kinds of talk.)

The talk we do with friends should, I contend, be viewed as a form of play. When adults are questioned about what they do with their friends, men emphasise shared activities such as playing football or pool, going to watch a match, going to the pub (Pleck 1975; Aries and Johnson 1983; Johnson and Aries 1983b; Miller 1983; Seidler 1989; O'Connor 1992). Women, by contrast, are more likely to deny that they 'do' anything. Here are two of the responses I received when I asked women what they did with their friends:

(23)

BEA: We don't 'DO' much of anything, we- we tend to TALK, I mean we- we- we talk

(24)

HANNAH: But for me just what I remember about the relationship is NOT like what we DID together, but just you know the amount of time we just spent sitting around and talking

The centrality of talk in women's friendships is well established (McCabe 1981; Johnson and Aries 1983a; Hey 1996; Rubin 1985; Gouldner and Strong 1987; Wulff 1988). It seems that, while women's 'play' centres on talk, men's 'play' is activity oriented. As one man said about his best male friend (reported in Sherrod 1987: 236): 'We don't act the same way my wife acts with her friends, but it doesn't mean we don't care – it's just different. We express a lot through racquetball.'

But talk is a vital component of all friendships. As I've argued elsewhere (Coates 1996a, 1998b), the fun of talk, for women friends, arises as much from *how* things are said as from *what* is said. But it seems that for men, *what* is talked about is very important, and playing with ideas, not to mention arguing about ideas, is what is construed as fun. 'Doing friendship', then, is a very different enterprise for women and for men, or at least for those women and men whose friendship patterns have been researched.

Conclusion

In this chapter I have demonstrated that men talking informally with their friends prefer to organise their conversation according to the one-at-a-time model outlined by SSJ. The one-at-a-time floor functions to keep speaker roles distinct, and to permit those with expert knowledge to hold forth, while at the same time guaranteeing the orderly exchange of turns. Conversation may, then, consist of serial monologues. Where all participants are more actively involved, talk is frequently structured by question–answer sequences, which also serve to demarcate speaker roles.

Friendship is a relationship of equals, but women and men draw on differential modes of conversational organisation to 'do' same-sex friendship. Men, through scrupulous adherence to a one-at-a-time floor, avoiding overlap and thus avoiding interruption, maintain equality by respecting each other's right to the solo floor, and acknowledging the individual ownership of ideas. Women, by contrast, draw on a collaborative mode of conversational organisation where their shared ownership of the floor symbolises collective rather than individual values, solidarity rather than separateness.

It is currently de rigueur to argue, as Sally Johnson (1997) does, that the similarities between the speaking practices of women and men outweigh the differences, and many of the researchers cited in this chapter are concerned to make this claim. Marjorie Goodwin, for example, writes about the all-female and all-male groups of children she worked with as follows: 'It will be seen that as important as the differences between groups are the interactional structures they share' (1990: 53). Indeed, the research evidence available suggests that men and women in English-speaking cultures have access to both a one-at-a-time mode of talking and a more collaborative mode (see, for example, Edelsky's (1981) original paper, where she demonstrates that a mixed group of colleagues can shift between these two modes). But what is fascinating is that the research I have carried out focusing on single-sex friendship groups shows that all-female groups of friends typically choose to organise talk using a collaborative floor, while all-male groups typically choose a one-at-a-time floor. In other words, it is clear that women and men share linguistic and interactional resources but that they choose to draw on these differentially.

While we need to avoid crude binary oppositions in our analysis of gender-related patterns of talk, we should also remember that we belong to societies where the hegemonic ideologies represent gender as binary.

As Bronwyn Davies puts it, 'Current understandings of what it means to be a person require individuals to take themselves up as distinctively male or female persons, these terms being meaningful only in relation to each other and understood as essentially oppositional terms' (1989: 234). We as actors actively engaged in the construction of our social worlds inevitably perform gender in our daily interactions as either 'being a woman' or 'being a man'. Even when we attempt to subvert the dominant patterns, our performance will usually be read in an either/or way, that is, as doing either masculinity or femininity, but not something other. And since one of the chief ways we do 'being a woman' or 'being a man' is through talk, it would not be surprising to find that interactive practices differ.

The evidence drawn on this chapter relates only to white, well-educated English-speakers. Until we have evidence from a wide range of speakers and cultures, broad generalisations cannot be made. But given that conversational organisation accomplishes far more than just the mechanics of turn-distribution, and has many important linguistic reflexes, if it can be shown that, in most social contexts, male speakers prefer a one-at-a-time conversational model, whereas women prefer a more polyphonic way of talking, then we will have demonstrated a significant gender-related difference in conversational practice.

Notes

1. Since the publication of Johnson and Meinhof's (1997) collection, there has been an upsurge in research on language and masculinity. Good examples are Benwell (2002), Charteris-Black and Seale (2009), Coates (2003a), Edley and Wetherell (1997), Kiesling (2011), Milani and Jonsson (2011).
2. But see Chapter 12, this volume, for an example of more collaborative all-male talk. David Graddol and Margaret Keeton (personal communication), working on the talk of boys in the classroom, have found a great deal of simultaneous speech in their data, but it seems that these boys are experimenting with the possibility of multiple strands of talk in a way that is playful and individualistic rather than genuinely collaborative.
3. Transcription conventions are given on pp. xiii–xv. The names of all speakers have been changed.
4. The corpus was meant to consist of friends talking informally in groups of three or more. But occasionally a conversation would consist of only two speakers because someone arrived late. This made a great deal of difference for male speakers, though not for female speakers. The difference between two and three participants in friendly conversation seems to be highly salient for male speakers. (But see Chapter 12 for some examples of young men talking more collaboratively.)

7

'So I Thought "Bollocks to It"': Men, Stories and Masculinities [2000]

My aim in this chapter[1] is to look at the way masculinity is constructed in conversational narrative, that is, in stories told in spontaneous conversation involving male friends. Narrative is an important resource for speakers in the construction of self (Bruner 1990; Kerby 1991; Linde 1993). Telling stories not only allows us to give shape to our lives and to maintain our sense of self; it also allows us the possibility of exploring alternative selves. And given that the self is gendered (Benjamin 1990; Jukes 1993: xxiii), then narrative is a key resource for speakers in the construction of gender.

The following extract is taken from a contemporary New Zealand song, a song written and sung by men, but which takes a critical look at contemporary masculinity.

(1) **How you doing?**

Mike: Oh how you doing? I haven't seen you for-
Kevin: Yeah, it's quite a while isn't it?
Mike: What are you up to these days?
Kevin: Oh, keeping busy, how about you?
Mike: Oh yeah, yeah. It's Kevin isn't it?
Kevin: What did you call me?
Mike: Kevin? It's Kevin isn't it?
Kevin: Yeah. John.
Mike: Mike.
Kevin: Mike!
BOTH: Yeah, Mike, that's it.
Oh how you doing? I haven't seen you for-
Oh how you doing? I haven't seen you for-
Kevin: Oh how you doing? I haven't seen you for-
Mike: It's quite a while isn't it?

Kevin: What are you up to these days?
Mike: Oh, keeping busy, how about you?
Kevin: Oh, you know. So where are you living anyway?
Mike: Well you'd hardly call it living. I lost my job. I'm having quite a few emotional problems ...
Kevin: Hamilton? Wellington? Palmerston North?
Mike: Grey Lynn.
Kevin: Oh. Yeah, it's nice out there eh!
Mike: Yeah it's nice.
Kevin: Yeah.
Mike: Grey Lynn, yeah.
BOTH: Oh how you doing? I haven't seen you for-
Oh how you doing? I haven't seen you for-

[from *Songs from the Front Lawn*]

This song sketches a meeting between two men, men who we are led to assume have been friends in the past. The men are portrayed as socially inept (they have trouble remembering each other's names), and they stick to platitudes and well-worn conversational routines. When one of them attempts to answer the question 'Where are you living now?' with an answer that involves self-disclosure rather than just bare facts, the other speaker quickly steers the talk back to the impersonal.

The song makes fun of masculine inarticulateness and inexpressivity – and I know from personal observation that it makes people laugh. The laughter seems to be the kind that arises from the shock of recognition, which suggests that this song contains some truth, however stereotyped its portrayal of male interaction.

In an attempt to find out whether the masculinity portrayed in the song corresponds in any way to the reality of men's lives today, and, more specifically, to try to get a better understanding of the way men talk to each other, I collected a corpus of all-male talk, consisting of 30 all-male conversations. These spontaneously occurring conversations were audio-recorded with the men's agreement and subsequently transcribed. Altogether the 30 conversations contain a total of 185 stories. Participants in all cases were friends: in other words, recordings were made of groups or pairs of men who had a well-established relationship.

The methodology employed in this research is an innovative form of participant observation: after contact was made with a group, they were asked to take responsibility for recording their conversations.[2]

The assumption was made that any self-consciousness induced by the presence of the tape recorder would be overcome by the strong normative pressure which such groups exert over their members (see Milroy 1987: 35). Participants were simply asked to record themselves when they were with their friends. Male participants recorded themselves in a wide range of settings: in their homes, in pubs, in a university office after hours, in a youth club, even in a garden shed in the case of one group of dope-smoking adolescent boys (and also in unexpected places like men's toilets and walking along the street to the chip shop). The pub was, however, by far the most popular setting for all-male talk, a finding which is not surprising, given that 'the pub seems to be a pivotal site for both the expression and reinforcement of traditional masculinities and gendered consumption' (Willott and Griffin 1997: 115).

Rather than look at the totality of men's conversational behaviour, I shall focus specifically on conversational narrative, that is, on the stories told by speakers to each other in the course of everyday conversation. Narrative provides the researcher with invaluable materials for exploring the presuppositions of cultural life – as Polanyi (1985: 112) puts it, 'story materials [can be used] as an entry into the cluster of basic interwoven ideas which lies behind and supports our daily lives'. In the case of the stories I shall look at in this chapter, my aim is to use these materials as an entry into the basic cultural ideas which lay behind men's lives in turn-of-the-century Britain.

Story-telling plays a significant role in friendly conversation. The writer Ursula Le Guin argues that 'Narrative is a central function of language' (1992: 39). Story-telling among friends not only allows us to catch up with each other's lives, with what's been happening to us, but, more importantly, it plays a key role in the construction of the self. If we accept that the self is gendered – in other words, if we accept there can be no sense of 'I' without the 'I' being either 'I a woman' or 'I a man' – then in friendly all-male conversation, one of the main functions of narrative is the construction of masculinity. I intend in this chapter to analyse the stories the men tell each other in order to explore some of the tensions arising from competing versions of what it is to be a man today.

Up to this point I have spoken of 'masculinity' in the singular. But this is a simplification: there is no singular masculinity – masculinity is fluid and variable and at any point in time there will be a range of masculinities extant in a culture, masculinities which differ in terms of class, sexual orientation, ethnicity, age, and so on. And these masculinities intersect in complex ways. Moreover, masculinity cannot be understood on its own: the concept is essentially relational. In other words, masculinity is only meaningful when it is understood in relation to femininity and to the totality of gender relations (Connell 1995: 68; Kimmel 1987: 12; Roper and Tosh 1991: 2). But bearing in mind these caveats, I hope the reader will tolerate my use of the singular form 'masculinity' as well as the plural 'masculinities' in this chapter.

So, let's look at my data to see what it shows us about the accomplishment of masculinity. In some ways, the masculinities portrayed and performed in the stories conform to the stereotypes. But some of what we find in these stories challenges the stereotypes in unexpected ways.

Four extracts

I want to begin by looking at four brief extracts from the stories in my corpus, extracts which I have chosen because I think that, despite their differences, they all draw on dominant discourses of masculinity.[3]

(2) **Car wouldn't start**
[*four young men aged 18/19 in garden shed in Surrey*]

can't believe my car
it's ((2 sylls)) [*really*]
mhm, speedo's fucked [*oh no*]
I was just about to- wind[screen]wipers are fucked [*oh right*]
and now the fucker won't start [*oh no*]
[...]
I mean last time I just banged the bonnet [*yeah*]
and I mean it started up straight away [*yeah*]
and this time I was banging it and kicking it and shouting at it ((xxx)) [*oh my god*]
so then I- .hh I had a look at the fuses
and the fuses were alright
so I pulled the wires off
and cleaned them all up
and put them back again [*%fuck it%*]
did that three or four times
it still wouldn't start so-
what a bastard
((xxx)) ((hope it)) starts first time tomorrow
<R laughs quietly>

(3) *extract from* **The Psion[4] swap**
[*three men in their 20s talk in a pub in Somerset*]

Yeah, like the most basic Psion he got was this one that he bought ages ago,
and he went and bought one from Argos
and totally swapped the cases over so he got like the new innards in his old case
and then took it back to Argos
and said he didn't want it any more. <LAUGHTER>
And then later on he changed it for the upgraded version again at Curry's,
took all the serial numbers off,
switched them over and the badges,
And this customer brought this back,
and he said "This is only a five twelve k".
"Oh that's strange it's meant to be two megabytes."
'Cos he- it was a five twelve k
but he put the two megabyte stickers on there and kept a five twelve k on his.
He was a dodgy bastard wasn't he?
he knew all the tricks though.
Yeah but look what's happened to him now
yeah now he's in prison.

(4) *extract from* **Tablets and drink**
[*two middle-aged men in a pub in Birmingham*]

and you know where Amble Road is?
I was takin that fucking corner
and everything went (2) woozy
y'know what I mean <FASTER>
so straight away ((then-)) pull into the fucking side
eh?
started seeing double vision
so I pulls in to the side
and I thought "Well I'll be alright in a couple of minutes" <FASTER>
I'd only had two pints.
The next thing I knew were fucking four o'clock in the morning
and the fucking copper was knocking on the doo- . on the windscreen.

(5) *extract from* **The good Samaritan**
[*two middle-aged men in a university office after work*]

and I was doing erm in 1969 a dialect survey
of the languages round about erm a town called Yola
and er . for our lunch with our interpreter one day we had sandwiches

and we decided after visiting this or that village in the area . to walk up to the top of one of these clusters of- of rocks and have our lunch.
This was about er four hundred miles or so from Ibadan,
erm about a hundred and fifty miles from any erm sizeable town,
pretty remote one might think.
It took us about half an hour to wend our way up this er jumble of very very large boulders,
and er we got close to the very top,
and the top was obscured from us by a boulder.
We walked round this boulder
and there sitting on the top . was er a European couple
with their backs to us.
As they heard us approach they turned round,
and lo it was my Vice Chancellor and his wife.

These stories obviously accomplish a lot more than gender: age is a significant factor in all these stories, and the first two stories perform being young as well as being masculine. Class is also a significant variable, with the differences between examples (4) and (5) being very much to do with the social class of the two speakers: the narrator of 'Tablets and drink' is a working-class Birmingham man for whom the pub is an extension of home; the narrator of 'The good Samaritan' is a highly educated middle-class man who has got into the habit of meeting his friend and colleague after work to chat – they have agreed to tape these conversations because, like all linguists, they can't resist collecting data!

But despite these disparities of age and class, there are some important commonalities. I shall discuss five of these in some detail: the topic of the stories, the gender of characters in the stories, the attention to detail, the use of taboo language, and the use of technical vocabulary and formal syntax.

First, the topics of these extracts are stereotypically masculine: they are about cars, about modern technology, about drinking, about travel. Other stories in my corpus have topics such as going out drinking, fighting, pornographic videos, sporting achievement. One of the functions of such topics is that they keep talk away from the personal: very few stories in my corpus involve self-disclosure of a kind parallel with that found in women's friendly talk (see Coates 1996a, 2003a).

Second, these extracts all portray a world peopled by male human beings. The only woman mentioned in these four extracts is the Vice Chancellor's wife. In the sub-corpus[5] of 67 stories that I have analysed, 94 per cent of the stories have male protagonists, and 71 per cent of stories depict an all-male world. This corresponds to Johnstone's findings for male narratives in Indiana, USA: 'when men are not the protagonists of their own stories, they tell stories about other men' (1990: 67).[6]

Third, these extracts display a great deal of attention to detail. For example, in example (2), the narrator talks about his car in detail: he mentions the speedometer, the windscreen wipers, the bonnet, and the fuses, and tells us how many times he cleaned the wires. In example (3), the narrator specifies *two megabytes* and *five twelve k* in relation to the Psion, details which position him as technically competent. In example (4), the narrator gives the name of the road at the beginning of the extract, tells us he had *only had two pints,* and specifies the time the policeman knocked on his windscreen; in example (5), we again get lots of detail about place and time. This is precisely what Johnstone (1990, 1993) found in her analysis of stories told by white middle-class males in Indiana, USA. This attention to detail constitutes an important strategy in men's conversation: it enables men to avoid talk of a more personal nature. That this is often a deliberate strategy is revealed by the following admission by David Jackson in his 'critical autobiography': 'I often turn to the sports page in the daily newspaper, concerning myself with the raw material for endless non-emotional non-conversations with other men ...' (1990: 221).

The detailed naming of objects, then, is one way the language of these stories accomplishes masculinity. The use of taboo words is another, one that is difficult to overlook, and which compares markedly with the language of the women's conversations and the language of the mixed conversations I have collected. To give an example, the word *fuck* and words deriving from it (*fucking, fucked, fucker,* etc.) appear 72 times in the stories in the all-male sub-corpus, 12 times in the mixed sub-corpus and not at all in the all-female sub-corpus. Examples (6–12) give some more instances of taboo language from the all-male data:

(6) **The Area Manager's call**
it's fucking crap here today

(7) **Oscar was very fucked off**
Oscar was very fucked off

(8) **The paint dispute**
he just fucking uses whatever's around

(9) **You can't not know your name**
Just one of those moments you know life's turned to shit like that

(10) **Lucky thirteen**
'cos I'd been driving like a dangerous cunt

(11) **Skin disease and stress**
he used to come out with so much bollocks like that

(12) **Quadruple Jack Daniels**
I was fairly pissed by the time we got to the fucking park if you remember

Taboo language in these stories functions in many ways: it gives verisimilitude to direct speech; it adds emphasis to points the narrator wants to foreground; but most importantly it performs hegemonic masculinity. Swearing and taboo language have historically been used by men in the company of other men as a sign of their toughness and of their manhood. Jock Phillips, in his classic account of early settlers in New Zealand, writes that swearing 'signalled the colonial man's readiness to live a hard and physical life and his unconcern for the genteel formalities of civilised life. It also showed contempt for the female world of manners' (1996: 32). Swearing has played this role for men all over the world, not just in the colonial setting: there is ample evidence that taboo language is used in all-male sub-cultures such as the army and in the rugby changing room as well as in male peer groups on the street as a way of constructing solidarity (Kuiper 1997; Labov 1972a; Moore 1993). Jackson (1990: 156) talks of the enormous pressure put on boys in Britain by the male peer group to swear and talk tough, while Gough and Edwards' (1998) analysis of the spontaneous talk of four male friends under the influence of alcohol demonstrates the ubiquity of taboo language in informal all-male talk.

Another highly significant function of the language in men's narratives is its role in maintaining emotional restraint. Male inexpressivity is recognised as a major feature of contemporary masculinity by commentators, and is increasingly seen as problematic (Pleck 1995; Seidler 1989). Jackson claims that 'the non-adult public arena was dominated by language routines that taught me to bury the language of personal feeling' (1990: 156). These language routines include swearing, boasting and talking tough, and men's narratives often function as boasts and construct a world peopled by swearing, tough-talking males. But emotional restraint is also accomplished through the use of technical vocabulary and formal syntax. 'The Psion swap' (example 3 above) is a good example of a story that uses technical language: the technical vocabulary is skilfully used to make the story convincing, but it also keeps the focus away from the personal and the emotional.

The use of more formal syntax as a way of accomplishing emotional restraint is more apparent in the narratives told by older well-educated men, who swear a great deal less than their working-class peers and also less than younger speakers of all classes. Example (5) is a good representative of the narratives told by these older middle-class men. First, some of the lines (determined largely by prosodic features, but also corresponding often to sentence boundaries) are long by normal narrative standards, for example, lines 3 and 4. Second, the verb is in the passive in line 10 (*the top was obscured from us by a boulder*); passives occur only rarely in narrative. Third, note the use of highly literate set phrases as this chunk builds to a climax: in lines 12–13 *and there sitting on the top was a European couple with their backs to us,* where the opening words *and there* followed by a non-finite clause starting with V + ing is readily recognised by English speakers as a rhetorical flourish often found at the climax of a story. The narrator then caps this in line 15 with his use of the archaic phrase *and lo* to introduce his climactic line *it was my Vice Chancellor and his wife*; this line uses a syntactic pattern which self-consciously mimics the language of the King James Bible. The overall effect of the language in this extract is to make the narrative stylistically very formal, and this has the effect of distancing the speaker from the addressee.

What emerges from this analysis of a few examples is that a variety of resources are exploited to accomplish dominant masculinity: topic choice, the virtual exclusion of women from the storyworld, and linguistic patterns, both lexical and syntactic. All these features contribute to emotional restraint, one of the key values inherent in dominant masculinity (Connell 1995; Jukes 1993; Seidler 1989; Tolson 1977).

Stories of achievement: men as heroes

Other than emotional restraint, the aspect of these stories which is most striking is their stress on achievement. Achievement is another central value of dominant masculinity. Story-telling has a key role to play in enabling male narrators to perform hegemonic masculinity through presenting themselves, or their male protagonists, as successful, as winners, as heroes.

Examples (13) and (14) are both tales of achievement and triumph.

(13) **The paint dispute**
[*three young men in their mid-20s are talking at Tim's flat about a difficult art student*]

did I tell you recently?
he rea- he u- u- used up all- he used up a-

like I had a palette with like loads of black paint on it
and he used it all up
and I said "Get me some more paint"
and he refused [*what?*]
I- I told him to get me some more paint and he was going- he was going to refuse
and he could tell that I was getting more and more serious about it
'cos he was getting more and more refusey about it
he y- y- YOUR paint?
it was MY paint [*yeah*]
he was a complete cunt about using other people's paint
and in- in the end I had to- er in the end I got REALly annoyed with him
and I kicked a chair into bits
and then he r- he sort of . ran- ran out of the studio
and stayed away for half an hour before coming back <LAUGHING>
back and sort of shaking my hand and being apologetic <AMUSED>
and then-
[*he still did- didn't get you more paint though?*]
well in fact he did
I mean he took a while about it 'cos he kept saying "I've got no money"
and I at one point lost my temper with him
I couldn't do it a second time
it was really pathetic
but in the end he gave- he gave me a tube of white.

(14) **Amazing left**
[*three 16-year-olds are talking in Julian's room at boarding school*]

in the June in the- in the final of the Ties
I did the most amazing left with this half-volley you will ever see.
((it)) came down
it was like quite- it was quite like- quite a- quite high but quite hard
it came down ((here))
I had someone running up
it was on my left so I didn't have time to ((xx)) change ((feet))
so I took it on the half-volley
and it just went flying <EMPHATIC>
and Neil ran on from an on-side position
and he was away
and he ((was))-
and it was just the most beautiful ball I've ever ever ever seen. <EMPHATIC>

In both these examples, the narrator presents himself as the protagonist in a story where he performs heroically, whether in contest with another person, or on the sports field. In 'The paint dispute', the narrator is relatively modest about his achievement: the evaluative clause *it was really pathetic* focuses on the inadequacy of Robin, the other student, rather than on Tim's victory. However, we are left in no doubt as to who came out on top in this dispute. Julian, in 'Amazing left', frames his story explicitly as a celebration of triumph with the phrase *the most amazing left* in line 2, and the final line *it was just the most beautiful ball I've ever ever ever seen.*

I also want to include an example from stories told by older speakers: a good example is a first-person narrative told by a middle-aged man about collapsing with acute appendicitis and having to survive with incredible stoicism a series of events which prevent him getting to hospital. The story is very long – 126 lines – so the following is only an extract from the epic tale.

(15) *extract from* **Appendicitis**
[*three middle-aged men in a pub after work*]

the next morning things were no better
so . I walked round the street a couple of hundred yards to the doctor's surgery
unfortunately . the doctor . lived out in Essex
and he'd been snowed in
so . I spent a couple of hours sitting around in his surgery
and then finally the receptionist says, "Look you know,
the doctor isn't going to be able to make it till this evening,
he's stuck in the snow,
would you mind coming back".
so I shuffled off around the street <LAUGHING>
and spent the day thinking . ((you know)) "This is really getting bad",
because .hh oddly enough the sort of classic appendicitis pain didn't appear until very late
you know "god only knows what is wrong with me,
but this is- this is definitely rough".
So I spent the whole day um-
finally five or so . o'clock came round
and I staggered around the street again to the doctor's surgery
and this time I got to see him
and I was standing in front of him
and I was going like this
sort of swaying in the breeze
and he said um "I need to get you a bed,
suspected appendicitis" he said.

Tony is then whisked into hospital, where it becomes clear that he has a ruptured appendix and needs to be operated on immediately if he is not to die. Like examples (13) and (14), it is a tale of heroism, but heroism of a different kind. The protagonist has to endure a terrible ordeal; he becomes increasingly ill, and circumstances, such as bad weather, conspire against him. He comes through the ordeal with stoic fortitude. As we see from these examples, heroic behaviour can mean winning a dispute, or making a perfect move on the sports field, or bearing pain and coming through an ordeal.

There are other stories in the men's conversations which deal with pain or illness. Typically, the narrator will only foreground the pain or the illness if it serves to illustrate how brave the protagonist was, or how successful in outwitting a significant other. In her analysis of the stories told by male and female speakers in a town in Indiana, USA, Johnstone (1990, 1993) found that the men's stories emphasised contest. Achievement in these stories, that is, the winning of the contest, was associated with the male protagonist acting alone. (By contrast, the women's stories emphasised *community* and the importance of acting in collaboration with others: women were portrayed as failing when they acted alone.) The stories in my corpus seem to support her findings: in (13), Tim acts alone – and violently – to make Robin replace the paint he'd used; in (14), Julian is clearly part of a team, but the story celebrates his solo contribution; in 'Appendicitis', the narrator portrays himself as battling alone against the odds.

Competition in story-telling

This focus on achievement in men's stories has a consequence that Johnstone (1990, 1993) does not discuss. It is that narrative activity in all-male groups can be face-threatening in a way that it is not in all-female groups. In other words, when men tell stories which present them as heroes, as the victors in conflict with various kinds of other, they are performing a particularly competitive version of masculinity which can be called one-upmanship. The result is that telling stories becomes in itself a competitive activity, with speakers competing to boast about their triumphs or their cock-ups. The 'Can you match that?' aspect of all-male talk is well illustrated by stories in my corpus: adolescent speakers compete to tell ever more extreme stories about getting drunk; young men in their 20s tell stories which exaggerate feats of aggression and getting the better of authority figures (e.g. about kicking down a door at work, about skiving off work, about a fight with a workmate); older men with a more working-class background tell stories about run-ins with the police, while older men with a more middle-class background vie with each other to appear widely read or well travelled or up-to-date in terms of technology and science – or even good wine.

In one story sequence, the narrator of the second story begins his story with the words *tell you what, I'll beat all of that,* which explicitly labels his narrative as a competitive speech act.

With younger speakers, this competitive element can be overt, with so-called friends ganging up on each other. The following extract comes from a series of boasting stories about drinking and getting drunk, told by three 16-year-old boys. It's the kind of narrative that Polanyi calls a 'diffuse story' because the story isn't told as a neat chunk, but instead 'blocks of story materials [are] interleaved with blocks of conversation in which points of the story are discussed or amplified' (1985: 66).

(16) *extract from* **Quadruple Jack Daniels**
[*three 16-year-old boys at public school*]

Henry: that evening you were in such a bad mood/ 'cos me and Robert were pissed and you weren't/
Robert: I'm serious you know/ I've never seen you pissed/
Julian: oh crap/
Robert: I've never seen you pissed/
Julian: how will that- hang on/
Robert: how have you ever been pissed? <R AND H LAUGH>
Julian: oh fuck off/
Robert: tell me now/ <MOCKING>
Julian: fuck you/

This is a particularly vicious bit of competitive talk. Note how none of the speakers mitigates the force of their remarks with any face-saving devices. In particular, Robert's attack on Julian's drinking ability is a face-threatening act, pure and simple. Julian responds by swearing, as a feeble attempt at counter-attack, but he is in an impossible situation since he can only lose face whatever he chooses to do: if he attempts to provide evidence that he has been drunk (which he does at another point), that still allows Robert the victory of having forced him onto the defensive.

A more subtle way of competing is to undermine another's story by adding a deflating comment at the end. In this way, the current narrator's heroism can be punctured so that the next narrator is free to take the floor. The talk following the story 'Amazing left' (example 14) is a good example of this: after the narrator's triumphant *it was just the most beautiful ball I've ever ever ever seen,* one of his co-participants at talk asks 'Who?' The narrator answers, with considerable bathos, 'Me'. The faux-naif question 'Who?' undermines the whole point of the story – if the addressees can claim not to know who the story is about, it fails as a piece of one-upmanship.

This strategy is also used by older speakers: a middle-aged middle-class male tells a long story about a Volkswagen Beetle which is swept off a bridge into a river somewhere in Africa but which proves to be watertight and starts first time once it's back on dry land. The story is well constructed, but the narrator's friend adds comments both during and at the end of the story which undermine the narrator. The final section of the story is given in example (17).

(17) *extract from* **Watertight Volkswagen**

The punchline of this tale was that he sent this er reel of film which he'd taken back for developing in Germany
and had addressed it to his wife
and it arrived when his wife's-
it arrived at his home
and his wife saw the pictures before a letter from him arrived explaining (.h) what was ((up))
she was no end surprised to see her husband's Volkswagen in the middle of a river
and no husband
and no husband
all was well <IN HUSHED TONES>
yes that seems to be the sort of thing one might attribute to the publicity department of Volkswagen

It is actually a very aggressive move to make a comment of this kind after a fellow-speaker has invested so much time (this is one of the longer stories in the corpus) and creative energy in building a story-world, in animating characters, in constructing a coherent plot. What the story-recipient is in effect saying is that he is not fool enough to think this is a genuine story, since in his view it is probably a fiction spread around by *the publicity department of Volkswagen*. He is relatively indirect in making this accusation – he uses the hedges *seems*, *sort of thing* and *might* and employs the impersonal pronoun *one* – but this is still a 'So what?' move, and a 'So what?' of a particularly sophisticated and middle-class kind.[7]

The struggle to express vulnerability

But now I want to begin to show how the picture is not as simple as this. While the stories we have looked at reproduce the dominant values of masculinity – emotional restraint, ambition, achievement and competitiveness – these values inevitably jostle for position with other, competing, values. We are all involved, whether we like it or not, in the ceaseless struggle to define gender (Weedon 1987: 98), and it is not the case that the men whose conversations I have listened to adopt the dominant discourses of masculinity at all times and without protest. Some of the stories reveal men struggling to reconcile competing discourses of masculinity.

The next story is a good example of this: in many respects this story performs conventional masculinity, but alternative discourses are voiced, and the discussion which follows the story shows the men struggling to reconcile these competing discourses. The story comes from a conversation involving four men, all carpenters, aged between 25 and 40, having a drink in a pub after work; the narrator is Alan.

(18) **The digger**

should of seen Jason on that digger though
yeah he . he come down the ((park)) part
where it's- the slope
then he's knocking down the front wall
and there was this big rock
and he couldn't get it out
so he put a bit more . power on the thing
and . and the thing- the digger went <<SCOOPING NOISE>>
it nearly had him out <LAUGHS>
he come out all white.

This story constructs a dominant version of masculinity, where masculinity is bound up with physical strength. It tells of a man knocking down a wall, and using a huge and powerful machine to achieve this. The point of the story, though, is that when Jason tries to employ more power to dig out the recalcitrant rock, he almost loses control of the machine.

The last line of the story, however, positions the audience slightly differently: Alan ends the story with the line *he come out all white*. 'To go white' is recognised as being a physical manifestation of fear, so Alan here portrays Jason not as a hero but as someone who nearly lost control of a powerful machine and who is frightened by the experience. Note that in lines 2–7 Jason is the subject of active verbs, but in lines 8 and 9, the climax of the story, the machine becomes the subject, with Jason becoming the object. This twist in the power relations between the man and the machine results in Jason *com[ing] out all white* in line 10.

As the following extract shows, two of Alan's co-participants orient to the narrator's evaluation of the story, but the third resists. The talk following Alan's story is transcribed here in stave format to allow the interplay of voices to be clearly seen.

(19) **The digger**

8	
Alan:	it nearly had him out/ <LAUGHS> he come out all white/
Chris:	<LAUGHS>
Kevin:	<LAUGHS>
John:	
9	
Alan:	
Chris:	<LAUGHS>
Kevin:	I bet that could be dangerous [couldn't it/
John:	(([hurt himself/))
10	
Alan:	
Chris:	
Kevin:	if it fell [on your head)) it's quite-
John:	[he- you know/ -
11	
Alan:	
Chris:	<LAUGHS> [<u>can I have some</u>
Kevin:	[it's quite big/
John:	[he crapped himself/ he [crapped himself/
12	
Alan:	
Chris:	<u>pot noodles please Kevin</u> <SILLY VOICE>
Kevin:	<LAUGHS> [no/
John:	[did he have to sit down
13	
Alan:	he- he- well . he was quite frightened [actually/
Chris:	
Kevin:	
John:	and stuff? . [I know/
14	
Alan:	'cos- 'cos- [well yeah/
Chris:	was it for you as well [mate?
Kevin:	
John:	I must admit-
15	
Alan:	well I still-
Chris:	did you go a bit white as well then did you?
Kevin:	
John:	god/
16	
Alan:	
Chris:	don't get
Kevin:	
John:	he was thinking "god please don't wreck it"/

17
Alan:
Chris: any blood on it/ <SARCASTIC>
Kevin: is that the one with all the loa-
John:

18
Kevin: lots of different things on it?

[*Discussion continues about different types and sizes of diggers*]

Kevin and John both orient to Alan's move to bring Jason's fear into focus: Kevin comments on the danger of such machines, while John surmises that Jason could have got hurt, and that he *crapped himself*, another physical manifestation of fear. Kevin's comments are met by taunting from Chris – at least, that is how I interpret Chris's remark *can I have some pot noodles please Kevin*. Chris uses a silly voice to say this and since at face value the remark is totally irrelevant, we have to use conversational inferencing to interpret it. Superficially this utterance is a polite request for food, the sort of thing you might expect somebody relatively powerless – a child, for example – to say to someone more powerful – a mother or a dinner lady. By saying this, is Chris implying that Kevin's utterances *I bet that could be dangerous couldn't it if it fell on your head, it's quite- it's quite big* would be more appropriate in the mouth of a caregiver or food-provider, that is, in the mouth of a woman? Certainly, Chris seems to be trying to humiliate Kevin, to position him as being cowardly, a wimp, as being un-masculine. Perhaps by producing an utterance as irrelevant as this, he is implying that Kevin's utterances are equally out of place. Chris clearly finds Kevin's view of Jason's near-accident threatening. However, Kevin does not seem to be intimidated: he laughs and says *No* to Chris, meaning 'No you can't have any pot noodles', which defuses the challenge by treating it humorously.

John continues to explore the theme of Jason and fear with his question to Alan: *did he have to sit down and stuff?* This leads to Alan, who was an eye witness, admitting: *he- he- well . he was quite frightened actually.* Note the hesitations and false starts in this response, as well as the presence of several hedges: Alan is clearly uncomfortable with his answer. Predictably, given his taunting of Kevin, Chris now has a go at Alan with the direct challenge *was it for you as well mate?*, that is, 'was it frightening?' Alan replies *well yeah*, with his *well* again signalling that this is a dispreferred response. Chris's subsequent question *did you go a bit white as well then did you?* ends with an aggressive tag. It is aggressive in that it demands an answer from Alan, and at the same time the repetition of *did you?* has overtones of motherese ('does he want his dindins, does he?'), which rudely suggests that Alan is behaving like a baby. Chris's question is highly face-threatening. His use of the phrase *go a bit white*, which picks up Alan's earlier utterance, mocks the euphemistic aspect of it and implies that to go white is un-manly. This question challenges Alan to align himself with Jason and, by extension, with un-manliness. Alan begins a reluctant response: *well I still-* before he is rescued by John's intervention: *god/ he was thinking "god please don't wreck it"*. John in effect answers for Alan with the claim that if Alan had gone white it was because he was worried about the machine. This utterance shifts the ground of the discussion by suggesting that the men's anxiety is to do with damaging the machine rather than with their own vulnerability. This interpretation of events is obviously more palatable to Chris, who here stands for hegemonic masculinity, but he still adds the sarcastic comment *don't get any blood on it* as if determined to wrong-foot Alan. But Kevin and John then steer the conversation into a discussion of exactly what kind of digger it was and how it compares to a fork-lift truck, an impersonal discussion involving lots of detail which re-establishes the solidarity of the group and their alignment with dominant norms of masculinity.

The tension and conflict in this short extract demonstrate how difficult it is for male speakers to discuss vulnerability, and how peer group pressure works to silence those who try to voice alternative masculinities. Alan, Kevin and John attempt to explore their feelings, and thus to push at conventional gender boundaries, but violations of gender boundaries will always be resisted, and will be met with sanctions ranging from ridicule, as here, to violence (Davidoff and Hall 1982: 29; Coates 2001).

Self-disclosure

Finally, I want to look at self-disclosure in all-male talk. As I've said, the majority of the stories in my corpus are first-person narratives, that is, the narrator and the chief protagonist are one and the same. First-person narratives in all-female talk very often involve self-disclosure, because the narrative will tell of an event that occurred in the speaker's life, usually very recently, which had some kind of emotional impact. Men's first-person narratives, by contrast, focus more on achievement and triumph, or on the more banal happenings of everyday life, and are not designed to reveal feelings or to lead into talk where feelings can be compared and discussed. The only stories I could really label as self-disclosing came in conversations involving older rather than younger men, middle-aged men who seem more solid in their masculine identity.

Example (20b) is an example of a story involving self-disclosure. The participants in the conversation that this story comes from were four middle-aged middle-class men in the pub after work (they were colleagues at a further education college). They are having a general discussion about peaks and troughs in social history. Example (20a) gives a brief chunk of this discussion to contextualise the story:

(20a)

Brian: we keep having this idea that things are going to get better/ which was an earlier part of the conversation/
Tony: yes/
Brian: it's paralleled by this- I think what tends to happen/ you- you ((just)) have peaks and troughs/ you know the thing goes- there's a wave/ it does- it doesn't suddenly turn into an exponential growth pattern/
Pete: right/
Brian: you know it goes up and it comes down again/ [you know and I think-
Pete: but [do you think- do you think- but do you think that there's a- within the p- peaks and troughs/ do you think there's a- there's a upward or a downward trend?

At this point Brian gives an example from his own life (note how it is Pete's question that allows Brian this opportunity):

(20b) **Suicidal**

→ well at the moment ((I mean)) this is partly personal
'cos I mean I- my own life sort of has been (*ah*) up and down
and I've . you know sort of- . if you'd t- if you'd had this conversation with me about a term ago
I mean I was just about as down as you could get
because I'm er- really was quite seriously suicidal
and . it HAS come up again
you know my life HAS improved/ (*mhm/ mhm/*)
((xx)) it hasn't actually got any better
but my attitude to it and psychologically I'm a lot straighter and clearer about what's going on
so it has picked up
and it was just literally a case of hanging on in there
I mean about . towards . about the middle of last term
I quite seriously- . I went out and I bought a big bottle of pills
they were codeine and aspirin mix

and a bottle of whisky
and I went and sat on Twickenham Green
and I was going to kill myself [*mhm*]
I was going to eat the pills and drink the whisky
er well it was only a little bottle of whisky <GREATER SPEED>
er sitting there y'know TOTALLY just about as depressed as you could possibly get
and then I just thought "you stupid sod"
so I threw away the pills
drank the whisky
and went home
[*everyone laughs*]
but y'know that was the turning point
I started coming up again <LAUGHING QUALITY TO VOICE>
[Pete: *good*/ Tony: *good/*]

This rare example of a man talking about a difficult moment in his life is introduced with some tentativeness. First, he warns his fellow conversationalists that he is about to talk about something *partly personal* (the hedge *partly* here is semantically nonsense, but functions to soften the force of his utterance and protect his addressees' face). Second, he ties his story in very carefully to the theme of 'peaks and troughs' which has been established in the preceding conversation. This careful tying in of his story to the more general conversational theme reveals his anxiety about telling the story, anxiety which is expressed in the many hedges which appear in lines 1–5 (three tokens of *I mean*, two tokens of *sort of*, and one each of *you know* and *really*). This density of hedging is unusual in men's talk (but is typical of all-female conversation where sensitive topics are under discussion). After this he seems to settle down to tell his story, perhaps reassured that his fellow-conversationalists have not raised any objections.

However, the reactions of the other men – laughing with Brian at line 25, then saying *good* after Brian's coda – express both relief and embarrassment. They do not seem very comfortable with Brian's self-disclosure, and this interpretation is borne out by a conversation which takes place the following week involving just Pete and Tony. They arrive at the pub ahead of the other two, and mull over Brian's self-disclosing behaviour the previous week. Example (21) gives an extract from this conversation:

(21) **Englishness**

Tony: I don't know Brian THAT well/ but every time I've met him/ he's been pretty . free with whatever happened to be on his mind at the time/

Pete: I don't know many people like that/ . you know who are able to sort of [*no*] just tap into . their- I don't know their situations their problems/ I know I take a long time to sort of er . warm to people I think=

Tony: =you . might wonder really how he . overcame the- the education that the rest of us obviously [succumbed to/ <LAUGHS>

Pete: [<LAUGHS> yeah/ %yeah%/ (1.0) I think I must be quite a typical Englishman in that sense/ being quite sort of er-

Tony: I k- I'm less English than I was/ <LAUGHS>

Pete: is that because you've been ab- abroad?

Tony: no/ [((xx))|

Pete: er [how did you- how did you manage to- to become less English?

Tony: I think it's because I decided that- . that (1.0) I ((really)) didn't like this way of relating to people very much/ and that . life actually would be . improved by . people being more open with each other/ . not that I'm . brilliant at it/ <QUIET LAUGH>

Pete: makes you vulnerable though don't you think? . um don't- don't you feel vulnerable? . sometimes?

Tony: yeah but . I suppose that . that's a useful reminder really isn't it/ ((I mean)) . vulnerability is er- (1.0) all the- all the- the- the masks and so on are supposed to keep vulnerability at bay/ but . .hh they only do this at a very high cost/

Pete: yeah/ I suppose that's another kind of pain isn't it/

Tony: yeah/

Pete: you know putting up barriers/ distancing yourself/ and maybe- . maybe more damage is done that way than actually=

Tony: =it's not impossible/

This is an extraordinary stretch of talk. I have found nothing comparable anywhere else in the conversations in the corpus. Pete and Tony not only address a topic that demands reflexivity, something men normally avoid; they stick to the topic and explore the issues that arise from it in a way that is relatively common in women friends' talk but is extremely rare in all-male talk. It is probably significant that there are only two speakers present: this conversation arises when two friends meet in the expectation that other friends will join them. When three or more males meet, it seems that peer group pressures make talk of this kind difficult, but where there are just two males, then a kind of intimacy is possible that is precluded otherwise.[8]

Peter and Tony make some fascinating observations on men's talk (though note that they gloss male inexpressivity as 'Englishness' and seem to overlook the gendered nature of the masks they are forced to wear). Tony argues for greater openness, which Pete responds to with a series of three questions: *makes you vulnerable though don't you think?* .

um don't- don't you feel vulnerable? . sometimes? Pete obviously feels vulnerable just talking like this, but wants to question Tony's assertion that it is better to be more open. Tony accepts that being open can make you vulnerable, but pursues his line of thinking by asserting that vulnerability is not necessarily bad but may be a useful reminder of our humanity. While feeling vulnerable can be uncomfortable, wearing masks all the time is a much worse option.

Tony here voices an alternative discourse which challenges hegemonic masculinity and asserts the value of emotional honesty and openness. The metaphor of the mask is a powerful one, and seems to express the experience of many men. Tolson, for example, describes conventional male interaction as follows: 'we would fall into the conventional "matiness" of the pub, a mutual back-slapping, designed to repress as much as it expresses. It was impossible to talk to other men about personal feelings of weakness or jealousy. A masculine "mask of silence" concealed the emptiness of our emotional lives' (1977: 10). It is this 'mask of silence' which Tony challenges in his bid for fuller, more honest interpersonal interaction.

Conclusion

In this chapter I have discussed only a fraction of the stories told in the conversations in my corpus. But I have tried to show how narrative is used in all-male talk to construct and maintain masculine identity. Conversational narrative is our chief means of constructing the fictions that are our lives and of getting others to collude in them. But storytelling also allows us to order or to re-order our everyday, normally taken-for-granted experiences. So while story-telling reinforces hegemonic masculinity, it can also provide a space where what is normally taken for granted can be questioned or challenged.

As we have seen, men's stories accomplish hegemonic masculinity through topic choice, language use and an emphasis on achievement and competition. We have also seen that male speakers struggle with issues of vulnerability, and struggle to come to terms with more 'feminine' aspects of themselves. Some of them explicitly struggle to form more meaningful relationships with each other, in place of the backslapping camaraderie typical of male friendship.

As Roper and Tosh put it: 'Despite the myths of omnipotent manhood which surround us, masculinity is never fully possessed, but must perpetually be achieved, asserted and renegotiated' (1991: 18). What I have tried to do in this chapter is to show some of the ways that conversational narrative is used by male speakers as a way of achieving, asserting and renegotiating the conflicting masculinities available to them at the turn of the century in Britain.

Notes

1. I would like to thank the following people for their helpful comments on earlier drafts of this chapter: Michael Bamberg, Wallace Chafe, Alison Kuiper, Dick Leith, Joanna Thornborrow.
2. I started using this methodology in 1985. Other sociolinguists who have collected conversational data using a similar approach are Rampton (1995) and Wilson (1989).
3. For transcription conventions, see pp. xiii–xv.
4. Psion is a company which manufactures mobile hand-held computers for commercial use.
5. In order to give some statistical backing to my observations, I've done a detailed analysis of a sub-set of the narratives in my conversational data: this sub-set consists of 67 stories selected to give full coverage of all 30 conversations. Stories chosen cover the whole range from minimal narratives of two lines to a very long story of 165 lines.
6. The following table summarises the gender of characters in the all-male sub-corpus of 67 stories (only 66 appear in the total here because in one story – 'Overheard between two cleaners' – the gender of the two cleaners is not clarified).

Table 7.1 Distribution of characters by gender in the sub-corpus

	Male	Female	Both	Total
Gender of protagonist	62 [94%]	3 [5%]	1 [2%]	66
Gender of other characters	47 [71%]	1 [2%]	18 [27%]	66

Note: Percentages have been rounded up to the nearest whole number, which means that totals are sometimes more than 100.

7. The worst thing that can happen to a narrator is that their story is seen as pointless; narrators need to avoid the 'So what?' challenge (see Labov 1972b: 363; Bruner 1991: 12).
8. The difference between two and three participants in friendly conversation seems to be highly salient for male speakers. A male friend of mine told me that he has two good friends who he goes running with, and that when he runs with either of them on their own, conversation is personal and engaging, but when all three of them run together, conversation is impersonal and stilted.

8

'My Mind Is with You': Story Sequences in the Talk of Male Friends [2001]

In this chapter,[1] I want to focus on the extent to which narrative construction involves collaboration between speakers, and how collaboration functions in informal friendly talk. Increasingly, conversation is seen as an achievement which involves 'the collective activity of individual social actors whose final product ... is qualitatively different from the sum of its parts' (Duranti 1986: 239). More specifically, narrative that occurs as part of spontaneous conversation is never a solo performance in the way oral narratives performed out in the public arena are (see Abrahams 1983; Bauman 1986; Labov 1972b). Conversational narrative is only possible when all participants in conversation jointly orient to someone telling a story. The terms 'narrator' and 'audience' set up a false picture of an active story-teller and a passive group of listeners, whereas the reality is that co-participants (the audience) are always co-authors in some sense. Commentators on narrative (for example, Goodwin 1986; Goodwin 1990; Ryave 1978; Sacks 1995) emphasise the fact that story-telling in conversation is a collaborative achievement, with narrative form and content being 'continuously reshaped by the co-participants, through their ability to create certain alignments and suggest or impose certain interpretations' (Duranti 1986: 242).

Where stories occur in sequence, the collaborative achievement of co-participants at talk is more overtly displayed. Story sequences are a common phenomenon in conversations of all kinds: a story can always be followed by another story, and a 'second story' (Sacks 1995) will be perceived as being in sequence as long as it is contiguous and has a topical link with the first story. In this chapter I want to focus on the role of story sequences in talk among male friends. Telling a second story involves co-participants in paying careful attention to what each other is saying. As Sacks (1995: 257) puts it, telling a relevant second story says

'My mind is with you'. This capacity of sequential story-telling to testify to the closeness of participants means that it can be a powerful way of 'doing' friendship.

Story sequences

In this chapter, I shall draw on a database of 30 all-male conversations. These conversations contain a total of 185 stories (for details of the methodology used, see Chapter 7, pp. 147–8).

When a narrative occurs in conversation, it can either stand alone, with normal multi-party conversation resuming after the story comes to an end,[2] or it can be followed by another story on the same theme. The tendency for stories to occur in clusters has been commented on by a wide range of researchers (Kirshenblatt-Gimblett 1974; Young 1987; Ryave 1978; Chafe 1994; Sacks 1995; Shepherd 1997). As Sacks puts it, 'stories come in clumps' and 'clumped stories have an apparent similarity between them' (1995: 249). Some commentators distinguish between clusters of stories which have no thematic link and *series* of stories which are thematically related. In this chapter I shall focus on the latter; that is, I shall focus on sequences of two or more stories in which 'the relations displayed between the two stories are not capricious and happenstance but are instead the product of the conversational participants' attention and careful management' (Ryave 1978: 121), and I shall refer to this structural pattern as a series or sequence of stories.

The decision as to what counts as a second story (a term coined by Sacks, 1995, to refer to a story that follows on thematically from a preceding story) is a subjective one. I have applied the two defining criteria of contiguity and thematic coherence very tightly. There are several examples in the database of stories which are on the same general topic but which are separated from each other by multi-party discussion among the participants, and I have not counted these as serial stories. An example is a conversation involving three college lecturers who are discussing men and clothes. This topic is sustained for nearly half an hour, and in the course of discussion five anecdotes are told. These range from personal stories about wearing a dinner jacket sprayed with glitter to a story about female students who couldn't afford dresses making their own ball gowns. In no case are two stories told one after the other; this is the main reason I have not counted them as constituting a sequence. But the other main reason is that these stories lack the quality displayed by 'true' second stories where the second narrator orients very carefully to the story told by the first narrator. In other words, these stories do not function as a display of closeness; they do not say 'My mind is with you.'

Story sequences in friendly talk

I shall look now in detail at one of the story sequences in my database to explore how the telling of second stories accomplishes solidarity. This sequence, the 'False identity' sequence, comes from a conversation involving three men in their 20s, Rob, Gary and Dan, who have met for a drink in a pub in Somerset. The sequence involves four stories. The men have been talking about their experiences in an electronics store where they have all worked at different times. An indirect reference to the practice of giving a false name when pressed by a customer triggers the following story from Rob.[3] (The full story sequence is given in full in an appendix at the end of the chapter.)

(1) **Avoiding sales**

There was one that I did,
was this customer,
was on the phone,
and I was setting up a satellite system that they wanted to buy,
not doing these satellites because it's a hell of a lot of discount on your number,
plus . a lot-
it's very time-consuming.
"Who shall I ask for when I come in?"
and I er- nearly said my name.
"Joh-n, Joh-n",
<D LAUGHS>
just came out,
"John"
<D and G LAUGH>
And then afterwards "I bet he'll have a go",
thought, "Oh fuck it"
<G LAUGHS>
I've done it a couple of times.
[G: *it's alright, I did that loads of times*]
"Who shall I ask for when I come in?"
"Jo- John".
<G LAUGHS>
I thought "look around and hope no one can see you".
John.

We can see how Gary aligns to this story, laughing at the climax of the story (lines 14 and 17) and again when Rob recycles the climax (line 22). His comment *it's alright, I did that loads of times* (line 19) is supportive in that it reassures Rob that what he has done is not abnormal (since Gary has done it *loads of times*). But perhaps Rob feels that this response focuses too much on Rob's mock anxiety about his action rather than on his self-presentation as 'a bit of a lad'. This could explain Rob's recycling of the last bit of his story in lines 20–24, which omits him worrying about the customer coming in (lines 15–16) and instead presents him as thinking *"look around and no one can see you"*, which has more bravado than the first version.

Dan, who produces a second story to follow this first story, mistimes the beginning of his story, because he assumes that line 18, *I've done it a couple of times,* is the last line of Rob's story (as Gary seems to do with his evaluative comment *it's alright, I did that loads of times*). Example (2) shows how the transition from the first story to the second story takes place.

(2)

1		
	Rob:	I've done it a couple of times/
	Gary:	it's alright/
2		
	Rob:	["who
	Gary:	I did that loads of times/
→	Dan:	bad as my mate [((xxxx
3		
	Rob:	shall I ask for when I come in?"/ Jo- John/
	Gary:	<LAUGHS>
	Dan:	xxxxxxxxxxxxxxxxxxxxxxx))
4		
	Rob:	I thought "look around and no-one
	Gary:	
	Dan:	he went out/
5		
	Rob:	can see you"/ John/
	Gary:	
	Dan:	so he went out last weekend right/

The opening line of the second story, *bad as my mate,* orients it carefully to the first, and announces that what Dan is taking as salient from the first story is that Rob did something 'bad'. 'Behaving badly' is a strong theme in the narratives of younger men in the corpus and is viewed as a positive way of doing masculinity (see Coates in press). Dan also announces that the chief protagonist in the story he is offering – who will play a parallel role to Rob in the first story – will be his mate. His next words are inaudible (because of Rob talking), and his utterance *he went out* is ignored by Rob, who continues with the end of his story.

Dan finally establishes a narrative floor with the line *so he went out last weekend right* and proceeds to tell the story 'You can't not know your name'. The story is given in example (3).

(3) **You can't not know your name**

Bad as my mate
[...]
So he went out last weekend right,
and he ended up going to Toff's.
'Cos he's underage he borrowed his mate's licence yeah,
and they always ask you your post code,
so he had that memorised right.
So he got to the door and he goes "Got any ID?"
Pulled up- pulled it out, give it to the doorman,
"What's your name?" <LAUGHTER>
And obviously like he'd been thinking about the post code over and over and over yeah
and he went "oh shit" <LAUGHTER>
"TA5 7ER . that's a funny name."
And he couldn't- he couldn't work it out right,
and he just stuttered after a while like that
going "yeah".
"What's your post code- post code?"
and he pulled that off perfectly
and he went "Alright I'll let you in like".
Just one of those moments you know life's turned to shit like that.
It's like . you can't not know your name, alright
you might not know your post code right
but you can't not know your name.

At this point Gary starts a third story on the same theme (of pretending to be someone you are not). The transition from Dan's to Gary's story is given in example (4).

(4)

1

Dan: you might not know your post code right/
Gary:
Rob:

Stave	Speaker	Utterance
2	Dan:	but you can't not know [your name/
	→ Gary:	[outside [of B's/
	Rob:	[fucking hell/
3	Dan:	
	Gary:	outside of B's/ Mike's driving licence/ "What's your
	Rob:	
4	Dan:	<LAUGHS> you can't think about it/
	Gary:	middle name?"/ shit/ um-
	Rob:	<LAUGHS>
5	Dan:	[it's too obvious isn't it?
	Gary:	[yeah but the thing is/ the worst thing was that
	Rob:	
6	Dan:	yeah/
	Gary:	Mike's parents fucked him about/ ((xx)) name/
	Rob:	

Gary's utterances *outside of B's/ Mike's driving licence/ "What's your middle name?"/ shit/* could be seen as an abstract for an upcoming story, or, more radically, it could be argued that they *are* the story. After all, given that we have had Dan's story, it is easy to make sense of Gary's telegraphic utterances: we assume that B's, like Toff's, is a club; that Gary, like Dan's mate, has borrowed a friend's driving licence as ID; that the doorman asks *What's your middle name?* (just as the Toff's doorman asked *What's your name?*), and that this question is problematic in some way since Gary's response (like that of Dan's mate) is *shit*. Dan's and Rob's laughter (stave 4) show that they have understood Gary's elliptical story. Dan adds the supportive comment *you can't think about it/ it's too obvious isn't it?* to show his alignment with the point of Gary's story (which matches the point of his own story perfectly), the point being that you can't hesitate when asked your name because you can't not know your name.

At this point Gary adds: *yeah but the thing is/ the worst thing was that Mike's parents fucked him about/*. This proposition – that Mike's parents fucked him about – provides the abstract for another story, one that Dan, rather than Gary, proceeds to tell. Perhaps Dan feels that Gary's statement on its own is insufficient for Rob, who does not know Mike as well as the other two, and who therefore may not be familiar with the story behind Mike's name and how his parents 'fucked him about'. Dan's story is given in example (5).

(5) **Mike's parents fucked him about**
For fucking sixteen or seventeen years of his life right
Mike's parents told him he had John Paul as his middle names
they said his middle names were John Paul right,
and when he turned seventeen or eighteen
they said it's Michael John Paul Honeyman
and they- and his Mum goes, "You haven't got any middle names by the way"
So all the things he'd applied for, right,
all his driving licence
everything had it on there, right,
and it was bullshit. <LAUGHS>

This story makes clear why Mike's name is an issue and why there could be doubt about what name might be on any given document. At the conclusion of Dan's clarificatory tale, Gary resumes his story; that is, he fleshes out what he had said before:

(6)
'cos I was- I was stood there
and he was like "What's your middle name?",
alright, well fuck,
has it got his middle name on there or hasn't it?
I said "Well I don't know,
if there's a middle name on there it'll be this,
if there isn't it's that".
<LAUGHTER>

Although I have talked so far of a series of four stories, it would be more accurate to say that this is a series of three stories with a fourth story embedded in the third. In other words, while the second and third stories ('You can't not know your name' and 'Mike's middle names') are both second stories in Sacks' sense, the fourth story ('Mike's parents fucked him about') is not: it does not 'follow on' from any other story but rather expands on a key point in the story 'Mike's middle names'. So this fourth story functions as part of the orientation (Labov 1972b: 364–366) of story 3. Story 3 could in fact be presented as follows (with Gary as the narrator and Dan's contributions given in italics):

(7) **Mike's middle names**
outside of B's,
outside of B's,
Mike's driving licence,
"What's your middle name?",

Shit.
<LAUGHS> *you can't think about it,*
it's too obvious isn't it?
yeah but the thing is,
the worst thing was that Mike's parents fucked him about [*yeah*]
((xx)) name.
For fucking sixteen or seventeen years of his life right
Mike's parents told him he had John Paul as his middle names
they said his middle names were John Paul right,
and when he turned seventeen or eighteen
they said it's Michael John Paul Honeyman
and they- and his Mum goes, "You haven't got any middle names by the way"
So all the things he'd applied for, right,
all his driving licence
everything had it on there, right,
and it was bullshit. <LAUGHS>
'cos I was- I was stood there
and he was like "What's your middle name?",
alright, well fuck,
has it got his middle name on there or hasn't it?
I said "Well I don't know,
if there's a middle name on there it'll be this,
if there isn't it's that". <LAUGHTER>

This story both exemplifies the careful work done to create second stories and the way speakers cooperate in talk. While Dan's embedded story is not part of the series of stories on false identity, it provides crucial background information for Gary's story. It thus helps Gary's story to be a successful second story, successful in the sense both that it works as a story (has a point) and that it works as a second story to the preceding story.

Second stories

Gary's story 'Matt's middle names' is a good example of the economy that can be found in second stories. Sacks (1995: 250) argues that while one criterion of what it is to be a 'story' is that it takes more than an utterance to produce, second stories are the exception to that rule. While Gary's second story here takes more than an utterance to produce, it is structurally quite different from the stories that precede it. Rob's first story has all the elements expected of a fully fledged narrative: it starts with an abstract (line 1), then provides orientation (who, where, when and other background information) in lines 2–7. The narrative core is told mostly through dialogue in lines 8–14, and is then repeated in lines 20–24. The story has a climax, in lines 11–13, clearly recognised by the laughter of Dan and Gary. It also has a clear point: the canonical script (that is, the unmarked script of everyday life – see Bruner 1991: 11) would have Rob giving his real name to the customer (and Rob alludes to this possibility in his story – *I nearly said my name* (line 9)), but he breaches the script by giving a false name. (For a story to be tellable, to have a point, it must involve a breach of the canonical script – see Bruner 1991; Polanyi 1985).

The story is evaluated through Rob's representation of his thoughts at the time: *thought, "Oh fuck it"* (line 16) frames the protagonist as someone who is prepared to risk the consequences of his deception; *I thought "Look around and hope no one can see you"* (line 23) presents him as well aware that what he has done is a breach of the canonical script but hoping to get away with it. This sense of 'getting away with it' is a significant theme in men's stories.

The second story in this sequence, 'You can't not know your name', is also a fully fledged story, with a narrative core and an explicitly made point. This means that this sequence of three stories consists of a first story, a second story that is structurally very like a first story and a third story which is structurally different from a first story. Why should these two 'second stories' (stories 2 and 3) differ like this? It seems to me that this variation in fullness between the two stories relates to how thematically coherent they are with the preceding story.

Let's look now in detail at the way these two stories achieve 'second storyhood' and also at the ways they differ. The first of them – 'You can't not know your name' – opens with the line *Bad as my mate*. This is a good example of the work required of second story-tellers if a story is to be perceived *as* a second story. It has been an important insight into serial stories in conversation that it is the work done by the second story-teller which creates the sense that the stories are in sequence (Sacks 1995; Ryave 1978; Young 1987). In other words, the teller of the first story cannot pre-ordain in any way that someone will tell a second story or what angle that second story will take. This may seem like stating the obvious, but given that analysts come at any given series of stories after the event – as part of a conversation on audio-tape or as a transcript on the page – it is easy to see them as structures involving two or more parts (stories), and to ignore the fact that the first story could have stood alone. As Young puts it, 'The appearance of thematic continuity is reconstituted backwards, the constitution of the pair of stories not being what is intended by the first but what is foregrounded by the second' (1987: 82).

Dan's words *bad as my mate* foreground 'badness' as the theme to be oriented to in Rob's story and so prepare his co-participants for a story which will parallel Rob's in telling about someone who behaved 'badly' in some way. The word *bad* not only orients to Rob's behaviour where he does not perform as the 'good' salesman, but also picks up the tone of *oh shit* which characterises stories of this kind which revolve around laddish pranks which have the potential for landing the protagonist in trouble. The syntactic structure *as ... as* (in the line [*as*] *bad as my mate*) explicitly sets up a comparison between the protagonist of this second story and the protagonist of the first, and foregrounds the parallelism between them in that both take on an assumed identity. But in other ways the stories are not parallel: they have very different settings – the first is set in the workplace during working hours; the second is set outside a club outside working hours – and the protagonists have very different motives for assuming a false identity. Moreover, Rob chooses a name, John, that belongs to no one in particular but which has the virtue of being a common name: his main aim is to avoid having to deal with a particular customer if he comes to the shop in person. By contrast, Dan's mate pretends to be a specific person, a friend who has a valid driving licence, and thus has no choice about what name he has to assume. These differences mean that Dan has to work hard to give his audience enough information to follow his story, since they can't infer this information from the previous story.

If we compare the second and third stories in the sequence ('You can't not know your name' and 'Mike's middle names'), we can see that they are topically very coherent. Both stories take place outside a nightclub, in both stories the narrative core involves the interaction between the protagonist and the doorman, and in both the point of the story is that 'you can't not know your name'. This very close parallelism means that the narrator of 'Mike's middle names' doesn't feel obliged to provide any linking utterance (to show the audience how he is orienting to the previous story). Instead he launches straight into his story, keeping rigorously to the structure set up by Dan in the previous story. He does not even use the pronoun 'I', so superficially this is a story without a named protagonist, but speakers will assume that where a story-teller ellipts the subject of narrative clauses, then the subject is likely to be 'I'.

The five lines that open Gary's story involve a great deal of ellipsis: not only is there no subject in these clauses; there are no verbs either. We hear lines 1–3 as orientation and lines 4 and 5 as narrative clauses because we supply past tense verbs as follows:

> *I was* outside of B's,
> *I was* outside of B's,
> *I had* Mike's driving licence,
> *The doorman asked* "What's your middle name?",
> *I thought* Shit.

We are able to do this because we have just heard the previous story. We can fill in the gaps from details that were given in full in 'You can't not know your name'.

You can't not know your name	**Mike's middle names**
1. So he went out last weekend right, and he ended up going to Toff's.	outside of B's
2. 'Cos he's underage he borrowed his mate's licence	Mike's driving licence
3. So he got to the door and he goes "Got any ID?" Pulled up- pulled it out, give it to the doorman, "What's your name?"	"What's your middle name?"
4. and he went "oh shit"	Shit.

The only changes that the second story introduces are: (i) the setting is a nightclub called B's not Toff's; (ii) the protagonist is the narrator, Gary, not Dan's mate; (iii) the driving licence belongs to Gary's friend Mike; (iv) the doorman asks him what his middle name is. The first three of these changes are trivial: the story hinges on the fourth change, the fact that it is Mike's *middle* name that needs to be known. The audience to the story 'You can't not know your name' can work out from their own cultural knowledge why it is that the protagonist is expected to know his name and why, in the circumstances, such a question might throw someone who was prepared for a harder question. However, in the following story, the reason that Mike's middle names are problematic is in-group knowledge, knowledge available to Gary and Dan but not necessarily to Rob. It is presumably for this reason that story 4, the embedded story 'Mike's parents fucked him about', is told.

What this discussion of a particular story sequence demonstrates is that it is not possible to make sweeping generalisations about the shape of second stories. They can only count as second stories if they are thematically coherent with the preceding story, but thematic coherence is an elastic concept. The second narrator may have to work quite hard to establish his story as a second story; or, as in the case of 'Mike's middle names', the second narrator may feel able to tell his story in an abbreviated form because it follows the pattern of the preceding story so closely. But whether a second story is more or less topically coherent with a first, telling a second story still accomplishes solidarity, since the achievement of a relevant second story demonstrates the close attention the second narrator has paid to the first story.

Story sequences and male solidarity

'Second story', then, is a term that covers a wide range of stories occurring in sequence, from more loosely connected stories to those with multiple close connections. While more loosely connected second stories require more careful linking work from narrators, more closely connected stories require careful inferencing and matching work from listeners. In other words, in all cases the telling of a second story is a collaborative achievement on the part of co-participants.

In the all-male conversations I've collected, nearly two-fifths (39 per cent) of the narratives told by men to their friends occurred as part of a sequence.[4] In other words, in a significant proportion of cases, men choose to follow a story with another story, a choice which carries a strong collaborative message.

This is interesting, given current understanding of masculinity and of male friendship. Contemporary accounts of male friendship (Greif 2009; Johnson and Aries 1983a, 1983b; Miller 1983; Nardi 1992; O'Connor 1992; Pleck 1995; Seidler 1989; Sherrod 1987) suggest that men's friendships are characterised by sociability rather than intimacy, with a focus on activity rather than talk. Social theorists link these characteristics of male friendship to emotional inexpressivity: 'masculinity is an essentially negative identity learnt through defining itself against emotionality and connectedness' (Seidler 1989: 7). Seidler goes so far as to claim that men's lives are structured by a particular relationship to language whereby 'language comes to be used as a weapon for the defence of masculine identity, rather than a mode of expressing connectedness with others, or honesty about emotional life' (1989: 7).

Recent research exploring the conversational practices of men friends lends support to the view of men as emotionally inexpressive (see Cameron 1997; Coates 2000; Curry 1991; Gough 1998; Gough and Edwards 1998). But while male speakers have been shown to avoid personal topics, mutual self-disclosure and collaborative turn-taking strategies, there is no doubt that male speakers express solidarity with each other through the use of linguistic strategies such as swearing, ritual insults, sexist and homophobic remarks and competitive banter (Cameron 1997; Gough and Edwards 1998; Kuiper 1997; Labov 1972a; Pilkington 1998). It is notable that these strategies simultaneously accomplish hegemonic masculinity (Connell 1995). What is interesting about the finding that male speakers will often choose to tell a second story is that this is a very different kind of way of accomplishing solidarity. Telling stories in sequence functions, among other things, to display mutual understanding. The capacity of male friends to tell stories in sequence suggests that male speakers *are* able to use language as a 'mode of expressing connectedness with others'.[5]

Conclusion

In this chapter I have explored the role of story sequences in talk among male friends. I have argued that telling a second story involves co-participants in paying careful attention to what each other is saying. By telling a relevant second story, a co-participant communicates 'My mind is with you' (Sacks 1995: 257). It could be that this aspect of sequential story-telling is valued by men precisely because it makes possible the display of mutual understanding. Most ways of displaying mutual understanding in all-male groups are taboo because of men's fear of appearing feminine, and the associated fear of appearing 'gay'. As Cameron puts it, 'men in all male groups must unambiguously display their heterosexual orientation' (1997: 61).

But men who meet as friends need strategies for 'doing' friendship. They need ways of showing mutual respect and understanding. Linguistic strategies such as the use of insults and taboo language may achieve solidarity, but at a cost, since such strategies are also highly face-threatening. The capacity of stories told in sequence to testify to the closeness of participants means that telling second stories can be a powerful way of 'doing' friendship. It is therefore not surprising that we find story sequences in conversations involving men friends: through their careful alignment to each other in their telling of second stories, co-participants at talk can display connectedness with each other, while at the same time telling stories of heroism or laddishness which construct and maintain hegemonic masculinity.

Appendix

The story sequence **False identities**

[*Asterisked portions of the conversation are spoken simultaneously*]

Rob: There was one that I did,
was this customer,
was on the phone,
and I was setting up a satellite system that they wanted to buy,
not doing these satellites because it's a hell of a lot of discount on your number,
plus . a lot-
it's very time-consuming.
"Who shall I ask for when I come in?"
and I er- nearly said my name.
"Joh-n, Joh-n",
<D LAUGHS>
just came out,
"John"
<D and G LAUGH>
And then afterwards "I bet he'll have a go",
thought, "Oh fuck it"
<G LAUGHS>
I've done it a couple of times.
Gary: it's alright, I did that loads of times
Rob: "Who shall I ask for when I come in?"
"Jo- John".
<G LAUGHS>
I thought "look around and no-one can see you".
John.
I've done it a couple of times.
Gary: it's all right. I did that loads of times.
Dan: bad as my mate **(xxxxxxxxxxxxx))**
Rob: **"who shall I ask for when I come in?"**
Jo- John.
Gary: <LAUGHS>
Dan: he went out.
Rob: I thought "look around and no-one can see you".
John.
Dan: so he went out last weekend right
and he ended up going to Toff's.
'Cos he's underage he borrowed his mate's licence yeah,
and they always ask you your post code,
so he had that memorised right.

So he got to the door and he goes "Got any ID?"
Pulled up- pulled it out, give it to the doorman,
"What's your name?"
<LAUGHTER>
And obviously like he'd been thinking about the post code over and over and over yeah
and he went "oh shit"
<LAUGHTER>
"TA5 7ER . that's a funny name."
And he couldn't- he couldn't work it out right,
and he just stuttered after a while like that
going "yeah".
"What's your post code- post code?"
and he pulled that off perfectly
and he went "All right I'll let you in like".
Just one of those moments you know life's turned to shit like that.
It's like . you can't not know your name, alright
you might not know your post code right
but you can't not know **your name**.
Gary: **outside** ++of B's++
Rob: ++fucking hell++
Gary: outside of B's
Mike's driving licence
"What's your middle name?"
shit, **um-**
Dan: **<LAUGHS>** you can't think about it/
Rob: **<LAUGHS>**
Dan: ++it's too obvious isn't it?++
Gary: ++yeah but the thing is++
the worst thing was that Mike's parents fucked him about
Dan: yeah
Gary: ((xx)) name.
Dan: For fucking sixteen or seventeen years of his life right
Mike's parents told him he had John Paul as his middle names
they said his middle names were John Paul right,
and when he turned seventeen or eighteen
they said it's Michael John Paul Honeyman
and they- and his Mum goes, "You haven't got any middle names by the way"
So all the things he'd applied for, right,
all his driving licence
everything had it on there, right,
and it was bullshit. <LAUGHS>
Gary: 'cos I was- I was stood there

and he was like "What's your middle name?",
alright, well fuck,
has it got his middle name on there or hasn't it?
I said "Well I don't know,
if there's a middle name on there it'll be this,
if there isn't it's that".
<LAUGHTER>

Notes

1. I would like to thank the following for their helpful comments on earlier drafts of this chapter: Michael Bamberg, Wallace Chafe, Alison Kuiper, Dick Leith, Joanna Thornborrow.
2. Conversations consist of two main components: discussion (multi-party-talk) and narrative (see Coates 1996a). All the conversations I have collected involve discussion, but the amount of narrative varies considerably (of the 30 all-male conversations, two involve only one story each, and one contains no narrative).
3. I shall follow the normal convention used by those who work on conversational narrative of presenting the story in numbered lines, each line corresponding to one of the narrator's breath-groups or intonation units, typically a grammatical phrase or clause (Chafe 1980).
4. This pattern is even more marked in all-female talk: women speakers tell stories which occur as part of a sequence in 62% of cases in my database.
5. Where self-promoting stories occur in sequence, then telling a second story can function as a competitive move. In one story sequence in the corpus, the narrator of the second story begins his story with the words *tell you what, I'll beat all of that,* which explicitly labels his narrative as a competitive speech act. Competitive story-telling only occurred in the younger groups in the database, where friendship links were less well developed.

9

'Everyone Was Convinced That We Were Closet Fags': The Role of Heterosexuality in the Construction of Hegemonic Masculinity [2007]

At any given time in a culture, there will be many competing masculinities in play, all available to be discursively reproduced by speakers. But of these competing masculinities, one will predominate. It is this form of masculinity – hegemonic masculinity – that I shall focus on in this chapter.[1] My aim is to explore the role of heterosexuality in the formation of contemporary masculinities in Britain, in particular in the formation of hegemonic masculinity, drawing on a database of spontaneous conversation collected over the last ten years or so.

The concept of hegemonic masculinity was developed by Robert Connell and his colleagues working in feminist sociology. According to Connell (1995), in order to carry off 'being a man' in everyday life, men have to engage with hegemonic masculinity. 'The concept of "hegemony" ... refers to the cultural dynamic by which a group claims and sustains a leading position in social life. At any given time, one form of masculinity rather than others is culturally exalted' (Connell 1995: 77). Hegemonic masculinity maintains, legitimates and naturalises the interests of powerful men while subordinating the interests of others, notably the interests of women and gay men. This position is not fixed but is always contestable: the masculinity occupying the hegemonic position is always open to challenge from alternative masculinities. It is an ideal, a normative construction against which males – whatever their class or ethnic allegiance – are measured and, almost invariably, found wanting (Kimmel 2000: 91).

Key components of contemporary hegemonic masculinity are hardness, toughness, coolness, competitiveness, dominance and control (Connell 1995; Wetherell and Edley 1998, 1999; Frosh et al. 2002). Although most men do not fit this ideal, the concept of hegemonic masculinity 'captures the power of the masculine ideal for many boys and men' (Frosh et al. 2002: 76).

One significant way in which hegemonic masculinity is created and maintained is through the denial of femininity. The denial of the feminine is central to masculine gender identity (Frosh et al. 2002: 77; Connell 1995: 78; Roper and Tosh 1991: 13; Segal 1990: 15). As Adam Jukes puts it, 'the exorcism of all one's identifiable "feminine" or "mothering" qualities is essential to assuming masculinity' (1993: 43). Such norms exert great pressure on males in our culture. Men avoid ways of talking that might be associated with femininity and also actively construct women and gay men as the despised other. In a research project involving in-depth interviews with boys in 12 London secondary schools, Stephen Frosh and his colleagues claimed that one of the canonical narratives about masculinity was the following: 'Boys must maintain their difference from girls (and so avoid doing anything that is seen as what girls do)' (2002: 77). Being different from girls is far more important for boys than being different from boys is for girls. In contemporary Western culture, we all recognise that 'being a sissy is a far more serious offence to the gender order than being a tomboy' (Kimmel 2000: 235).

Avoidance of the feminine is viewed by psychoanalysts in terms of mother–son relations. As Jessica Benjamins puts it, repudiation of the mother results in 'a kind of "fault line" running through the male achievement of individuality' (1990: 76). This fault line is implicated in the 'othering' of women and of gay men. Identity construction involves by definition the construction of out-groups as well as the construction of in-groups. We know who is 'we' because 'we' is 'not them' and 'they' is 'not us'. 'The dual others to normative heterosexual masculinities in schools are girls/women and non-macho-boys/men' (Frosh et al. 2002: 62). For adult males, the othering of gay men and the denial of homosexuality are particularly salient. Many researchers believe that hegemonic masculinity and heterosexual masculinity are isomorphic (Kiesling 2002; Gough and Edwards 1998; Cameron 1997; Curry 1991; Herek 1987). It is certainly the case that, at the beginning of the twenty-first century in westernised cultures, 'heterosexual meanings have come to saturate dominant notions of adult "femininity" and "masculinity"' (Thorne 1993:155).

Data

The conversational data in this chapter were collected as part of a wider research project exploring gender differences in language use in Britain. Participants come from a wide range of geographical locations, including urban contexts such as Belfast and Birmingham, suburban contexts such as the Wirral and Surrey, and more rural locations such as Somerset. They belong to a wide range of class and age groups; the majority are white. The database resulting from this project includes all-male, all-female and mixed talk.[2] This chapter focuses on the all-male data: 32 all-male conversations, audio-recorded with the men's agreement and subsequently transcribed. Participants in all cases were friends: in other words, recordings were made of groups or pairs of men who had a well-established relationship.[3]

An example

At any given time, according to Connell, one form of masculinity rather than others is 'culturally exalted' (1995: 77). This is the masculinity he calls 'hegemonic masculinity' and is the ideal against which contemporary British men measure themselves. To illustrate the kind of masculinity that is 'culturally exalted' at this time in Britain, I shall look at a typical man's story from my database. Example (1) is a story told by Rob during conversation with friends in the pub. It is one of a series of stories about the workplace – this one focuses on a colleague who had an alcohol problem.[4]

(1) **The fight**
[three lower-middle-class men in their 20s in a pub in Somerset talk about an alcoholic engineer at work]

he came in this one time,
drunk,
and he started ordering me about.
With kind of personality I've got
I told him to piss off,
I wasn't taking any of it.
So I was making these um alarm bell boxes,
the alarm boxes,
you put this bell on and you wire these-
can't remember how to do it now anyway but-
wiring these up,
and he come out,

and he sss, sss, sss, <MIMICS NOISE>
what he did was he threw this knife at me,
this is honest truth,
threw a knife at me,
and then- and there was this cable,
you know um like on the workbenches where you connect the cables into these three points,
a bare wire,
he fucking chased me with it,
and I thought "Fuck this",
and he kept like having a go and teasing me,
and I just smashed him straight round the face with a bell box in front of the boss,
crack,
got away with it as well,
I said "Look", I said, "he's thrown knives at me",
it sounds like something out of a film but it's honest truth.
[...]
Honestly it was unbelievable.

'The fight' is a typical first-person male narrative (see Coates 2000, 2003a). It is typical in that it contains the following features: the story constitutes a boast; the narrator presents himself as a lone protagonist who gets involved in conflict, conflict which involves physical violence; the narrator presents himself as a winner; the story is infused with an awareness of power, both the narrator's physical power in relation to the drunken engineer and also the boss's institutional power, which means the narrator can boast that he *got away with it* (line 25). Other minor points to note are that all the characters in the narrative are male; the setting is the workplace; the narrator goes into detail about technical things such as alarm boxes and cables; the language used includes taboo words (e.g. *piss off, fucking*) and sound effects (e.g. *sss, crack*).

Rob's story focuses on action, and, through his story, he presents himself as a winner, someone who will not be pushed around, someone who stands up for himself, and also as someone who gets away with things. His story foregrounds the workplace as a key arena for action, and the storyworld he creates is populated entirely by men: women do not exist in this world. The story, 'The fight', is a performance of masculinity; moreover, it is a performance of hegemonic masculinity. By this, I mean that Rob uses his account of his fight with the drunken engineer to align himself with dominant norms of masculinity, norms which are exemplified by characters in popular films such as *Rambo* and *The*

Terminator. Stories like 'The fight' are canonical stories of male achievement. When they are told by male narrators to other men, they perform hegemonic masculinity in two ways: first, they perform hardness, coolness, dominance and control (as I have argued, these are key components of hegemonic masculinity); second, they function to maintain difference from women.

What this story accomplishes unambiguously is saying 'I am a man.' The narrator's heterosexuality is not foregrounded in the story, and in this respect the story is typical of those I have collected. Heterosexuality does not have to be foregrounded; it is an assumed component of hegemonic masculinity. Thus, in stories such as 'The fight', 'compulsory heterosexuality is taken for granted as the cultural norm' (Frosh et al. 2002: 63).

Hegemonic masculinity and heterosexuality

I shall now move from canonical stories like 'The fight' to an examination of stories which throw light more overtly on the links between hegemonic masculinity and heterosexuality. I shall look in turn at the following: homophobic talk and talk about homosexuality, the exclusion of women from men's storyworlds, misogynistic talk, boasting to women, collaborative story telling.

Homophobic talk and talk about homosexuality

Hegemonic masculine discourses are both misogynistic and homophobic. Deborah Cameron spells out the norm as follows: 'men in all-male groups must unambiguously display their heterosexual orientation' (1997: 61). Younger males in my corpus are openly homophobic at times. Example (2) is a story told by Lee, a 20-year-old male student from an upper-working-class background, to a friend about an evening out with his friend Bill.

(2) **Queerie**

and er night before I left to come here right
I um ((xx)) Bill ((xx)),
I told you this.
I was driving down the road
and I've just seen this long hair little fucking mini-skirt.
I've beeped the horn,
this fucking bloke's turned round,
I've gone "aaaggghhh!" <SCREAMS>
<LAUGHTER>

Bill's gone "what what what?",
"it was a bloke",
I've gone, "turn round, turn round",
and he's turned round
and you could just see these shoes hiding under this car
and he must've thought we were just gonna literally beat the crap out of him.
[...]
I've driven past,
opened the window,
"come out, come out, wherever you are,
here queerie, queerie, queerie".

This story does important work in terms of establishing the narrator's identity: he positions himself as uncompromisingly heterosexual both through his initial interest in the person with long hair wearing a mini-skirt, and also through his horrified reaction when he realises this person is actually a man. His fantasy that the cross-dresser feared they would *beat the crap out of him* hints at the violent feelings unleashed by this encounter. The story ends with the narrator presenting himself as venting his fury at this subversion of conventional gender boundaries by shouting taunts and insults at the man (whether this actually happened or not is beside the point). This story demonstrates how powerful narrative can be as a tool of self-presentation and self-construction: the narrator is at an age when his sexual identity is still fragile, and the function of this story is to establish his credentials as a 'normal' heterosexual man.

The next example, example (3), is an extract from a conversation between two 17-year-old boys at one of Britain's most prestigious public schools. They are discussing another boy, called Prendergast. Again, these boys are still working to develop a more solid sense of their own masculinity, and this extract shows them struggling with what that means.

(3) **Talking about Prendergast**
[*Henry's study-bedroom at boarding school*]

Julian: Prendergast had tea in Mason's room
and threw stuff out of the window
Henry: yeah
Julian: were you there?
Henry: yeah
Julian: was he being a massive twat?

Henry: no not really [...]
you know he was just being normal
he was going- he was talking about . being raped by Ralph, yeah?
Julian: yeah
Henry: and he was going on about how he didn't see it-
think it was actually that disgusting
Julian: he is gay! <INDIGNANT TONE>
Henry: and then- and then we said [...]
"didn't you think it was absolutely disgusting?"
he was sit- he was just sitting there like not answering,
he was just sort of avoiding the question.

This discussion of an absent third person allows them to explore their attitude to homosexuality. Homosexuality is a live topic in British public schools, as it is in all all-male institutions such as the army and men's prisons. With no women in this social world, and with the dominant discourses insisting that males are biologically programmed to 'need' sexual gratification (Hollway 1983), the taboos against homosexuality have to be very strong, and in such institutions 'compulsory heterosexuality' (Rich 1980) is rigidly affirmed. The specialised language of such institutions is very revealing: the slang of an in-group is a powerful bonding mechanism, and areas of 'lexical density' centre on women, sexual activity, homosexuality and race. The misogyny and homophobia of such groups can literally be measured by the enormous numbers of pejorative words coined in these areas (see Moore 1993; Looser 1997).

In this extract, Henry seems prepared to explore what it means to be 'raped'[5] and to mull over Prendergast's claim that this experience was not necessarily disgusting. Julian, however, is quick to say *he is gay* (line 13). What this statement asserts is that if someone describes a sexual encounter with someone of the same sex as not 'disgusting', they must be homosexual. This is a defensive move, and shows Julian's anxiety to close down discussion. He wants to draw a clear line between people who are gay and who consider same-sex activity to be not disgusting, and 'normal' people who *do* consider same-sex activity to be disgusting. Henry's story threatens to breach that neat dichotomy, since Prendergast appears to be a 'normal' boy like Julian and Henry and yet he seems to be saying that his sexual encounter with Ralph was just 'an experience'. Henry's response to Julian's outrage is noticeably disfluent: he in turn feels threatened, and he has to re-establish his credentials as a member of the 'normal' camp. He does this by claiming that he and his friends had asked *"didn't you think it was absolutely disgusting?"* (line 15), a question that presupposes that it was 'absolutely disgusting'.

But despite Julian's strong reaction here, other parts of this conversation between these two friends, Julian and Henry, reveal a persistent homoerotic theme. For example, before Henry embarks on the story about Prendergast, a remark of Julian's casts light on the way the two boys are sitting in Henry's study-bedroom.

(4) *talk preceding* **Talking about Prendergast**

Julian: ow ow like . OK the neck massage is great [*Henry laughs quietly*]
but not when done by your feet [*Henry laughs*]
Julian: ng ng ng...
Henry: ng ng ng... [*both boys mimic the sound of an electric guitar*]

To judge from Julian's words, Henry has his feet on Julian's neck while they talk. The evidence that they are both relaxed about this physical contact is provided by their making those noises so typical of teenage boys, sounds imitating an electric guitar solo (made, presumably, while they pretend to play a guitar).

Later in the same conversation, Julian actually steers the talk round to a time in the past when they were suspected of being 'fags' (i.e. homosexuals).

(5) **Closet fags**

Julian: I'd- I'd forgotten about that little . episode in M
when everybody was convinced that we were closet fags
Henry: um that- but that- ((I mean)) that just- that ((was))- that's finished
Julian: that was just 'cos every second minute I was .
popping along to your room [...]
yeah it's also like the way-
you know it's what Robert dines off
is the fact that .hh Lynch climbing into your bed
and like no insult but I really couldn't
climb into your bed in the morning
Henry: **yeah that- that was fairly** that was unfortunate I agree
Julian: I really couldn't climb into your bed in the morning
Henry: <LAUGHS>
Julian: I'm sorry, it would have to be very cold
Henry: <LAUGHS> yeah that was unfortunate,
does he still go on about that?
Julian: <u>yes</u> <BORED DRAWL>

Henry: really?
Julian: yes <BORED DRAWL>
Henry: %god%

[*NB: utterances appearing between asterisks ** were spoken at the same time*]

This chunk of talk does very important work in negotiating their relationship. They establish that they are not 'closet fags', even though people thought they were. They look at why people made this assumption, and also consider the problems caused for Henry by Lynch's escapade, which according to Julian is still a topic of conversation. Julian's light-hearted banter about why he chooses not to get into bed with Henry in the morning suggests that while it is important for him to state that this is *not* what he wants to do, he still chooses to talk about what he would not do, and to say it twice. He even jokes *I'm sorry, it would have to be very cold* (line 14), implying that in certain circumstances he *would* get into bed with Henry.

For younger speakers, the work of asserting their heterosexuality, that is, of asserting non-homosexuality, is an important part of their everyday construction of themselves as men. These few examples show that this can vary from virulent homophobia (as in example 2) to more relaxed discussion and negotiation of sexual identity (as in the last example). In all these examples the dominance of heterosexual masculinity is apparent, as is the tension between heterosocial and homosocial norms.

Exclusion of women from the storyworld

Another aspect of men's talk that I want to look at is the virtual exclusion of women from the storyworld of men's stories. In both women's and men's storyworlds, the most common character is the narrator themselves. In other words, first-person narratives are the preferred form for all speakers. In relaxed circumstances we tend to tell stories about ourselves more than we tell stories about significant others (in my database, first-person narratives constitute 72 per cent of women's narratives and 68 per cent of men's). This suggests that women's storyworlds will have a bias towards female characters and men's towards male characters. But nearly all stories involve other characters beside the protagonist, and third-person stories focus on a character who is not the narrator (even though the narrator may be a participant in the events narrated). In other words, there is plenty of scope even in first-person narratives to portray a world which contains both men and women.

But, as we have seen in earlier examples, men's stories often involve no women. The story, 'The fight', discussed above, is a good illustration of this. The main character is the first-person narrator, who tells a story about a fight with a (male) workmate, a fight witnessed by the (male) boss. There are no women in this storyworld. Overall, only 28 per cent of the men's stories include women, as Table 9.1 illustrates. This contrasts with the storyworld typical of female narrators, where men are more often present than not (88 per cent of stories in the all-female conversations involve both men and women).

Table 9.1 Gender of characters in stories told in all-male and all-female conversation

Gender of characters	Men's stories	Women's stories
All characters are male	72%	1.5%
All characters are female	1.5%	10%
Characters are both male and female	26.5%	88%

The exclusion of women from the storyworld of men's stories is a disturbing aspect of all-male narrative. These narratives do important ideological work, maintaining a discourse position where men are all-important and women are invisible. This seems to be another aspect of the denial of the feminine.

Misogynistic talk

It is generally assumed that one of the topics of all-male talk is women, and that much of this talk is misogynistic. In this section I shall examine two explicitly misogynistic stories from my database, but it is important to note that the conversations I collected contain relatively little misogynistic material compared with those collected by male researchers for a variety of research projects. These research projects involved men talking in the 'locker room' before and after sporting events, boys talking about sex, men meeting for a drink and a chat, and men talking about drink and violence (see Curry 1991; Gough and Edwards 1998; Tomsen 1997; Wood 1984). Much of this material is more sexist and homophobic than anything I have collected. For example, the men's talk in my database does not involve explicit talk about male genitalia (Gough and Edwards 1998), sustained talk about women in terms of body parts (Gough and Edwards 1998; Wood 1984), or fantasies about rape (Curry 1991; Wood 1984). This might mean that male speakers unconsciously censor themselves when the researcher is female. On the other hand, it could suggest that men are more constrained by hegemonic norms when designing their talk for the ears of a male researcher. Certainly, the more 'macho' elements of hegemonic masculinity are more in evidence in data collected by male researchers, just as they are more in evidence in my data in the all-male conversations than in the mixed conversations.

The two stories I shall focus on here come from the subset of stories told by men which actually include women as characters. I've argued that in conversation men and boys avoid ways of talking that might be associated with femininity, and also actively construct women as well as gay men as the despised other. Misogyny certainly seems to inform men's portrayal of women in some of the stories where women *do* appear.

(6) **This girl called Debbie**
[*two male friends aged 19/20, upper-working-class, narrator = Lee*]

I know this girl called Debbie
well I used to know her
and er-
why did you stop knowing her?
dickhead <LAUGHTER>
anyway first time I met her I was sitting in someone's garden having a joint with this bird with my legs like that
having a chat with her
and suddenly I just felt this like warmth all over my leg
I've looked round and she's-
no joke I swear to god she had her fucking tits hanging over my leg
I just went "ooh" like that
and this girl's just gone.

(7) **The vibrator**
[*seven male friends aged mid-20s, lower-middle-class, narrator = Gary*]

I went to this customer's house the other day with um-
I was told to go there basically by um the corporate sales director for the Dixon's Stores group [*yeah*]
he phoned me up and he said "You've got to go to this customer
'cos she's been like trying to write letters to Sidney Smith [*the Managing Director*]" and stuff like this [*yeah*]
so I get round there and there's like nothing wrong with her computer at all
whinging bitch
it was quite funny when I was walking out though
'cos I was walking out-
the computer's in her bedroom
I was just sort of looking around
looked down on the floor under her bedri- bedside cabinet
and there was this fucking great vibrator
<LAUGHTER>
I sort of looked at her and she looked at me and she was like "oh fuck"

<LAUGHTER>
it's not the sort of thing you leave about when you got the engineers coming to do the PC is it?
she had kids as well though
fucking kids walking around
bloody great vibrator with a sucking cap on the end of it
was she very nice looking?
no she's a big fat pig [*oh*]

Both these stories function as boasts and perform hegemonic (heterosexual) masculinity. Both stories are first-person narratives, and both storyworlds include a female character. But in both the woman is presented in sexual terms. In 'This girl called Debbie', the eponymous Debbie is hardly a rounded person: the point of the story is that the narrator felt her breasts on his leg. For the narrator and his friend, it seems that the recounting of such an event is regarded as tellable. This reveals a lot about the internal world of young men – for them, accounts of such encounters are a significant means of bolstering their sense of their own masculinity. It doesn't seem to matter what the woman Debbie was like as a person, since what matters in Lee's construction of himself as a heterosexual male is this contact with part of a woman's body. The reduction of women to body parts is a well-documented phenomenon which objectifies women and strips them of human status (see Gough and Edwards 1998; Haywood and Mac an Ghaill 1997; Renold 2000).

In example (7), 'The vibrator', the narrator is more sophisticated in his self-presentation. He presents himself as a reliable employee (who carries out promptly the orders of an important senior male) and as a responsible citizen upholding moral standards (see lines 17–18: *she had kids as well though, fucking kids walking around*). However, he simultaneously presents himself as a patriarchal male who treats women with contempt, with his backstage comments *whinging bitch* and *a big fat pig,* and as a sophisticated, sexually experienced man who knows about vibrators. This complex self-presentation performs masculinity on many levels. But yet again, the woman in the story is unimportant as a person: she is presented in stereotypical terms as a technically incompetent complaining customer – *whinging bitch* – and as a sexual being. While the narrator's attitude to her sexuality is one of disapproval, what matters is that he consigns her to this sexual pigeonhole.

When women are not defined in sexual terms, they tend to be peripheral characters in men's stories, appearing most commonly as wives or mothers. While such references to women are not explicitly misogynistic, they hint at an underlying – androcentric – worldview where women are of little importance. A good example is the following brief extract from the story 'The good Samaritan':

(8) *extract from* **The good Samaritan**
we walked round this boulder
and there sitting on the top . was a European couple
with their backs to us,
as they heard us approach they turned round,
→ and lo it was my Vice Chancellor and his wife.

The point of this subsection of the story is the unexpected meeting between the narrator – a linguistics lecturer – and his Vice Chancellor. The Vice Chancellor's wife is an incidental character.

Another example comes in the story 'Strap 'er on':

(9) *extract from* **Strap 'er on**
this bloke called Phil at work
lives in Taunton
[...]
→ and he calls his Mum our Gladys

The reference to the mother is included because the narrator is building up a picture of his strange colleague, Phil: the mother is not a character in the story in any proper sense. The world depicted by the narrator, where Phil behaves in a crazy way, is peopled by men apart from this fleeting reference.

Boasts in front of women

My database contains all-female and mixed talk as well as all-male talk. I shall now turn to the mixed conversations in my database, that is, to conversations where men and women are talking to each other. I want to show how men's stories in mixed talk function as a form of heterosexual display.

The first example is an extract from a long story and is part of the story's opening. The story is told by Tony to his friend Emily; they are both in their early 20s.

(10) **The fire alarm**
have I told you that story about um . me on cricket tour? [*no*]
got no relation to what I've been saying but- [*E LAUGHS*]
no, I'll tell you anyway.
this must've been when we were about thirteen

and we stayed at this really posh school
it was in the summer holidays
'cos it was like the cricket season obviously <LAUGHS>
and um- and we're all like in a corridor
[...]
and um- and we're just like pissing about in the corridor playing cricket
[...]
I've bowled this ball
and it's hit the top of this chair which we used as a wicket
and it's gone-
it's only a tennis ball
and it's hit like . the main alarm [*E LAUGHS oh dear*]
and it's evacuated the-
I'm not joking
must be about a hundred and fifty people in this building [*E LAUGHS*]
and um . this is like two in the morning [*bloody hell*]

This story is clearly a boast, just like 'The fight'. Stories are often boasts, but the narrators in all-male talk are overtly competing with each other to tell the best story; they use story-telling as a way of jockeying for position. However, in a story such as 'The fire alarm', the male narrator is not competing with his female friend in terms of individual prowess. Tony does not expect Emily to respond with a story about her own sporting achievements. Tony tells his story to impress Emily and to be indulged by her.

Men's assumption that women will indulge them and listen to their stories of youthful escapades is borne out in this particular conversation. The conversation contains a total of 20 narratives. Of these, 15 are told by Tony, 4 by Emily, and 1 is a joint effort. Not only does Tony dominate the conversation in terms of narrative, he uses these narrative opportunities to construct a dominant form of masculinity and is supported in doing this by Emily.

Let's look now at a story from a different type of conversation, one involving a middle-aged lecturer (Michael), his female partner (Suzanne) and a close male friend (Bill) during a meal at Michael and Suzanne's house in Islington. This story is also a boast; it emerges from general conversation about wine and wine-drinking. Example (11) is just an extract from the opening of the story; the storyteller is Michael. (Michael's words are printed in normal font; Suzanne's in italic capitals; Bill's in italics.)

(11) **Buying wine in Cornwall**
funnily enough we went to an inn in Cornwall

which had a most impressive display of . wine bottles on the wall [*mhm, MHM*]
um . well you may see Bill after you've finished
and um .
these were empty bottles
no no, they were full I mean
and they had a- a-
and- and . it was recommended as a place to eat by various guidebooks
so we had a meal there
and got chatting to the owner
'cos I thought his wine was very good
and very reasonable- very reasonably priced [*yes*]
and so well we have a list
so er -
[...]
paradoxically . I- I've ordered um four cases of wine from Cornwall

While this narrative displays the emotional restraint typical of well-educated middle-aged men (Jackson 1990: 156; Seidler 1989: 63; Pleck 1995), it is still in essence a boast. The narrator/protagonist presents himself as someone who cleverly spots that a Cornish inn-keeper has a good palate and orders four cases of wine from him. This is a narrative of achievement, but achievement in a social context where being a hero is acted out in terms of wine connoisseurship rather than engagement in physical contest with another man (as in 'The fight').

After Michael has finished his narrative, Bill tells a minimal narrative about wine-buying which aligns him very positively with Michael's point of view and performs solidarity between the two men. It also functions to position him as another wine connoisseur. Example (12) gives Bill's story and Michael's response to it. (Bill's words are in italics; Michael's in normal font.)

(12) **Oddbins in Upper Street**

well I went to the Oddbins in Upper Street to get the bottle that I brought
I wasn't wildly impressed with what they had there [no, it's um-]
they're trying too hard in too many directions
yeah, ((that's)) my sense
you see whereas with this chap [in Cornwall] he just- . he buys what he likes
[...]
I thought we'll . see if his palate is as extensively good as-
it was certainly good on the Chablis and- and on Côtes du Rhône
so I was thinking well- if it extends across the range
I'll put you on the mailing list

The chief recipient of the story 'Buying wine in Cornwall' is, at first glance, a male. But a better analysis of examples (11) and (12) is to see them as a performance of masculinity by two male friends to a female audience. These two examples show how complex recipient design can be, with the primary narrator–recipient duo (Michael and Bill) being attended to in turn by another recipient, Michael's partner. The fact that the primary duo consists of male speakers, while the secondary recipient is female, is highly salient to the narrative's design. Suzanne, apart from helping to clarify a particular point in Michael's story (not shown in example 11), does not make any contribution to the narrative, but her silent presence is vital to our understanding of what Michael and Bill are doing, which is in essence a form of masculine (heterosexual) display (see Dunbar 1996). So in examples (10), (11) and (12), men and women collude in the construction of hegemonic masculinity and in the maintenance of conventional gender relations.

Collaborative story-telling

I have argued that telling stories to a female audience allows men to indulge in a form of heterosexual display. But telling stories in mixed company also allows men to discuss topics which they avoid in all-male talk – topics such as death, fear, concern for small animals. Even more striking, it allows men to tell stories collaboratively. This is something that occurs only rarely in all-male talk, though it is common in all-female talk. Collaborative story-telling is symbolic of closeness and connection – it is presumably avoided by men in talk with other men because displaying closeness with another male is dangerous and could be construed as 'gay'.[6]

But in mixed talk involving heterosexual couples, men and women share in the telling of stories. I'm going to focus on two examples which occur in sequence. They come from a conversation involving two couples, Diane and Ian, and Jean and Martin. What is remarkable about this sequence of two stories is that both stories are collaboratively constructed, with Jean and Martin telling the first and Diane and Ian telling the second.

(13) **Kittens 1**

[*Jean's words are in normal typeface, Martin's in italics*]

we looked out of our window today
we saw two little kittens didn't we?
[I thought "what the hell is that doing out there"
[*dashing past the window yeah, tiny*

**'cos I thought i- it was too young to be out
one of them was like that
just chucked in the garden**
***only one of them that big and one was just a little bit bigger there*
*it just- they had the- ***
I thought [“((xxxxxxxxxxx))”
[*chasing each other round the garden*
I knocked next door,
I said “have you got two new kittens?”,
and he said “yeah”,
and I said “Have they escaped or something or what?”,
“They're alright as long as they don't go that way”,
like pointing to the road,
I thought well can't really guarantee that really can you?
no the road is a- it's a busy road.

Jean and Martin's story is followed directly by another one, told by Ian and Diane, again on the subject of kittens. The story is initiated by Ian, who makes the topical link with the first story, but Diane provides the second line, and from then on they construct the story collaboratively, with occasional contributions from Jean and Martin. Example (14) gives an extract from this (longer) story. ('Jazz' is Ian and Diane's cat.)

(14) **Kittens 2**
[*Ian's contributions are in normal typeface; Diane's in italics; Jean's in italic capitals*]

it's like that stupid bat who lived next door to me in . Allen Close
she had a cat that could [*never have been more than five weeks old*
[she- she had a . ((little)) cat that big
no way maybe even four weeks old
like that
NOT WITH THE MOTHER? [no] OH THAT'S AWFUL
((there)) there and sh- she put it out for the day
[((xxxxxxxxxxxxxxxx))
[*((put it out there))*
and Jazz used to bring it home
[she just put it out
[*and it is so tiny*
it couldn't even get through the cat flap
it couldn't [reach up into the cat flap
[*that's how . tiny he was*
[...]
he was completely black and just absolutely . adorable wasn't he?
and on one day “bug doosh” <SOUND EFFECT>

through there [in the cat flap ((2 words))
[*and one day he actually got through*
and i- he was- he was hanging through the cat flap with his little paws dangling
[he was like <RUNNING NOISE>
[*but . he couldn't get the rest of his body through*
and he got through the cat flap
and that was it
he used to come [in and out and then out
[*they went up and down the stairs*
[they w- it didn't want to go
[*we used to feed him and everything*
and she used to put it out all day like
I mean this thing was like . just could not survive
I used to get in from work and ((take it from)) the door and feed him and everything

'Kittens 2' is a classic example of collaborative narration. The story is co-narrated by two speakers who share the floor to give an account of a shared experience, using repetition of words and phrases and simultaneous speech to tie their contributions together.

Example (14), like (13), shows that male speakers can perform alternative versions of masculinity in certain contexts. Ian and Martin both choose to collaborate in narratives where the topic is kittens and where key themes are care for and concern about vulnerable creatures. Such themes are not characteristic of narratives produced in all-male talk. What seems to be crucial about the circumstances of this conversation is that both men (Ian and Martin) are in stable partnerships with women, and the four speakers are also friends with each other.

But if we examine Ian and Diane's contributions to 'Kittens 2' carefully, we can see that as co-narrators they still take up conventional gender positions relative to each other. Diane's contributions draw on a nurturing or maternal discourse; examples are *Jazz used to bring it home* (line 10), *we used to feed him and everything* (line 29), *I used to get in from work and ((take it from)) the door and feed him and everything* (line 32). They also pay attention to the kitten's adorability and smallness: *he was [...] just absolutely adorable wasn't he?* (line 17), *that's how tiny he was* (line 15), *with his little paws dangling* (line 21). Ian contributes more narrative clauses than Diane (compare lines 11 and 12, where Ian's narrative clause *she just put it out* is said at the same time as Diane's evaluative line *and it is so tiny*). Ian's contributions focus more on the kitten achieving its goals: *and within the week he learned how to get there* (from the omitted central section), *and he got through the cat flap and that was it* (lines 24–25). So Ian and Diane simultaneously perform coupledom through collaborating in story-telling and also maintain gender distinctions through subtle differences in the perspectives they adopt as co-narrators.

The mixed conversations are full of collaborative narration, involving heterosexual couples, fathers and daughters, mothers and male family members, as well as mothers and daughters, sisters, female friends. But there are no examples in the mixed conversations of men collaborating with other men to tell a narrative. Why should men avoid collaborative talk in the company of male peers and in mixed company? It seems to be the case that, given the homophobia which informs hegemonic masculinity, men avoid ways of talking which display closeness with men for fear of being accused of being gay. Conversely, in mixed talk it seems that men choose to co-construct talk with a female partner to display their non-gayness. In other words, the phenomenon of men co-narrating stories with a female partner confirms that heterosexuality is at the heart of dominant versions of masculinity. When male speakers co-narrate a story with a woman partner, they are performing heterosexual coupledom and so are also by definition performing hegemonic masculinity.

Conclusion

In this chapter, I have explored the links between heterosexuality and hegemonic masculinity in contemporary Britain. I have used examples from a database of spontaneous conversation to illustrate the form of masculinity which is 'culturally exalted' at this point in history in Britain, and to demonstrate that this hegemonic form is unambiguously heterosexual.

The last 20 years have seen a huge outpouring of books focusing on masculinity. These books are the result of work in a wide range of disciplines: sociology, anthropology, psychology, media studies, literary criticism. But whatever their disciplinary framework, many of these analyses have conflated gender and sexuality without question. This is because heterosexuality is an intrinsic component of the dominant ideology of gender. 'This ideology holds that real men axiomatically desire women, and true women want men to desire them. Hence, if you are not heterosexual you cannot be a real man or a true woman ...' (Cameron and Kulick 2003: 6–7). But this link between sexuality and gender – between sexuality and masculinities and femininities – is too often overlooked. It is one of the aims of this chapter to flag up this link and to argue that the analysis of gender entails an analysis of sexuality.

This chapter has focused on hegemonic masculinity, but it is important to remember that the hegemonic position is only one among many competing masculinities; it is always contestable. One of the issues exposed by this chapter is the constant tension between hegemonic, heterosexual masculinity and the subversiveness of gay alternatives. 'Homosexual desire', as Connell puts it, '... is certainly a bodily fact, and one that disrupts hegemonic masculinity' (1995: 58). Lynne Segal has argued that the stability of contemporary heterosexual masculinity depends on the obsessive denunciation of homosexuality (1990: 137). While homophobia has – obviously – a huge impact on gay experience, it also structures the experience and identities of heterosexuals, since heterosexual men live in fear of being 'perceived as unmanly, effeminate or worst of all gay' (Kimmel 2000: 238). It is for this reason that we see men in their everyday talk striving to align themselves with the heterosocial norms as part of their performance of themselves as men.

Notes

1. This chapter is based on the keynote lecture I gave at the conference 'Love Is a Many Splendoured Thing: Language, Love and Sexuality' held at Kingston University in April 2002. I subsequently gave a revised version of the chapter at the 10th Lavender Languages and Linguistics Conference at the American University, Washington DC, in February 2003. I am grateful to participants at these two conferences for helpful feedback. I am indebted to Margaret Gottschalk, Linda Thomas, Kira Hall, Helen Sauntson and Sakis Kyratzis for comments on the written version of the chapter.
2. The following table gives details of the database:

Number of:	**All-female**	**All-male**	**Mixed**
Conversations	22	32	18
Speakers	36	48	52
Hours of talk	15 hrs 5 mins	18 hrs 45 mins	12 hrs 0 mins

3. For details of the methodology used, see Chapter 7, pp. 147–8.
4. Transcription conventions are given on pp. xiii–xv.
5. The boys' use of the word 'rape' is problematic: there is no way of knowing exactly what had taken place between 'Ralph' and 'Prendergast', but frequent listening to this passage on the tape suggests to me that the word does not have the same (extremely negative) meaning as it would have in, for example, a feminist context. Henry's choice of this word may be influenced simply by his wish to imply that Prendergast had not *chosen* to take part in this sexual encounter.

6. Interestingly, Deborah Cameron (1997) looks at an example of all-male talk that does display collaborative features, but she shows how it is simultaneously competitive (two of the men dominate discussion), and the predominant topic of conversation is non-present students who are despised for being 'gay'. In other words, her example of collaborative talk involving men is explicitly homophobic, so the males involved need not fear being accused of displaying homosexual tendencies.

Part III

Gendered Talk in Other Contexts

10
Language, Gender and Career [1994]

In this chapter,[1] I want to argue that gender-differentiated language use may play a significant role in the continued marginalisation of women in the professions, particularly in terms of career progress and development. It is now widely accepted that women and men talk differently,[2] that is, that women and men make differential use of the linguistic resources available to them (Thorne and Henley 1975; Thorne, Kramarae and Henley 1983; Coates 1986; Graddol and Swann 1989). There is a great deal of evidence to suggest that male speakers are socialised into a competitive style of discourse, while women are socialised into a more cooperative style of speech (Kalcik 1975; Aries 1976; Coates 1989, 1991, 1996a). Maltz and Borker (1982), using an ethnographic approach, argue that same-sex play in childhood leads to girls and boys internalising different conversational rules, with boys developing adversarial speech, and girls developing a style characterised by collaboration and affiliation. Support for such a distinction comes from more psychologically oriented research on gender identity and moral development (Gilligan 1982; Gilligan et al. 1988) and on gender differences in epistemological development (Belenky et al. 1986), which characterises the feminine orientation as focusing on the relationship, on connection, and the masculine orientation as focusing on the self, on separateness.

In public life, it is the discourse patterns of male speakers, the dominant group in public life, which have become the established norm. The isomorphism of male discourse patterns and public discourse patterns is the result of the split between public and private spheres; it was at the beginning of the last century that the division between public and private became highly demarcated in Britain. This demarcation involved the exclusion of women from the public world. In other words, in the early nineteenth century, patterns of gender division changed: 'men were firmly placed in the newly defined public world of business, commerce and politics; women were placed in the private world of home and family' (Hall 1985: 12).

One significant consequence of the gendered nature of the public–private divide is that the discourse styles typical of, and considered appropriate for, activities in the public domain have been established by men. Thus women are linguistically at a double disadvantage when entering the public domain: first, they are (normally) less skilful at using the adversarial, information-focused style expected in such contexts; second, the (more cooperative) discourse styles which they are fluent in are negatively valued in such contexts.

As women start to enter the professions in greater numbers, there are calls for women to adapt to the linguistic norms of the public domain. A commentator writing in the *Independent* newspaper (20 December 1990) criticises women for not 'fighting back' in public debate; she argues, 'If women genuinely want to succeed in these [public] spheres, they can learn to hold their own. And learn they must if they wish to have a voice' (Daley 1990). The possibility that adversarial talk might not always be the most appropriate or effective does not cross this writer's mind; if women want to succeed in the public domain, then women will have to change. This view is endorsed by women who have themselves been successful in the public domain. In a forceful article in the *Daily Telegraph*, Mary Warnock (Mistress of Girton College, Cambridge, and former chair of the Warnock Committee) is highly critical of women's behaviour on committees: 'I wonder whether women themselves realise quite how bad they can be as members of boards' (Warnock 1987). She lists what she sees as women's shortcomings, such as their proneness 'to think they are entitled to make fey, irrelevant, "concerned" interventions' and 'to disregard economic considerations for "human" ones'. She urges women 'to adapt to what is required', implicitly accepting the male-dominated discourse patterns of conventional committee meetings.

Women who succeed in adopting a more competitive discourse style in public meet other problems. Jeanne Kirkpatrick, former US ambassador to the UN, describes the dilemma faced by women in high positions, where there is a clash between gender and work identities:

> There is a certain level of office the very occupancy of which constitutes a confrontation with conventional expectations ... Terms like 'tough' and 'confrontational' express a certain general surprise and disapproval at the presence of a woman in arenas in which it is necessary to be – what for males would be considered – normally assertive. (quoted in Campbell and Jerry 1988)

In other words, women are in a double-bind: they are urged to adopt more assertive, more masculine styles of discourse in the public sphere, but when they do so they are perceived as aggressive and confrontational.

In contrast with this, a different point of view is now starting to be heard, a point of view which emphasises the *positive* aspects of women's communicative style. There is space here for only three examples. A female environmental engineer working for the Bonneville Power Administration of Portland, Oregon, claims: 'As a woman, you can communicate in a different way which is helpful in a sphere usually analytical' (quoted in Barker 1988). Carol Tongue, talking about her work as MEP for London East, contrasts 'the friendly and supportive meetings of the women's committee' of the European Parliament with 'the all-male environment of industrial affairs', another committee she serves on (quoted in Lovenduski 1989). The writer Jill Hyems, interviewed for Channel 4 television (*Ordinary People*, 6 February 1990) expressed a preference for working with female producers and directors 'because there are a lot of short cuts, one's speaking the same language'.

These conflicting views are indicative of the lack of consensus and the social confusion about women's role in the public arena. The long struggle to give women equal access to professions and to careers is now giving way to the struggle over whether women have to adapt to androcentric working practices. Victory in terms of equal opportunities may turn out to be pyrrhic as we come to recognise that the price demanded by the dominant group is acceptance of dominant-group norms.

The language of the professions

In this section, I want to examine in greater detail the language used in the public domain. The talk which takes place between professionals and clients, such as doctor–patient talk or teacher–pupil talk, can be seen as prototypical professional discourse. The distinguishing feature of such encounters is that they are *asymmetrical*: the professional uses language not only to carry out particular professional tasks, such as giving clients medical or legal advice or instructing pupils, but also to construct and maintain power relations.

So what is this discourse like? What are the linguistic features which characterise professional talk? In this chapter, I shall focus on three features – questions, directives and interruptions – in order to illustrate the language used by professionals in their work. Examples will be drawn from the domains of law, medicine and education.

Questions

In the discourse of the public sphere, questions function as *information-seeking* devices. This is illustrated in example (1), an extract from an asymmetrical encounter between magistrate and defendant. (Questions in these examples are underlined.)

(1) [*Magistrates' court dealing with arrears and maintenance*]
Magistrate: Are you paying anything at all?
Defendant: No I haven't been able to at all sir

(Harris 1984: 15)

In this example, one of the participants asks a question in order to gain information. But questions don't just seek information; they are also used to establish power and status. Discourse analysts have identified questions as potentially powerful forms, as they oblige the addressee to produce an answer, and to produce an answer which is conversationally relevant (see Grice 1975). The following extract, taken from doctor–patient interaction, shows how the doctor's questions constrain what the patient can say.

(2)
Doctor: What brings you here today?
Patient: My head is killing me
Doctor: Have you had headaches before?
Patient: No

(Beckman and Frankel 1984: 693)

The doctor's second question here – 'Have you had headaches before?' – is close-ended, and effectively narrows the focus of the consultation from the outset.

Not surprisingly, questions are asymmetrically distributed in asymmetrical discourse: powerful participants typically ask many more questions than less powerful participants, as Table 10.1 demonstrates.

Table 10.1 Distribution of questions in professional discourse

		% of questions asked	
Field	**Research**	**Professionals**	**Laypeople**
Medicine	Todd (1983)	85%	15%
Medicine	West (1984b)	91%	9%
Medicine	Frankel (1991)	99%	1%
Law	Harris (1984)	97%	3%
Education	Barnes (1971)	97%	3%

In some contexts, such as the law court, the asking of questions by less powerful participants is explicitly disallowed:

(3)
Magistrate: I'm putting it to you again – are you going to make an offer – wh- wh- to discharge this debt?
Defendant: Would you in my position?
Magistrate: I- I'm not here to answer questions – you answer my question
(Harris 1984: 5)

Through the use of questions, powerful participants are able to control the topic of discourse. Recent analysis of doctor–patient interviews (Mishler 1984; Fisher 1991) shows how the structure of such interviews constrains patients' ability to tell their stories coherently. Doctors' choice of questions does ideological work, promoting the values of medicine and the status quo, and silencing the alternative values of the patients' life experience.

Directives

A directive can be defined as a speech act which tries to get someone to do something. Directives can range from the bluntness of imperative forms (e.g. 'Shut the door') to more mitigated forms (e.g. 'Could you possibly shut the door?'). Typically, powerful participants will demonstrate their power (i.e. their ability to ignore the face needs of their addressees) by using direct commands. Those given in example (4) below are from the classroom; those in example (5) are from the doctor's surgery (imperatives underlined).

(4)
(a) Raise your hand, any children whose name begins with this letter (Mehan 1979: 163)
(b) Now don't start now, just listen (Stubbs 1983: 51)

(5)
(a) Lie down
(b) Take off your shoes and socks
(c) Pull off a shirt [taps patient on knee] for me
(d) Sit for me right there
(West 1990: 92)

To show how directives are embedded in discourse, here's a more extended example from the medical domain:

(6)

Doctor: ... if you don't flow, call me, then I will give you an injection, don't take any more tablets then
Patient: Uh huh
Doctor: I'll give you an injection and I'll uh, get you started with your menstruation and I'll give you a different type of pill
Patient: Okay
Doctor: Okay?
Patient: All right
Doctor: But meanwhile stay on the pills. Don't you get into trouble
Patient: Right

(Todd 1983: 169)

The doctor's use of unmitigated forms here emphasises the power asymmetry of the situation. He clearly feels that since what he is saying to the patient is 'for her own good', there is no need for him to protect her face needs.

Sometimes less aggravated forms are chosen, as the following examples from classroom discourse illustrate:

(7)

Teacher: I could do with a bit of silence (Stubbs 1983: 51)

(8)

Teacher: Can you come up and find San Diego on the map?
Pupil: [goes to board and points]

(Mehan 1979: 54)

Covert imperatives such as (7) and (8) constitute a more subtle exercise of power, but like bare imperatives, they assume a universe where the speaker ('I') is all-powerful, and the addressee ('you') has no power. The use of more aggravated directives helps maintain a universe where professionals are constructed as repositories of wisdom and clients are viewed as objects to be helped, rather than as subjects in their own right.

Turn-taking and interruptions

The Sacks, Schegloff and Jefferson (1974) model of turn-taking in conversation views simultaneous speech by two or more participants as an aberration. Their rules for turn-taking are designed to ensure that (i) one speaker speaks at a time and (ii) speaker change recurs. In terms of this model, interruptions are seen as 'a violation of a current speaker's right to complete a turn' (Zimmerman and West 1975: 123), while overlaps are merely cases of slight mistiming or over-eagerness on the part of the next speaker. So example (9) below would be viewed as an overlap:

(9)
J: because they've only got to win two seats =
R: two = yes I know
(Coates 1991: 299)

However, if speaker R had begun to speak any earlier, this would have constituted an illegitimate bid for the floor, that is, an interruption.

The Sacks, Schegloff and Jefferson model of turn-taking works well for language in the public domain. Normally, one speaker speaks at a time and speaker change recurs. Simultaneous speech represents a breakdown in the system, and is nearly always the result of the more powerful participant in asymmetrical discourse interrupting the less powerful, as the following examples illustrate. (A double slash // indicates the start of an interruption.) The first comes from doctor–patient interaction:

(10)
Doctor: Swelling or anything like that that you've noticed?
Patient: No, not th//at I've noti-
Doctor: // tender to the touch? pressing any?
Patient: no, just when it's – sitting
Doctor: OK =
Patient: =er lying on it
Doctor: Even lying. Standing up? walking around [singsong]
Patient: No // just
Doctor: // not so much, just – lying on it ...
(West 1984b: 61–2)

The next example comes from a legal context, and demonstrates what happens when a defendant attempts to provide more than a brief response to the magistrate's questions:

(11)
Defendant: I realise entirely that it's up to me to
Magistrate: // are you paying anything
Defendant: counterbalance that by paying // you know I know (xx)
Magistrate: at all // are
Defendant: no I haven't been able to – at all sir – // no I

Magistrate: you supporting anyone else
Defendant: get(xx) not at all, no – I live on

Magistrate: and how much do you receive then
Defendant: my own sir fourteen

Magistrate: well can't you spare something of
Defendant: pounds thirty-five

Magistrate: that for your children – um // when did you last
Defendant: yes – I would do //(xx)

Magistrate: pay anything

(Harris 1984: 15–16)

Interruption is used as a strategy by powerful participants in discourse to gain the floor and to control the topic of conversation. Research on doctor–patient interaction (Frankel 1983; Beckman and Frankel 1984; West 1984a, 1984b) has revealed how physicians regularly intrude into patients' turns at talk. At first sight, such intrusions may seem warranted by the external constraints of medical examination and treatment. 'But when these inquiries cut off the patient's utterance-in-progress, particularly when that utterance-in-progress is the presumed necessary response to a prior necessary question, then the physician is not only violating the patient's right to speak, but is also systematically cutting off potentially valuable information that is necessary to achieve a diagnosis' (West and Frankel 1991: 186). This comment is presumably equally applicable to other professional contexts where the professional's interruptions cut off the client's response. Example (11), from law rather than medicine, is a case in point. Professionals need to learn to listen; otherwise they, as well as their clients, have much to lose.

Women's discourse patterns in the professional sphere

As we saw in the previous section, the language of the professions, like all-male discourse, tends to be information-focused and adversarial in style, favouring linguistic strategies which foreground status differences between participants. Women's talk in the private sphere, by contrast, is interaction-focused, favouring linguistic strategies which emphasise solidarity rather than status. This dichotomy is in part functional: the chief goal of discourse in the public domain is the efficient exchange of information; that of discourse in the private domain is the creation and maintenance of good social relations. However, those working in the professions need to be sensitive to the interpersonal function of language: interaction in any context involves more than the exchange of information.

Analysis of all-female discourse patterns is beginning to establish which linguistic features have a significant role in the construction of cooperative discourse (see Coates 1989, 1991, 1996a). For example, women typically use questions and directives in different ways from men, in ways that differ from how they are normally used in formal public discourse. Moreover, turn-taking strategies in all-female talk do not always correspond to those assumed by current models of turn-taking (e.g. Sacks, Schegloff and Jefferson 1974). Simultaneous speech (that is, two or more people speaking at the same time) is common in all-female interaction, yet it is rarely a sign of conversational malfunction. On the contrary, it seems to function as a way of symbolising joint activity.

In the public sphere, there is evidence to suggest that some women have resisted adapting to the androcentric discourse norms which prevail there. Instead, they are employing their own more cooperative speech style. In this section I shall examine a few examples of this phenomenon: Fisher's (1991) work on the questions used by nurse practitioners; West's (1990) analysis of directive–response sequences in doctor–patient talk; Atkinson's (1993) exploration of simultaneous speech in the talk of home-helps with elderly clients; and Nelson's (1988) description of the collaborative interactive patterns adopted by teams working in a university writing centre.

Nurse practitioners and the use of questions (Fisher 1991)

Sue Fisher compares how nurse practitioners and doctors communicate with women patients during medical encounters. The nurse practitioner is a relatively new health care professional in the United States, who claims to provide care differently from doctors by 'adding caring to curing'. Fisher describes two cases, comparable in all respects except that one patient is seen by a doctor, while the other is seen by a nurse practitioner. The patients were both young women in their 20s who had vague, non-specific complaints. Fisher focuses on the role of questions in structuring the discourse. The (male) doctor uses questions 'which pay little linguistic attention to the life context of patients' symptoms, with an emphasis on technical information and a technical fix even when the medical complaint is marked as social' (Fisher 1991: 161). The (female) nurse practitioner, on the other hand, 'probes for the life context of the patient's symptoms and emphasises the social rather than the technical' (ibid.). The doctor's questions are narrowly focused in such a way as to constrain the range of answers possible and to keep control of the discourse (see section on 'The language of the professions'). The nurse practitioner, on the other hand, uses questions to open up the discourse, to get the patient to explore her feelings and to give a full picture of the situation. When the patient describes how she got a job to get her out of the home, the nurse practitioner comments:

(12) You know that's a real growth step for you, to realise those needs and then to go take some action, to do something about them. Do you see that as a growth step? (Fisher 1991: 169)

Notice how the question that this utterance ends with (*Do you see that as a growth step?*) allows the patient to accept or reject the professional's assessment. The nurse practitioner constantly encourages the patient to talk about her symptoms in the context of her emotional and social life, through the use of sensitive questions. The professional is inevitably the dominant interactional partner, and questions are used as a way of controlling topics. But professionals can use this control in very different ways. Throughout the encounter the nurse practitioner accepts the patient's definition of the situation and validates her opinion. The doctor is committed to a traditional discourse, in which motherhood is seen as a full-time job, while the nurse practitioner supports an alternative discourse in which women take control of their lives. The nurse practitioner's use of questions arises directly from her different conception of her role.

Women doctors' use of directives (West 1990)

Candace West analysed directive–response speech sequences between doctor and patient, drawing on Marjorie Goodwin's (1980, 1988, 1990) work on gender differences in children's use of directives. West discovered that women and men doctors issued directives in very different ways. Moreover, women doctors are more likely than men to use directive forms which elicit a compliant response from the patient. While male doctors preferred to use imperative forms, or statements in which they told patients what they 'needed' to do, or what they 'had' to do, female doctors preferred to use more mitigated forms. For example, women doctors often made directives in the form of proposals for joint action, using the form *let's*:

(13) Okay! well *let's* make that our plan

(14) So *let's* stay on uh what we're doing right now, OK?

They also used the pronoun *we* rather than *you* in their directives:

(15) Maybe what *we* ought to do is, is stay with the dose of di(avameez) you're on

Where a woman doctor did use *you*, she typically mitigated the directive by the use of modal forms such as *can* or *could*, as well as *maybe*:

(16) one thing you *could* do is to eat the meat first
(17) and then *maybe* you *can* stay away from the desserts and stay away from the food in between meals

West measured the compliance rates for different types of directives for male and female doctors. Male doctors' bare imperatives (e.g. 'lie down') elicited compliant responses in 47 per cent of cases in which they were used, while their statements of patients' needs elicited only 38 per cent compliant responses. As West puts it, 'the more aggravated the directive, the less likely it was to elicit a compliant response' (1990: 108). Female doctors' proposals for joint action using *let's* elicited compliant responses in 67 per cent of the cases in which they were used. Suggestions for action ('you could try taking two every four hours') had a 75 per cent success rate. Overall, the women doctors used far fewer aggravated directives than the male doctors, and their overall rate of compliant responses was 67 per cent, compared with the male doctors' 50 per cent.

This study shows women using more collaborative interactive strategies in the medical profession. The women doctors used more mitigated directive forms, thus minimising status distinctions between themselves and their patients. The more egalitarian relationships they established with their patients emphasised doctors' obligations as well as patients' rights. The evidence from this study is that such an approach has better outcomes for patients than more traditional approaches which emphasise asymmetry in doctor–patient relationships.

Simultaneous speech in talk between home-helps and elderly clients (Atkinson, 1993)

Karen Atkinson has carried out long-term participant observation of the interaction between young home-helps and elderly clients. The majority of carers who look after the elderly are female, as are most of the elderly population. Thus, the inter-generational talk occurring in home-help–elderly person dyads tends to be all-female. Despite the asymmetry of both age and status, Atkinson has observed a significant amount of simultaneous speech in such dyads, similar in kind to that found in the talk of female friends. The following is an example from her data:

(18) [*elderly client (EC) talks to home-help (HH) about new gadget for arthritis*]

1	
EC:	now if my knee [b] got bad again/
HH:	yeah yeah now that'd

2	
EC:	that might be worth it/ . ((your)) knee
HH:	be lovely ((there)/ yes yeah where

3	
EC:	you would use it on yourself/ yes/
HH:	you can use it . yourself/ that's it, yeah/

This short extract from one of Atkinson's 60 audio-recorded conversations between young female home-helps and their elderly female clients illustrates the way overlapping speech is used in these interactions. Speakers perform as a single voice, saying the same thing in different words ('now that'd be lovely'/'that might be worth it', staves 1 and 2) and even saying the same thing at the same time ('yourself', stave 3). Speakers use minimal responses ('yes', 'yeah', 'that's it') to confirm that what one has said has the support of the other. In terms of the conventional norms of turn-taking (where one-speaker-at-a-time is the rule), virtually all the simultaneous speech occurring here should be labelled 'interruption', since the overlapping segment involves more than the last syllable of a speaker's turn. But in all-female conversation, as this example demonstrates, such categories are inappropriate: participants do not view conversation as a battle to hold the floor; the floor can be (and often is) jointly held. When EC says 'you would use it on yourself' in stave 3, she is not trying to seize the floor from HH, but is agreeing with HH and saying the same thing in her own words. These 'conversational duets' (Falk 1980; Coates 1991, 1996) are a key characteristic of all-female discourse.

It seems that young female home-helps are bringing to their job as carers the collaborative speech styles typical of symmetrical all-female talk. This suggests that gender solidarity may be over-riding age and status differentials. While this may be good professional practice, we should note that professions which are female-dominated (such as nursing, certain kinds of social work, nursery and infant teaching, caring for the elderly), and which are therefore capable of supporting more cooperative speech styles, have lower status and prestige than those which are male-dominated (such as medicine, law, university teaching).

Interactive patterns in teacher-research teams (Nelson 1988)

Marie Nelson observed and recorded the interactive patterns of five successive teacher-research teams working in a university writing centre in Washington DC. These teams were made up of graduate Teaching Assistants (TAs), who were mostly female. Nelson's research shows how the women successfully used the interactive patterns familiar to them, while the occasional male TAs adapted to these interactive patterns and were positive about the experience. The members of the team enjoyed the trust and closeness engendered by close collaborative work. One of the rare male TAs commented:

> I just love being in here with all you women. You make it such a nice place to work. You're so warm and supportive that I never feel stupid when I make a mistake. It's different in here from how I've seen people do things before. Most graduate students are so competitive. (Nelson 1988: 202)

Transcripts of team discussion sessions confirm the claim that women's interactions are rooted in emotional expressiveness, and are cooperative rather than competitive. They show what Miller (1976) calls 'productive conflict', that is, conflict which is beneficial to all participants, as opposed to conflict which results in one winner and many losers.

The success of this collaborative venture is borne out both in the achievement of the teams in helping students to write better, and in the comments of participants on how much they had gained from the experience. One graduate TA, who subsequently worked for a large corporation, described the contrast between the competitive ethos of the large corporation and the collaborative ethos of the university research teams:

> The corporation emphasises only negative aspects of performance, but we female teachers have been used to stressing the positive first. Our emphasis has always been on what students do right – to help students build on what they do well instead of discouraging them. In addition, we've all been used to using collaborative methods. (Nelson 1988: 220)

Nelson discusses the problems women face in trying to maintain their collaborative style in more competitive environments, and argues that we must try to overcome these problems since the interactive patterns into which women are socialised 'offer substantial benefits to academic and professional teams' (1988: 203).

Conclusion: women, language and career

The studies described in the previous section are only a few of a growing number of research projects which demonstrate the positive aspects of incorporating cooperative discourse styles typical of women into the public domain. Troemel-Ploetz (1985) compares male and female TV interviewers and shows how female interviewers encourage more open and more equal discussion through their interactive strategies. Graddol and Swann (1989: 178–81) describe how some firms are trying to encourage the promotion of women and to introduce more 'feminine' styles into management. Campbell (1988) argues that women's presence on high-powered committees has had beneficial effects. She quotes Tessa Blackstone, Master (*sic*) of Birkbeck College, London, who said of her experience as a member of the Central Policy Review Staff: 'Women are less competitive for a start and there's less confrontation in a group that's got women in it ... I just think that organisations that have women are more in touch with the society in which they work' (Campbell 1988).

On the other hand, women attempting to pursue careers in the public domain will continue to encounter problems. If they adopt a more adversarial, more 'male', interactive style, they are in danger of being labelled 'unfeminine'. If they attempt to retain a more cooperative style of interaction, they risk being viewed as ineffectual. Moreover, in mixed interaction male speakers will use their competitive discourse skills to dominate female speakers (see, for example, Edelsky 1981; Troemel-Ploetz 1985; Woods 1989). Men dominate mixed interaction even when a woman has higher status: West's study of doctor–patient interaction has been referred to extensively in this chapter; her analysis of interruption makes depressing reading. While male doctors were rarely interrupted by patients, and used interruptions to control the progress of the medical interview, women doctors were interrupted, especially by white male patients (West 1984b).

As women enter the workforce in greater numbers and with higher expectations, it remains to be seen whether the more cooperative discourse style which women are skilful in will be welcomed in the public sphere as a new resource, or whether it will be challenged. More overt forums of discrimination against women are slowly being eradicated. But the fact that women are still having difficulty progressing in their chosen careers suggests that other, covert means of discrimination are still at work. The androcentric norms of public discourse are alien to most women. This discourse is extremely powerful in promoting and maintaining the competitive ethos of the world of work. If the dominant elite insist that women must acquire a public 'voice' in order to take their place in the public sphere, then society as a whole will be the loser. Some (female) professions already benefit from the use of more collaborative discourse styles. It is time the value of such discourse patterns was acknowledged.

Postscript

Although this chapter was written many years ago (it was first published in 1994), and adopts a (now obsolescent) difference approach to gender, I have included it here in its original form because things haven't changed as much as might have been expected: workplaces continue to be gendered and women still encounter obstacles in their pursuit of a career. Issues of gender inequality have not gone away[3] and it is clear that language continues to play a part in sustaining inequality. Moreover, the linguistic features I focused on in this chapter are still relevant for any analysis of power and dominance in interaction.

What has changed is that research analysing professional discourse and workplace language has increased exponentially and a great many papers have been published since 1994.[4] This more recent research covers a much wider range of cultures than earlier research, and includes Brazil (Ostermann 2003), Japan (Reynolds 1991), Canada (Ehrlich 2006), Austria (Menz and Al-Roubaie 2008), Denmark (Holmgreen 2009) and New Zealand (Holmes and Stubbe 2003; Holmes 2006) as well as many investigations in the UK and the USA. This more recent research also covers a wide range of workplaces: for example, hospitals (Menz and Al-Roubaie 2008), law courts (Ehrlich 2006; Conley and O'Barr 2005), police stations (Ostermann 2003; McElhinnie 2005), broadcasting studios (Walsh 2006), call centres (Cameron 2000), Parliament (Shaw 2006), scientific contexts (Xie and Shauman 2003) and various professional and white-collar workplaces (see especially work done by Janet Holmes and colleagues on the Wellington Language in the Workplace Project). I will give a brief summary of five of these research projects here.

A comparative study by Ana Cristina Ostermann (2003) demonstrates that working in an all-female space can make a huge difference to women's ability to act effectively. Ostermann compares two institutions that work with victims of domestic violence in Brazil. Both workplaces are all-female, but the interactional patterns found in them are very different. Those used at the feminist crisis intervention centre were more cooperative and functioned to produce solidarity. By contrast, those used by women police officers were less cooperative and more face-threatening, and turn-taking was less smooth. It seems that female police officers, working in a male-dominated system, use more distancing and controlling interactional strategies, in part because they fear that using interactional patterns seen as more typical of women will disadvantage them in the symbolic market of the police system. Ostermann shows that these two groups of women professionals belong to distinctive Communities of Practice, with distinctive ideologies, and their ways of interacting with victims of domestic violence differ accordingly.

In a completely different context, Sylvia Shaw (2006) looks at the experience of women Members of Parliament (MPs) in Britain. Parliaments have been, until very recently, an arena reserved for the male voice. Women MPs have to learn the norms of this Community of Practice, in particular the official rules for formal debate. To be accepted as a core member of the Community of Practice, a new member must demonstrate they have mastered these rules. An important way to 'do' power in parliamentary debate is to hold the floor. Shaw analysed floor apportionment and established that women MPs had trouble holding the floor, even when it was legally theirs, because male MPs frequently break the rules, making illegal comments (such as 'Rubbish') without being censored by the Speaker (who moderates parliamentary behaviour). In five debates, male participants made 90 per cent of all individual illegal utterances, suggesting that this kind of rule breaking is seen as normal by male MPs, while women MPs are disadvantaged because they are reluctant to break the rules. Women MPs find themselves subject to contradictory expectations: they are expected to be as good as the men, but simultaneously to demonstrate that women in Parliament can 'make a difference'. They are in a no-win situation, either adhering to the rules of parliamentary debate (thus marking themselves out as peripheral members of the Community of Practice) or flouting the rules like the men and becoming part of the 'bear pit'.

The tension between dominant norms of femininity and acting effectively in the workplace is taken up by Janet Holmes and Stephanie Schnurr

(2006), but with the interesting twist that they look more broadly at femininity and its performance by both women and men in the workplace. They draw on data collected as part of the Wellington Language in the Workplace Project to explore the ways in which participants manage and interpret the notion of 'femininity' in workplace discourse. They show how using good 'relational practice', that is, subtle discursive work that attends to collegial relationships and ensures that things run smoothly, is an asset in the workplace. Such behaviour is normatively feminine, and associated with collaborative linguistic strategies typically linked with women. But in some workplaces (labelled more feminine by participants), Holmes and Schnurr found examples of men as well as women using such strategies, which were treated as unmarked in these contexts. These tended to be organisations which dealt directly with clients or with people-oriented social issues or with education, and not IT companies or manufacturing organisations, which were assessed as more 'masculine'. Overall, Holmes and Schnurr demonstrate that there are multiple femininities in the workplace, some affiliative, but others more contestive. (These findings are supported by Baxter (2010), who found that, in male-dominated and gender-divided corporations, women leaders have to develop an extraordinary linguistic expertise just to survive, whereas in what she calls 'gender-multiple' corporations, their linguistic expertise helps them to be highly regarded and effective leaders.)

In her analysis of the linguistic practices of two businesses situated in Nottingham, UK, Louise Mullany (2003, 2007), like Holmes and Schnurr, demonstrates that discourse strategies normatively associated with femininity or masculinity are used by both women and men. However, Mullany's interviews with participants reveal that there is some hostility to women who use language normally associated with powerful men. A more assertive female manager was described by her co-workers as 'bossy', 'bombastic' and 'dragon-like'. Her assertive management style is negatively evaluated by her peers and by her subordinates. So although she is regarded as an effective manager by the company, her deviation from the hegemonic norms of feminine behaviour mean that she attracts criticism in the workplace. Here we see evidence of male resistance to the growing number of women in the workplace and to their rise to managerial positions. Overall, then, the overarching ideology in these workplaces is one that supports stereotypical views of women and men, and which therefore does not support women in positions of power and seniority.

Susan Ehrlich (2006) looks at the language used in a Canadian court room, in a trial about sexual assault, and shows how 'a feminist perspective, when manifest in a public context, can be distorted or rendered invisible by the androcentric discourses that often dominate in these contexts'. Ehrlich analyses question-and-answer sequences in transcripts of the courtroom discourse to shows how lawyers' questions to a large extent determine what witnesses can say. The Crown Attorney (in support of the complainant) invokes a feminist sense-making framework, and shows how the woman complainant was worried about being alone with the defendant and how she went along with many of his suggestions because she was frightened that he might become violent. The complainant's strategies of resistance were not precursors to consensual sex, but the trial judge and the appeal court judge both fail to recognise the complainant's account as representing resistance – they only recognise resistance when it takes the form of persistent physical struggle. As Ehrlich comments, feminist discourse has difficulty making itself heard in public institutions like law courts.

These studies suggest that there has been some progress, with some workplaces facilitating a wide range of linguistic strategies, some historically seen as more masculine, some as more feminine. In certain contexts, women's interactional patterns can be used to good effect, particularly in all-female workplaces with a feminist agenda (see Ostermann 2003) or in workplace labelled more 'feminine' by workers (see Holmes and Schnurr 2006). But it is still largely the case in the twenty-first century that women are expected to adapt to androcentric norms. And it is still the case that women who successfully adapt to characteristically male linguistic norms run the risk of being perceived as aggressive and confrontational, as un-feminine, while those who choose to use a more affiliative, cooperative style risk being marginalised. Moreover, in the public sphere, feminist discourses are often ignored or simply not heard. Judith Baxter summarises the current position as follows: 'Women still struggle for acceptance within institutional settings such as government, politics, law, education, the church, the media and the business world' (2006a: xiv). Sociolinguistic interest in language use in public contexts and in continuing gender inequalities in the workplace means that the speaking practices of the public sphere are being scrutinised as never before. However, whether this will lead to change remains to be seen.

Notes

1. This chapter arises from work I carried out as a member of the Women and Career research group based at the Sociology Department, University of Nottingham.

2. The reader should bear in mind that when this chapter was written (the early 1990s) it was uncontroversial to make claims such as this. I took the decision to leave the chapter as it was, as a representative of sociolinguistic work adopting a difference approach, and to add a Postscript which would bring the reader up to date (see pp. 223–6).
3. The Global Gender Gap Index 2011 (published by the World Economic Forum in Geneva) reveals that the UK is now ranked sixteenth in the world, and has fallen steadily since 2006, when the country was ranked ninth.
4. There is space here to refer to only a small number of contemporary research projects, so this account is inevitably selective.

11
Having a Laugh: Gender and Humour in Everyday Talk [2006]

This chapter will explore the way gender is constructed in humorous interaction, drawing on a database of spontaneous talk involving all-female, all-male and mixed groups.[1] I shall take the theoretical position that gender is not fixed but is accomplished in interaction with others. Humour is a normal component of everyday talk and serves (among other things) to reproduce gendered stereotypes, ideologies and identities. I shall examine humorous talk in a wide range of contexts, including the home, the pub, the classroom and the workplace, but concentrating on informal contexts and on humour's role in creating and maintaining solidarity among speakers.

Language and humour

After many years of relative neglect, humour is now the focus of attention in a range of work being carried out by social psychologists, sociolinguists and conversation analysts, and in a variety of contexts. These contexts include the workplace (Holmes 2000; Holmes et al. 2001; Holmes and Marra 2002; Mullany 2003), the classroom (Kehily and Nayak 1997; C. Davies 2003), medical settings (DuPre 1998; Astedt-Kurki et al. 2001; Sullivan et al. 2003) and TV discussion groups (Kotthoff 2003), as well as informal settings such as the home (Norrick 1993, 2004; Gibbs 2000; Hay 2000; Everts 2003). It now seems to be widely accepted that conversation is one of the key locuses of humour and that shared laughter nurtures group solidarity.

Many researchers have drawn on Bateson's (1953) idea of a 'play frame'. Bateson argues that we frame our actions as 'serious' or as 'play'. The notion of a 'play frame' captures an essential feature of humour – that it is not serious – and at the same time avoids being specific about the kinds of talk that can occur in a play frame: potentially anything can be funny. In this chapter I will not discuss joke-telling, which involves set formulae, but will focus on conversational humour, defined as 'a play frame created by the participants with a back-drop of in-group knowledge' (Boxer and Cortes-Conde 1997: 278).

For a play frame to be established in talk, conversational participants must collaborate with each other. As Holmes and Hay observe: 'Successful humour is a joint construction involving a complex interaction between the person intending a humorous remark and those with the potential of responding' (2003: 131). Collaboration is an essential part of playful talk, since conversational participants have to recognise that a play frame has been invoked and then have to choose to maintain it.

Humour often lies in the gap between what is said and what is meant. When a play frame is invoked, we have the choice of joining in the play and responding to what is said, or of reverting to the serious mode. Kotthoff (2003) compared ironic humour in TV discussions with ironic humour in dinner-time conversations and found that, in the TV discussions she analysed, the speakers preferred to return to the serious mode, whereas 'In informal situations among friends, the preferred strategy is to continue in the humorous key and respond to the said' (2003: 1408). In other words, in relaxed friendly talk, speakers collaborate in talking about one thing while meaning something else, thus maintaining a play frame. What is said often draws on metaphorical language. One of the strengths of humour is that it allows us to explore what we know in new ways, and even, by using other words, to explore things which are difficult or taboo.

Gender and humour

Until recently, claims that women and men differed in terms of humour seemed to rest on stereotypes and androcentric ideas about what was funny. As Crawford remarks, 'Women's reputation for telling jokes badly (forgetting punch lines, violating story sequencing rules, etc.) may reflect a male norm that does not recognise the value of cooperative story-telling' (1995: 149). In other words, women may be regarded as lacking a sense of humour because their humour is being judged by androcentric norms.

But sociolinguistic research exploring gender variation in humour has begun to delineate some differences between male and female speakers. Using questionnaire data, Crawford and Gressley (1991) argue that male and female speakers are more alike than different in their accounts of humour preferences and practices. However, male participants scored higher on hostile humour, jokes and slapstick, while female participants scored higher on anecdotal humour. Where men preferred formulaic humour – the set routines of jokes, for example – women preferred to tell funny stories.

Drawing on data from the USA and Argentina, Boxer and Cortes-Conde (1997) discuss the use of self-denigrating funny stories to present a positive self-image, a strategy used more by women than by men in their data (1997: 284). They argue that gender 'strongly conditions the type of verbal play that occurs in everyday talk' (1997: 290) and summarise their findings as follows: 'We note clearly differences in the data between the male propensity to use verbal challenges, put-downs and story telling ... and female attempts to establish symmetry' (1997: 290).

Jennifer Hay (2000) explored the *functions* of humour in conversation. The conversations came from 18 New Zealand friendship groups. She found that women were more likely to share funny personal stories to create solidarity and that creating solidarity seemed to matter more to women than to men in both single-sex and mixed talk. Hay comments that 'appearing witty seems more central to a male personal identity than to a female identity' (2000: 733).

Looking at talk in the workplace, Holmes et al. (2001) found some clear gender differences. First, women initiated more humour, especially in all-female meetings; second, there was strong correlation between the number of women present at a meeting and the frequency of humour (i.e. the more women present at any time, the more humour); third, the gender of the Chairperson was significant: female chairs instigated more humour and also instigated more collaborative humour; finally, women-only meetings involved the most humour, while men-only meetings involved the least humour.

To summarise, there is evidence from both questionnaire data and spontaneous conversational data that there are differences in the humour typical of women and men. In particular, men seem to prefer more formulaic joking, while women share funny stories to create solidarity. In the remainder of this chapter, I shall explore the correlations between the different functions of humour and the gender of the speaker, and I will draw on a range of research data to see what support there is for the sociolinguistic research findings outlined above.

The functions of conversational humour

Humour is a highly significant part of everyday interaction and is a useful tool for the speaker because of its multi-functionality. As Mary

Crawford says, 'Humour is a flexible conversational strategy ... With it [people] can introduce taboo topics, silence and subordinate individuals, create group solidarity, express hostility, educate, save face, ingratiate, and express caring for others' (1995: 152). More simply, Jennifer Hay (1995) identifies three main functions of humour:

1. to emphasise power differences
2. to provide self protection – used in self defence or to cope with a problem.
3. to create or maintain solidarity within the group

Using Hay's three-part distinction, I shall illustrate the different kinds of humour found in talk, to show how women and men have different preferences. I shall look briefly at examples of the first two functions listed here, before devoting the rest of the chapter to an exploration of the solidarity function of humour and the contrast between men's and women's patterns of humorous talk.

Humour's role in emphasising power differences

The first example is taken from Griffin (1989). Four people are on a train together: three are women who know each other well and work in the same field (they are all reference librarians). The only man is the companion of one of the women. The women are talking about their work when the man interrupts with a joke:

(1)

Woman 1:	
Woman 2:	[*talk about their work as reference librarians*]
Woman 3:	
Man:	what's the difference between a feminist and a bin liner? A bin liner gets taken out once a week.

(2.0)

The joke produced no laughter – on the contrary, the women became silent. The man then started a new topic, a topic unrelated to the women's work talk, and took an active part in the ensuing conversation.

Example (2) comes from a very different context, a secondary school classroom. The pupils are participating in a problem-solving activity called 'The Desert Survival Situation'. This brief extract comes from discussion involving the whole class.

(2)

Rebecca: But it's pointless trying to stay in one place. You have got to try and survive. You can't just stay in one place [*general hubbub as she speaks, some heckling from one boy*]

Teacher: Hands up everyone. Hands up.

Rebecca: Until someone will, might come long, you've got to at least try. And without a compass, you don't know where [you are going.

Damion: [Yeah, but ... Yeah, but ...

Teacher: Damion

Damion: I think that, sorry, just a minute [*pretends accidentally to fall off his chair. Everyone laughs.*]

(Baxter 2002: 91)

Damion is one of the most popular boys in this class and here we see how he uses humour to maintain his dominant position. Damion appears to have something to add to the discussion but once he succeeds in gaining the teacher's and the class's attention, he pretends to fall off his chair. His clowning around interrupts Rebecca's contribution and makes him the centre of attention. Baxter argues that disruptive humour of this kind is a key strategy for dominant male speakers who want to stay in the limelight.

Both these examples show how male speakers can exploit humour to assert power. In both cases the male's disruptive humour means that he gains the floor while other speakers (female in both these examples) are silenced.

Humour used for self-protection

A second function of humour is to protect the self. I shall illustrate this function with two examples of talk produced in the context of a breast clinic involving women patients and female radiology technicians in charge of the mammograph equipment. Having a mammogram (i.e. an x-ray designed to check for tumours indicating breast cancer) is not exactly a pleasant experience – the woman patient has to strip to the waist and have her breast clamped in a machine to be x-rayed.

(3)

Radiology technician: need your arm outta your right sleeve

Patient: sorry, I'm just standing here waitin' for mother to tell me what to do!
[*both laugh*]

(DuPre 1998: 93)

(4) [*patient to technician as she arranges her breast ready for mammogram*]
Patient: there's not very much to put on there
[*compression begins*]
Patient: you're going to squash what I have left!
[*laughter*]

(DuPre 1998: 93)

In both these examples, the female patient says something humorous which results in laughter. The humour here performs an important face-saving function and reduces physical stress. DuPre (1998) argues that patients may be anxious about a procedure that can reveal breast cancer; they often find the procedure uncomfortable if not painful (which also causes stress); and some patients are embarrassed at having to expose their breasts to a stranger. Humorous exchanges like the ones reproduced here mitigate the discomfort and the anxiety. The humour, of course, also functions to create solidarity between the patient and the technician.

Humour and solidarity

The creation and maintenance of solidarity is the main function of humour in everyday conversation between equals. The main goal of most informal talk in the private sphere is the establishment and maintenance of good social relationships. The exchange of information – the main goal of most interaction in the public sphere – is still important, but is relegated to a secondary position. This being the case, it is not surprising that humour emerges as an important component of conversational interaction between friends.

Sociolinguists tend to see solidarity as something associated with women's talk, not men's. It is argued that men pursue a style of interaction based on power, while women pursue a style based on solidarity and support. Janet Holmes (1998) even raised the possibility that this pattern could be seen as a sociolinguistic universal. Summarising research on the links between gender and conversational discourse, Cheshire and Trudgill come to the following conclusion:

> it seems clear that, other things being equal, women and men do have a preference for different conversational styles. Women – in most western societies at least – prefer a *collaborative speech style*, supporting other speakers and using language in a way that emphasizes their ***solidarity*** [my emphasis] with the other person. Men, on the other hand, use a number of conversational strategies that can be described as a *competitive style*, stressing their own indi-

> viduality and emphasizing the hierarchical relationships that they enter into with other people. (1998: 3)

While this claim may be true as a summary of conversational practices in general, when it comes to the talk of good friends, creating solidarity is clearly an important function of talk for men as well as for women. In my view, Cheshire and Trudgill's claim that women prefer a more collaborative style while men prefer a more competitive style does not entail that women are more concerned with solidarity than men. As I shall show, speakers in all-male talk often achieve solidarity through using conversational strategies which can be labelled competitive or adversarial.

All-male talk

'Having a laugh' is something which young males value very highly, to the extent that it is claimed that '"having a laugh" is central to being acceptable as masculine' (Frosh et al. 2002: 205). In the classroom, one of the ways that boys 'do' masculinity is by fooling around. Boys try to be cool and to avoid the label of 'nerd' or 'boffin'. Damion, the boy who falls off his chair to make the class laugh in example (2), is a good example of someone who is 'cool' and who knows how to have a laugh. Coupland et al. (2005) asked school students to evaluate certain boys as storytellers in relation to seven dimensions, dimensions which had emerged from observation of and discussion with adolescent peer groups. One of these dimensions was 'Do you think this speaker is a good laugh?' The most popular boy was evaluated as 'a good laugh', and this boy's use of the phrases 'having a laugh' and 'taking the mick' in his talk 'establish his community's investment in non-serious, non-literal interactional styles' (Coupland et al. 2005: 82).

A boy interviewed by Kehily and Nayak (1997) describes the everyday classroom ethos as one where the 'normal' student is saying 'What can we do for a laugh today?' This boy claims he has had to change to fit in with this ethos: ''cos I was fairly quiet in the classroom and for a while everyone was callin' me gay' (Kehily and Nayak 1997: 83). Long-term ethnographic research in London schools by Stephen Frosh and his colleagues (2002) revealed the pervasiveness of this ethos – 'having a laugh' and being cool make it very difficult for boys to engage seriously with academic work.

Labov's famous study of vernacular culture in Harlem (Labov 1972a) examined, among other things, the use of ritual insults among Black adolescents and pre-adolescents. In that culture, verbal duelling has evolved into a kind of art form, with young male speakers demonstrating their prowess on the street in what is known variously as 'sounding' or 'signifying'. Young British males now engage in very similar rituals of verbal duelling or 'jocular abuse' (Rampton 1995: 171–9), known colloquially as 'cussing' or 'blowing' (see, for example, Frosh et al. 2002; Rampton 1995). Many of the insults involve obscenity, and a large proportion insult the addressee's mother. Example (5) is a (non-obscene) example from Labov's work, from the group known as the Cobras:

(5)
C1: Your momma's a peanut man!
C2: Your momma's an ice-man!
C3: Your momma's a fire-man!
C4: Your momma's a truck driver!
C5: Your father sell crackerjacks!
C6: Your mother *look* like a crackerjack!

(Labov 1972a: 346–7)

Among grown-up males, too, talk often takes the form of an exchange of rapid-fire turns, as in example (6), collected by Jane Pilkington in a bakery in Wellington, New Zealand. Sam and Ray disagree over whether apples are kept in cases or crates:

(6)
Ray: crate!
Sam: case!
Ray: what?
Sam: they come in cases Ray not crates
Ray: oh same thing if you must be picky over every one thing
Sam: just shut your fucking head Ray!
Ray: don't tell me to fuck off fuck (...)
Sam: I'll come over and shut yo-
Jim: yeah I'll have a crate of apples thanks [*laughingly using a thick-sounding voice*]
Ray: no fuck off Jim
Jim: a dozen ...
Dan: shitpicker! [*amused*]

(Pilkington 1998: 265)

Here we see Sam disagreeing with Ray, Ray disagreeing with Sam, Jim disagreeing with Ray, and Dan criticising Jim. But, as Pilkington stresses, the participants here and in other similar exchanges seem to be enjoying themselves and their talk contains much laughter. It is friendly sparring, not a quarrel.

An example of verbal sparring from my own database involves two school students arguing about whether or not another student speaks French (this example also shows that research participants remember from time to time that their talk will be listened to by a female researcher, as the boys' reference to 'she' reveals in the last two lines):

(7)

Julian: but the boy speaks French
Henry: he does not . do you want this knife embedded in your face?
Julian: do you want that tape-recorder inserted up your rectum?
Henry: <LAUGHING> she'd get some pretty interesting sounds then
Julian: yeah she would actually

Although these three examples come from very different contexts (a New York street, a New Zealand workplace, and a British public school), in all three we see all-male groups organising talk in a stylised way which seems to relish conflict and where speakers normally limit themselves to a single utterance per turn. In both, there is evidence from paralinguistic and prosodic features such as laughter that such talk is perceived as enjoyable, as fun. These examples give support to Cheshire and Trudgill's claim that men prefer a more competitive style, but it is clear that such examples show speakers constructing masculinity in a way which builds solidarity in the group.

If we turn to the private talk of friends in pairs or small groups, competition is not so evident. The conversational data I've collected comes not from the street, the workplace or the classroom, but from places where friends meet in their spare time. In example (8), two men friends have met to have lunch together and in their talk they play with the idea of a parallel world in which Chris had become an academic rather than a solicitor:

(8)

Chris: I would've been going down the shops for more . leather elbow patches for my cardigan
Geoff: <LAUGHS> yes and you would've been running a 386 machine and gasping at the graphics that that would produce
Chris: a 386! I would've had a Style Writer or something
Geoff: <LAUGHS> "what's wrong with the old pen and paper?" <OLD MAN'S VOICE>

The two friends here collaborate in constructing a play frame which mocks the idea of the unworldly academic, rather in the style of the Monty Python 'sardine tin in the road' sketch. Each contribution takes a more extreme position and Geoff's laughter demonstrates their amusement at this sustained bit of joking. (Of course, by mocking the technological naivety of academics, they position themselves as technologically sophisticated.) Their ability to co-construct this joking fantasy is evidence of their shared understanding of each other – this builds solidarity between them.

The next extract, 'Jonesy and the lion', is a third-person narrative. It comes from a conversation involving three male friends in their 20s and early 30s, Eddie, Geoff and Simon. They are talking in Simon's flat about a man who Eddie and Geoff used to know. Eddie is the narrator (Geoff's comments are in italics; Simon's are in italic capitals).

(9) **Jonesy and the lion**

God that reminds me talking of lion cages d'you remember Jonesy?
oh yeah Jonesy yeah
well he lost his job at the um-
he worked at an army camp but lost his job there
[...]
but the one I was thinking of was when he was at er- he worked at the zoo
[...]
and somebody said that they needed some electrical sockets in the lion's cage
and they said that that would be his next task to put some electrical sockets in the- in the lion's cage
but- <LAUGHS> but then <LAUGHS> what he did
he just went and picked up the keys from the office one day
and he went IN to the lion's cage <LAUGHS>
[*G laughs*]
and started drilling
and this lion . became sort of <LAUGHS> quite aroused by the er- by this drilling
OH NO <LAUGHING>
and he ended up being chased around the cage by the- by the lion
OH NO
and then the-
and well by this time there was quite a commotion in the zoo generally
THERE WOULD BE <LAUGHING>
so the um head or- the head keeper discovered what was going on
so he was outside the cage you know
doing um whatever er lion um tamers do to keep the lion away from this guy

and eventually they managed to get him out of the cage
so um-
HE WASN'T HURT?
no he wasn't hurt
so there you go
he's just mad <LAUGHS>
and it's just a miracle really
that he's still alive
but um he's always <LAUGHS> been mad like that

The story focuses on an eccentric character, Jonesy, who Eddie describes as 'just mad'. The story gives an account of an episode when he acted in a very eccentric, not to say dangerous way. This portrait of someone as different, as 'other', serves to construct solidarity: the three friends are bonded by their shared amusement at the crazy behaviour of Jonesy. They position themselves as an in-group clearly distinct from people like Jonesy, and in so doing they reinforce their own group norms.

Like all speakers, men tell stories about themselves as well as about others as part of conversation. But while women's narratives often contribute to sustained reciprocal self-disclosure (see Coates 1996a; Kalcik 1975), men's story-telling is often more of a performance for humorous purposes. The next example, 'Closing time' (example 10), is a good illustration of this point. This story comes from a conversation involving three young men in their 20s, talking over a drink at a pub in Somerset. The narrator is Rob.

(10) **Closing time**

Yeah, convinced the boss that it's worth me opening until (.) um (.) all day,
but but really I wasn't gonna open all day,
I was closing up.
But the trouble is his wife walked past one day didn't she.
"Where are you going?"
"Oh I'm just popping out for a bit"
"Why've you turned all the lights off?" and everything,
"Oh I'm gonna save electricity." <LAUGHTER>
And she didn't like her husband anyway.
So (.) I got away with that,
She never said nothing to him. <LAUGHTER>

This example is a typical masculine story in that it focuses on a lone protagonist who succeeds against the odds. What is salient here is how the protagonist gets away with something (*I got away with that,* line 10), rather than how heroic he's been. In this respect, example (10) belongs to that subset of male achievement stories which paradoxically tell of things going wrong, yet which function as boasts. Rob simultaneously gets away with skiving at work (so getting one up on the boss), while quick-wittedly persuading the boss's wife of his innocence. Part of the humour of this story derives from Rob's ability to tell the story through dialogue: his creation of the voices of himself and the boss's wife makes for a vivid and concise account of what happened. As his friends' laughter testifies, this is a successful story, a story which bonds the young men in their sense of laddishness. They are not heroes, they get into scrapes of all kinds, but in the end they come out on top.

All-female talk

'Having a laugh' is not such an overt characteristic of female subculture, but having fun together is an aspect of friendship that women cherish. In fact, one of the things that struck me very forcibly when I transcribed the tapes I collected of all-female conversations was the amount of laughter involved.

In my interviews with the women who participated in my research, several mentioned fun. Sitting over a cup of tea or a glass of wine in a private space was seen as a classic locus of good talk, and was explicitly contrasted with sitting round a table in a more public space such as a restaurant. The following extract comes from an interview with three women friends. (The extract has been transcribed using stave notation; see the transcription conventions on pp. xiii–xv.)

(11)

1

Jen: where do you like to talk? [...]

2

Sue: I mean in- in someone's house it's easier to talk than= =out/
Liz: =out=

3

Liz: oh I don't know we have been
Anna: yes we would never- we wouldn't-

4

Sue: [we have but I don't know that it's the same=
Liz: out for a meal
Anna: we [have in the past/ =no=

5

Sue: =I mean you can't shriek with laughter can you
Liz: =no it isn't as relaxing=

6

Sue: when you're out= =you [have to be very controlled= =yeah you
Liz: =no= [well you CAN =you CAN=

7

Sue: can but you get chuckled out
Jen: <LAUGHS>

This extract hints at other aspects of women's talk, and suggests that the home is preferred because it's a place where women feel uninhibited about expressing themselves. It also suggests that women's behaviour is still policed.

I asked participants in my research to tell me what talk with friends was like. This was Mary's answer:

(12) We probably laugh a lot and find things that are in common ... so that you would- you would pick up on one thing and then the person reinforced that by saying well the same thing happened to them, or it happened in a different way, then you'd have a laugh because it's a shared thing.

Mary's words make an explicit link between laughter and solidarity: she claims that women establish common themes and take it in turns to tell stories arising from these themes, and that this results in a sense of shared understanding. Laughter, she argues, arises directly from the sense of a shared understanding.

To illustrate women's sense of humour, let's look at a few examples. Example (13) is a third-person narrative; it's a story told by a woman to two friends about her eccentric mother.

(13) **My mother and the jogger**

She took- she's got these two Dobermans who are really unruly but very sweet.
She took them for a walk on the beach one day,
and this was at the height of the Rottweiler scare,
and this jogger's running along the beach at Liverpool,
and Rosy, her dog that she can't control,
decided to run along after the jogger
and bit him on the bottom.
And this man was going absolutely mad,
and my mother started off by being nice to him
and saying, "I'm terribly sorry, she's only a pup and she was just being playful" and so on,
and he got worse,
so the more she tried to placate him,
the more he decided he was gonna go to the police station and create a scene about it.
So she said, "Let me have a look",

and she strode over and pulled his- <LAUGHS> pulled his tracksuit bottoms down,
and said, "Don't be so bloody stupid, man, there's nothing wrong with you,
you're perfectly all right".
At which point he was so embarrassed he just jogged away.
<LAUGHTER>

This story constructs solidarity among the three friends by focusing on a non-present other, the narrator's mother. The mother is presented as an eccentric, a woman capable of doing the outrageous. The narrator implicitly contrasts the eccentric mother with the three (sensible) friends. The narrative positions the mother as 'other', while the three friends are bonded as the in-group who are not like this woman (in the same way that Eddie, Geoff and Simon are bonded by the story of Jonesy, example 9). At the same time, the story celebrates the mother as a woman who demonstrates agency, and a woman who inverts the normal order of things – at the end of the incident it is the man who is embarrassed and the woman who is triumphant. This overturning of normal expectations is another reason the story is so funny. So humour here both maintains notions of 'normal' femininity, while at the same time subverting those norms by celebrating a woman behaving badly.

More commonly, women narrators tell funny stories about themselves. Example (14) comes from a conversation involving four schoolgirls in their early teens. The story is told to Hannah by Becky (with Claire's help – Claire's contributions are in italics) about an incident involving Becky, Claire and the school librarian which took place in school on a day when Hannah wasn't there:

(14) **Knicker stains**

It was so funny when you weren't there one day.
Well we were in the library, right?
and we were in that corner where all the erm the picture books are.
Claire's putting on some lipstick,
I was putting on some lipstick,
and and and they said "oh what are you doing in that corner?",
and she said we were smoking ((xx)),
no I said we were checking for people who were smoking,
and he said- and he said "are you sure you weren't having a quick smoke yourself?",
and I said, "yes I must admit it",
and I meant to say, "Look at my nicotine stains",
and I held up my fingers like that,
and I said, "Look at my knicker stains".
((xx)) we were rolling about the tables.
It was so funny.

Notice how the evaluative clause 'it was so funny' frames this story, appearing both as a prelude to the story and as the final line. The telling of this story is followed by chaotic talk and laughter, with Jessica saying that she had told the story to her mother, and her mother too had been reduced to hysterics.

This story is about a funny (or embarrassing) slip of the tongue, and depends for its impact on Becky telling us what she *didn't* say, that is, *Look at my nicotine stains.* The punch line, the words she actually said, *Look at my knicker stains,* only has such an impact because we know what she was trying to say. Overtly the friends treat this as yet another ridiculous story which they can laugh over – it fits a tradition of women's funny stories where a female protagonist finds herself in an impossible or humiliating or embarrassing position.

The next example comes from a conversation between three friends, all students at Melbourne University.[2] At this point in the conversation, Amanda tells her two friends (Jody and Clare) that the mother of a friend of theirs is proposing to marry the man she has been having an affair with for a month. All three friends are horrified at the news, but they use humour to good effect to express their critical view of heterosexual marriage, of the particular man talked about and, by implication, men in general, and to have a laugh about an earlier joke about Clare, sex and the computer.

(15) **It's probably heterosexual**

1
J: oh yuk that's gross/ I thought at least she could have come to her

2
A: =mhm=
J: senses after a few weeks of whatever they do together=

3
A: =probably heterosexual for one thing/
J: =I hate to think=
C: <LAUGHING> =Jody!=

4
A: mhm/
J: he's got a bloody mobile phone/ he wears it round his waist/
C: <LAUGH> well we KNOW what they do then

5
A: you're the
J: in his little pocket/ . little leather pouch for his
C: DON'T we?/

6
A: techno-sex guru Clare/ you can hardly talk/ <LAUGHS> ——————>
J: mobile phone/ WHAT!? <LAUGHS>
C: <LAUGHS> ——————————————————>

7

A: <LAUGHS>
J: um this side of Clare hasn't come out yet/ <LAUGHS>
C: <LAUGHS>

8

A: cyber [sex/ there's nothing virtual about it
J: [virtual sex?
C: yeah/ <LAUGHS> no/

9

A: let me tell you/ <LAUGHS> [...]
J: <LAUGHS> [...]
C: <LAUGHS HYSTERICALLY> [...]

10

A: I mean the man has a mobile phone <LAUGHING> so [one thing leads to
J: [he's an architect/
C: <LAUGHS——————>

11

A: another [...] <LOW LAUGH>
J: [...] would you want to marry this man?= would you want
C: =no

12

A: =would you want to bloody .
J: to be in the same room as this man?=
C: =no

13

A: [USE THIS MAN'S MOBILE PHONE? <LAUGHS>
J: [<LAUGHS——————————>
C: [yeah <LAUGHS——————————>

Jody's words *whatever they do together* in stave 2 are initially received with only a minimal response from Amanda. But Jody chooses to re-focus attention on the idea of 'whatever they do together' by adding *I hate to think*. This reframes the phrase: *whatever they do together* is now marked as both humorous and sexual. Clare's recognition that a play frame has been introduced is marked by her laughing protest, while Amanda maintains the frame with the joke *(it's) probably heterosexual*, a joke which inverts the normal pattern of heterosexual unmarked/ homosexual marked.

Amanda's joke is picked up with relish by the other two speakers: Jody launches into a series of utterances which talk about the man's mobile phone, with heavy sexual innuendo. Clare responds to Amanda's comment in kind, with the utterance *well we KNOW what they do then DON'T we* in a mock-patronising reference to the act of sexual penetration – the implication here is 'boring!' and/or 'predictable'. At the same time, she cohesively ties in Jody's reference to mobile phones by saying, in effect, that what we imagine them doing involves a mobile phone in some unspeakable way. This reading is confirmed by Amanda's subsequent teasing remark to Clare: *you're the techno-sex guru Clare you can hardly talk*, in which the reference to *techno-sex* can be understood only if Clare's utterance has something to do with techno-sex. The mobile phone joke recurs throughout their talk, and the play frame is maintained throughout the succeeding conversation, with the young women constantly sending up the normative discourse of Romantic Love.

The final example shows how conversational participants can draw on what has been talked about in a serious frame earlier in conversation. Sue tells her two friends that she has brought the school rabbit home for the weekend. They talk briefly about the rabbit before the conversation moves on through other topics to a discussion of marriage and relationships. Sue tells a story about a couple she knows where the wife has forbidden the husband to play his guitar, or even to have a guitar in the house. This raises issues about obedience and appropriate behaviour in relationships, and after some more serious talk about the husband's wild youth and near-alcoholism, Sue re-introduces the rabbit theme. The example below represents a very small part of the discussion of the obedient husband.

(16) **Relationships** (*final section*)

1
Anna:
Liz: oh [bless him= [he does[n't have much of a life=
Sue: [he's- =yeah [((he's just))[

2
Anna: =he doesn't [by the sounds [of it/
Sue: =he doesn't real[ly/ <LAUGHING>[he's like the RAbbit/

3
Liz: [he is really isn't he/ [she should
Sue: yeah <GIGGLE> I think [I should bring him- [I think I should

4
Anna: [introduce them/
Liz: get him- <GIGGLING> [I wonder why she doesn't [get him a RUN in
Sue: bring him home for [weekends/<LAUGHS>

5
Anna: introduce them [((then you'll be able to-
Liz: the GARden <GIGGLING——————> [I'll be all ((6 sylls))
Sue: ((xxxx)) bring

6
Anna:
Liz: ——————> get him a few
Sue: him home at)) weekends and let him go out in a run/ yeah/

7

Anna: <LAUGHS——————

Liz: lettuce leaves/ he'd be quite happy/ "thank you Ginny" [name of wife]

Sue: <LAUGHS——————

8

Anna: ——————>

Liz: <LAUGHS———>

Sue: ———> oh don't/ poor thing <SOLEMN TONE>/

9

Liz: it's strange isn't it the life some people lead/

Sue:

At the beginning of this extract, the three friends ponder the obedient husband's life. Liz's utterance *oh bless him he doesn't have much of a life*, spoken in a mocking, quasi-maternal tone, switches the talk from serious to play, and Sue maintains the play frame with her laughter and the comment *he doesn't really*. Sue then introduces a new dimension with her simile *he's like the rabbit*, and warms to her theme, continuing, *I think I should bring him home for weekends*. Liz joins in with the suggestion that the bossy wife should get the husband/rabbit a run in the garden, while Anna suggests the two 'rabbits' could meet. Liz fantasises that the husband/rabbit would be happy with a few lettuce leaves and adopts an ingratiating voice to mimic the husband thanking his wife for the lettuce. This is a very good example of Kotthoff's (2003) claim that the co-construction of humour relies on participants responding to what is said (playing with the theme of rabbits, of bringing pets home for the weekend, of making runs in the garden), rather than to what is meant (wives and husbands should have a more equal relationship and shouldn't order each other round). The repetition of the rabbit theme makes the talk of these friends textually cohesive. By reverting to the rabbit theme and using 'rabbit' as a metaphor for *obedient husband*, these friends are able to play with the parallels that this throws up and to say some pretty devastating things about the obedient husband.

In all these examples, we see how women achieve solidarity though the sharing of funny stories and the co-construction of humorous talk. The creation of solidarity is an inevitable consequence of this kind of talk since interactants who collaborate in humorous talk, 'necessarily display how finely tuned they are to each other' (C. Davies 2003: 1362).

Conclusions

In this chapter, I've argued (following Hay 2000) that humour has three main functions: first, humour can emphasise power differences; second, humour can provide self-protection; and third, it can be used to create or maintain solidarity within the group. I've shown how these three functions do not seem to be evenly distributed between male and female speakers: male speakers use humour as a way of exerting dominance, female speakers use humour as a form of self-protection, and both male and female speakers use humour to create solidarity.

As the examples we've looked at demonstrate, humour is used by women and men as a tool of gender construction. Men constitute themselves as masculine by engaging in verbal sparring and insulting each other. Competitive behaviour of this kind counts as 'having a laugh' in male subculture. Men's humorous stories focus on non-present others who do idiotic things (like going into a lion's cage to fix a switch) or on their own laddish escapades where they managed to 'get away with' something. These stories focus on actions rather than feelings and function as boasts. Women, by contrast, constitute themselves as feminine through telling funny stories which focus on people and on relationships between people. Their playful talk explores the meaning of relationships and finds humour in embarrassing experiences and the betrayals of the female body.

So it appears that humour, language and gender are linked in multiple and complex ways. Humour is a tool of gender construction for both women and men. Paradoxically, the unique properties of humour also make it a valuable tool of gender *de*construction. The straitjacket of hegemonic gender norms can be resisted in humorous talk. In their laddish tales of getting away with things, men exploit the indirectness of humour to acknowledge the possibility of vulnerability and failure. In their disclosure of personal disasters and their reflections on the behaviour of abnormal 'others', women friends use humour to explore the problems of the gender order and also to experiment with less 'nice' selves. Behaving badly, if only in fantasy, is one of the things that humour makes possible for female speakers in informal friendly talk.

As Boxer and Cortes-Conde have pointed out, 'we all enjoy a good laugh' (1997: 293). By exploring the linguistic features of humorous talk, my aim has been to improve our understanding of what it means to 'enjoy a good laugh'. In this chapter, I have argued that having a good laugh is important to both male and female speakers, in particular because of its capacity to construct solidarity. But what counts as 'a good laugh' varies along gender lines, to the extent that it can be claimed that conversational humour plays a key role in both the construction and the deconstruction of contemporary masculinities and femininities.

Notes

1. This includes data collected by others and also data that I have collected over the last 20 years, from both single-sex and mixed groups (for analysis and discussion of this data, see Coates 1996a, 1999a, 2003a).
2. The entire transcript of this humorous chunk of conversation can be found in the appendix to Coates and Jordan (1997). I would like to thank Mary-Ellen Jordan, who collected the Melbourne data and who collaborated with me in analysing it.

12

Turn-Taking Patterns in Deaf Conversation [2001]

In this chapter,[1] we intend to analyse the turn-taking patterns of Deaf[2] signers and to compare them with the turn-taking patterns found in spoken interaction. Turn-taking in the conversation of hearing people has been the subject of considerable attention, but the way conversation is organised by Deaf conversationalists has received less attention. One of the more interesting findings of recent years in research on spoken interaction is that speakers have the choice of two modes of conversational organisation (Edelsky 1981). In the first, speakers take turns to hold the floor, with one speaker's turn ideally following on from the previous one without any perceptible gap and without any overlap (this model is sometimes referred to as the 'no gap, no overlap' model – see Sacks et al. 1974). In the second, speakers share the conversational floor, which means that overlapping talk is one of the main characteristics of this mode of talk. A subsequent finding, again arising from research into spoken interaction, is that in informal conversation involving friends, male speakers seem to prefer the no gap, no overlap way of talking, while female speakers seem to prefer the all-in-together mode (Coates 1994, 1997a, 1997b).

Our two research questions are: first, are these two modes of conversational organisation applicable to sign language interaction? and, if so, is there any evidence of gender difference in the use of these two modes? These questions are provocative, given the fact that, where the medium of communication is visual rather than sound-based, participants can attend to only those sources of talk that they can see. This should pose no problem in a simple conversational dyad. However, where there are more than two participants, not all participants can be seen at all times by everyone in the group. This makes demands on participants in signed conversation which are not present in hearing conversation, and would appear to make the all-in-together mode problematic. Indeed, both Baker (1977) and Mather (1996) claim that Deaf speakers[3] will not initiate signing unless eye contact is established.

By examining a small corpus of spontaneous conversation involving Deaf friends, we hope to clarify the ways in which Deaf speakers systematically organise talk, and to relate these strategies to what is known about conversational organisation in the hearing community.

The data

The research reported in this chapter is based on data collected over the last four years. One of the co-authors (RSS) negotiated with pre-existing friendship groups (we chose pre-existing friendship groups because we hypothesised that if the all-in-together mode is used in Deaf conversation, we would maximise our chances of finding it by concentrating on informal talk among status equals). These negotiations resulted in two groups of British Sign Language (BSL) users being video-recorded at a University location.[4] Two video cameras were used: one camera filmed two of the signers as they sat closely next to each other, and the other camera filmed the other two, who also sat closely next to each other, opposite them. This arrangement meant that while all signers could turn to see any one person holding the floor, they could not see everyone directly all the time. The implications of this are discussed below. The resulting pictures were then combined into a single split-screen image recorded onto standard VHS tape, as can be seen in Figure 12.1. The women were filmed with the screen split vertically. Improvements were made when we filmed the men by splitting the screen horizontally, giving the men a little more lateral space.

As we can see from Figure 12.1, the seating arrangement (especially for the women) was far from ideal. Usually, Deaf conversationalists deliberately place themselves at some distance from each other, to gain the best view of all participants. A distance of six feet is commonly regarded as an ideal distance for sign conversation (Siple 1978). The constraints in this research were practical ones imposed by the field of view of the cameras, the split screen requirements and the length of the cables connecting the equipment. The women signers were directly next to their neighbours and approximately five feet away from those opposite. The men signers were slightly further away from their next-door signer but the same distance from their opposite neighbour. However, this unnatural arrangement serendipitously created a signing environment

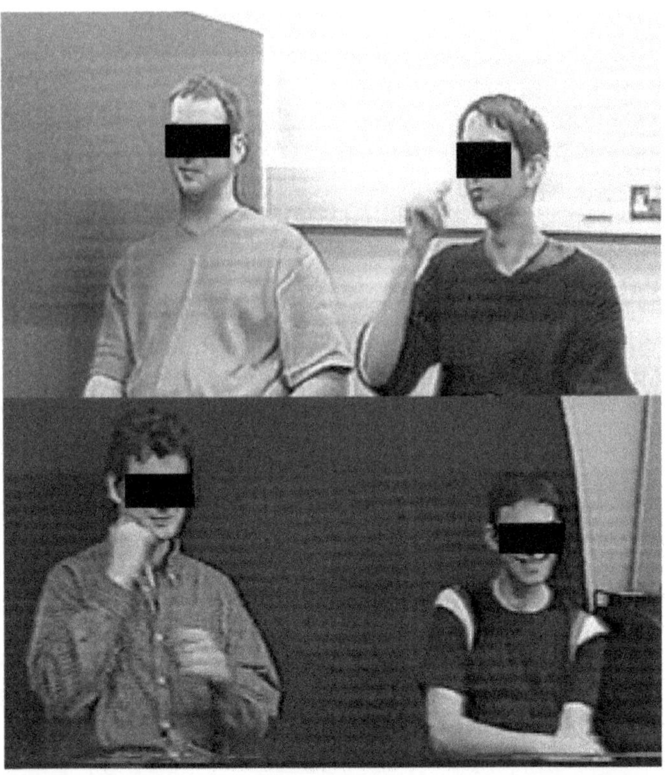

Figure 12.1 Female and male conversation layouts (altered to respect the anonymity of the participants)

that allowed us to see what happens when easy visual contact with all participants is hindered.

This methodology is obviously far more intrusive than the single microphone required for the audio-recording of spoken conversation, but the evidence of our recordings is that participants soon adjusted to the constraints of the recording environment. The choice of pre-existing friendship groups as informants guarantees that interaction is relaxed and informal: any self-consciousness induced by the presence of the recording equipment is overcome by the strong normative pressure which such groups exert over their members (see Milroy 1987:35).

Each group consisted of four friends, all university undergraduates, aged in their 20s. The four young Deaf women had known each other for 18 months, since they started university, and had become close friends. They were all following the same course, shared most classes, and saw each other daily (two of them shared a flat). They came from a variety of ethnic and cultural backgrounds but all identified with the British Deaf community. The four young Deaf men were also good friends and had attended the same school before coming to university. They were studying different courses but saw each other regularly and shared many social activities.

The groups were told that we were interested in comparing the way Deaf and hearing friends interact in groups when they talk. Gender differences were not mentioned. Participants were asked to bring their lunch to the room where the recording equipment was set up, and to talk for the duration of their lunch hour (they were subsequently paid for participating in the study). Almost four hours of usable conversational data were collected.

Turn-taking in conversation

Ever since Harvey Sacks directed attention to the question of sequencing in conversation (in his lectures in the early 1960s – see Sacks 1995), turn-taking has been a central concern for those studying conversation. A model to explain the orderly sequencing patterns found in many conversations whereby one speaker speaks at a time and speaker change recurs was outlined in Sacks et al. (1974). More recently, Edelsky (1981) suggested that speakers might draw on two models of turn-taking in their everyday interactions: a one-at-a-time model (like the one put forward by Sacks et al.), and an alternative all-in-together model. She calls these two models the single, or singly developed, floor, and the collaborative, or collaboratively developed, floor. The main characteristic of the single floor is that one speaker speaks at a time: in other words, in a single floor speakers take turns to speak. By contrast, the defining characteristic of the collaborative floor is that the floor is potentially open to all participants simultaneously.

The fundamental difference between the two floors, then, is that one is inhabited by only one speaker at any one time, while the other is inhabited by all participants simultaneously. This difference has important consequences for other aspects of conversational organisation. For example, minimal responses in a one-at-a-time floor signal, among other things, support by co-participants for current speaker's solo occupancy of the floor, while minimal responses in a collaborative floor are a resource for co-participants to demonstrate their continued shared occupancy of the floor. More dramatically, overlapping speech has a completely different meaning in the two floors: in a one-at-a-time floor, overlapping speech of any duration (more than a single word or syllable) signals conversational malfunction, since current speaker's right to the solo floor is being challenged; in a collaborative floor, by contrast, overlapping speech is a palpable symbol of participants' active engagement in a shared conversational space. In other words, in a collaborative floor the notion of 'interruption' is meaningless, since speakers share the floor and therefore do not need to compete to seize it.

The concept of 'turn' also has different significance in the two models of conversational organisation. The turn is the fundamental unit in the one-at-a-time model, since this model is, at heart, a turn-allocation system (Sacks 1995: 624ff). Turns are conceptualised as tied to individual speakers: speakers take the floor one-at-a-time, each speaker's occupation of the floor constituting a single turn. Turns/speakers follow each other in an orderly fashion, with no gap and no overlap between them. In the collaborative model, the turn has less significance, since the shared construction of talk has priority over individual turns. A turn at talk in the collaborative model may be shared between two or more speakers, and turns at talk may occur at the same time rather than in sequence.

Edelsky's (1981) paper arose from an analysis of five university subcommittee meetings involving seven women and four men, some of whom were close friends as well as colleagues. She observed that these meetings fluctuated between talk which was more firmly oriented towards the business they were meant to discuss, and talk which strayed from the agenda. The chief goal of committee meetings is to get through a certain amount of pre-specified business. The kind of talk achieving this goal involved a single floor with one speaker speaking at a time, sometimes at considerable length. But there is another goal at meetings where members of a committee work together on a daily basis and are in some cases friends as well as colleagues: the goal is to maintain good social relations. This more interpersonal goal was achieved in the meetings analysed by Edelsky through the collaborative floor.

Edelsky observed that, not only did speakers alternate between two conversational floors in the data she had collected, but also women's and men's participation in talk varied depending on which floor was in use. In the more formal talk produced with a single floor in operation, male speakers talked more than their female colleagues; in the more informal talk where speakers moved away from the agenda, women's and men's contributions to talk were more evenly balanced. This gender difference suggests that, whereas male speakers were able to dominate when a single floor was in operation, more symmetrical talk resulted when a collaborative floor was used. Edelsky's research looked only at mixed groups in the public sphere. In research exploring single-sex talk in the private sphere, Coates (1994, 1997a, 1997b) has established that women talking with same-sex friends tend to adopt a collaborative floor, while men talking with male friends tend to adopt a single floor. In other words, in informal talk with friends, male speakers prefer a mode of turn-taking which parallels that used in formal public meetings, while female speakers prefer a mode of turn-taking which parallels that which occurs in less formal, more solidarity-oriented sections of public talk.

It should be pointed out that the term 'collaborative floor' as coined by Edelsky (1981) is a technical term and carries no value judgement. The two floors she posits are not better or worse than each other but simply different. All conversation is cooperative, in Grice's (1975) sense, and conversation involving a one-at-a-time floor may also exhibit a high degree of collaboration among participants. Indeed, this is true of Edelsky's original data. Edelsky's terminology simply tries to capture the fact that a collaborative floor has to be collaboratively developed by all participants, whereas a one-at-a-time floor is singly developed by a solo speaker.

All the research on conversational turn-taking to date is based on the talk of hearing people using spoken language data (usually English). There have been some studies of interactive patterns in Deaf talk, but these do not refer explicitly to particular turn-taking models. However, researchers implicitly assume a one-at-a-time system. For example, Cokely and Baker (1980) describe the use of conversation regulators in Deaf interaction (strategies like waving a hand or tapping a fellow speaker to get attention). They explain that the signer may use regulators to begin signing, to maintain the floor or to indicate to the addressee that they are ready to relinquish the floor. Addressees may use regulators to signal that they accept the signer's right to the floor and are ready to receive the signing (see also Smith 1999; Smith and Sutton-Spence 2006). Similarly, Siple (1978) and Swisher et al. (1989) in their work on peripheral vision in Deaf interaction discuss the social norm requiring that the addressee or addressees maintain eye gaze on the signer's face during signing.

Such accounts of Deaf talk presuppose that only one signer at a time holds the floor. The writers distinguish between the signer – a person holding the floor – and the addressee – a person or persons not holding the floor, and the floor is conceptualised as a conversational space that is occupied and then relinquished in an orderly way by one participant at a time. Such accounts, in other words, conform to the model of turn-taking expounded in Sacks et al. (1974).

However, the assumption that Deaf conversation always and exclusively follows a one-at-a-time pattern is not based on hard evidence. Informal conversation involving Deaf speakers has not been formally researched until now. Studies of Deaf interaction have focused on more formal talk, particularly on classroom talk. Mather (1996), for example, described visual and tactile initiation regulators between adults and children in a classroom situation and between signing dyads in formal situations. Baker (1977), in her seminal work on conversational regulators used in American Sign Language, also based her observations on formal talk. Both these studies focus on turn-initiation strategies rather than on the wider question of turn-taking and conversational organisation.

Baker and Mather are both emphatic that a signer 'cannot' initiate a turn without eye contact with the addressee. By 'cannot', they clearly mean that optimum communication will not occur without the elaborate attention-getting they describe. However, there is in reality no physical reason why the signer cannot sign while no one is watching. In other words, we must understand Baker's and Mather's use of 'cannot' to mean 'it would not normally make communicative sense' for a signer to initiate a turn without eye contact with the addressee. While the attention-getting strategies described in these studies may be useful in formal situations such as the school classroom, if they were to be used each time a signer wished to contribute to a small informal group, conversation would be slow and laborious and spontaneity would be lost. So one of the questions addressed in our research is how strategies for eye contact work within the conversational organisation of Deaf friends, and what the role of peripheral vision might be.

In the next section we will look in detail at some extracts from the conversations we have recorded to establish how BSL users organise turn-taking in relaxed spontaneous conversation, and whether the strategies typical of signing friends are similar to or different from those of hearing friends.

Examples from the conversations

The conversational extracts used in this chapter have been transcribed using stave notation. This means that all participants' contributions are to be read simultaneously, like instruments in a musical stave. Any sign, or portion of a sign, appearing vertically above or below any other sign, is to be read as occurring at the same time as that sign. This system allows the reader to see how the utterances of the different participants relate to each other. These transcripts give a sign-by-sign rendition into English: this provides the reader with something which is reasonably faithful to the original, but which is not always easy to interpret. A freer translation is given immediately after each transcript. (Details of transcription conventions are given in the appendix at the end of the chapter.)

The two extracts we shall look at in this section have been selected not at random but because they seem to us to be typical of the men's and women's talk respectively. In other words, they are meant to be representative of the conversations we have recorded. The first extract comes from a conversation between the four men. They start to talk about a match they hope to watch, and about individual football heroes:

(1) **Ronaldo**
[*signers = Robert, James, Nick and Sid*]

1 ———————————————————————
R: UM UM UM. SIMONE ARRIVED ENGLAND LAST NIGHT. HE SAID "I-DIVED TO-GET
J:
N:
S:
2 ———————————————————————
R: BECKHAM SENT-OFF". COME ON!
J: WOW!———
N: THAT'S-TERRIBLE. TODAY <taps Sid>
S: <nods>
3 ———————————————————————
R:
J:
N: TODAY "RONALDO CAN PLAY IF FIT" HEADLINE. GAME LAW SAYS IF HE FLIES I-MEAN
S:
———————————————————————

4
R:
J:
N: HE MUST FLY-TO THIS COUNTRY 24 HOURS BEFORE. RIGHT?
S: <nods>

5
R:
J: WHAT?
N: CAN PLAY. BUT RONALDO NOT HERE NOT-YET. [....] 2 YEARS AGO
S:

6
R:
J: BUT YOU'RE-RIGHT
N: ONE KOHLER SAID "I'M NOT COMING". HE-PLAYED————. WHAT A FUCK-UP!
S:

7
R:
J: TOO-MANY TOO-MANY
N: I THINK THERE TOO-MANY HICCUPS TOO-MANY. DEFINITELY WILL
S:

8
R:
J: INTERESTING.
N: HOT GAME IF MANCHESTER UNITED PLAY WELL. PROUD ENGLAND.
S: <points to Nick> I THINK RONALDO

9
R:
J:
N:
S: I THINK WHAT I HEARD TALK ABOUT RONALDO USES HIS TEETH OPEN BEER BOTTLE

10
R: <laughter>
J: <laughter>
N: <laughter> THAT'S-TERRIBLE. GREAT. <Nick continues to talk about Ronaldo's girl-friend>
S: <laughter>

Gloss

James: Simone arrived in England last night. He said "I dived to get Beckham sent off". Well, really.

Nick: That's terrible. Today I saw the headline "Ronaldo can play if he's fit". The game law says if he flies, I mean, he has to fly to this country 24 hours before, right?, he can play, but Ronaldo isn't here yet. [...] Two years ago. Kohler [football player] said, "I'm not coming" and played anyway. What a fuck up! I think there are too many hiccups.

James: Too many, too many.

Nick: Too many. It definitely will be a hot game if Manchester United play well. England will be proud.

Sid: I heard talk about Ronaldo that he uses his teeth to open beer bottles. <Laughter>

Nick: That's terrible.

In this extract the four young men begin to talk about the football star, Ronaldo. This topic is initiated by Nick, in response to Robert's remarks about Simone (another footballer). As the transcript shows, there is a consistent pattern of signers holding the floor one-at-a-time. In terms of Sacks et al.'s (1974) model, we can say that signer change is managed in an orderly way, with next signer starting to sign at a transition relevance point (TRP), that is, at a point where current signer's utterance is finishing. (Participants in conversation are very skilful at predicting TRPs: they use syntactic, semantic and prosodic clues to anticipate the end of a signer's turn – see Baker 1977; Cokely and Baker 1980.) Good examples of signer change occur in stave 2, where Robert's turn ends and Nick's begins, and in staves 9–10, where Sid's turn ends (signalled by laughter from all four participants) and Nick's begins (Nick then continues to hold the floor).

The Sacks–Schegloff–Jefferson model predicts that speaker change will occur without any noticeable gap between speakers and without any overlap. In the case of this extract, we can see that there are no gaps between turns. However, there are some cases of overlap. This is uncontroversial where it involves no more than a word or syllable at the end of current speaker's turn (Zimmerman and West 1975). This very minor type of overlap can be seen in stave 2, where Nick's first sign, THAT'S-TERRIBLE, overlaps with James's sign, WOW. Nor is overlap controversial where it is minor in extent and where the overlapping signer is not making a bid for the floor. For example, James' WHAT? (stave 5), signed while Nick is signing, is a request for clarification, not a bid for the floor, and James' comment INTERESTING (stave 8) overlaps with Nick's last word, WELL, but is clearly a form of agreement token, not the start of a new turn.

Agreement tokens are the most common reason for overlap in this short extract. Participants may express agreement by signs which function as minimal responses (e.g. YOU'RE-RIGHT, stave 6; INTERESTING, stave 8), by signs which repeat earlier signs (e.g. TOO-MANY, stave 7), by gestures (e.g. nodding, stave 2) or by laughter (stave 10). The only place in this extract where overlap involves more than a word or syllable, and where the signer who starts to sign while someone else is signing is clearly making a bid for the floor, occurs in stave 8, where Sid's opening words I-THINK RONALDO overlap with Nick's PROUD ENGLAND. It is likely that Sid assumed that Nick's turn had finished with the words IF MANCHESTER UNITED PLAY WELL. Certainly James produces his agreement token INTERESTING to coincide with the end of this clause. So Sid begins his turn ('self-selects' in Sacks et al.'s (1974) terminology) at the same time as Nick adds a final comment to what he has already said. Evidence that these participants at talk are themselves disconcerted by the resulting overlap is provided by Sid's disfluency at this point: he is forced to repair his utterance, repeating I-THINK and reformulating what he has to say. In other words, Sid's disfluency here gives us a warrant to argue that these signers are orienting to a turn-distribution system which specifies that one speaker should speak at a time.

The second extract we shall analyse comes from the all-female friendship group. The four friends – Tanya, Trish, Nancy and Frances – start to talk about Pamela Anderson, one of the stars of the TV soap 'Baywatch'.

(2) **Pamela Anderson**

1 ———

TA: HEARD PAM YOU? <turns to N> DREADFUL! HEAR PAM
TR: YES-RIGHT———
N: PAM? BEAUTIFUL GIRL?
F: WHO?

2 ———

TA: <runs Baywatch style> HER TREATMENT HUGE-CHEST MASSIVE-BOOBS FUNNY SEE
TR:
N: BIG-CHESTED? <nods>
F: HEY <waves at TA> HEY———

3 ———

TA: PAM ME HEY NO HEY
TR:
N:
F: SHE DIFFERENT HUSBAND TOMMY TATTOO-ON-FINGERS HOW I-DUNNO

4 ———

TA: YES-RIGHT RIGHT YOU KNOW DIVORCED TATTOO-FINGERS
TR: YES-RIGHT ——— <reaches out to F> SCRUB-KNUCKLES———
N:
F: HOW DIVORCE I-DUNNO

5 ———

TA: I-DUNNO. YOU? <toF>
TR: ——— AH <nods> TATTOO-OFF-FINGER HEY——
N:
F: I HEARD CAN NEW LASER———OFF-FINGERS—

Gloss

Trish: Have you heard about Pam? It's terrible, I heard Pam-
Frances: Who?
Nancy: Pam? Beautiful woman? Big chest?
Tanya [imitates the Baywatch running style] She had treatment for a huge chest. Maaa-sive boobs. It's funny, I saw Pam ...

Frances:	She's got a different husband. Tommy. Got tattoos on the fingers. I don't know. I think they're divorced.
Tanya:	Yes, you're right, they're divorced.
Trish:	I think she scrubbed the knuckles.
Tanya:	I don't know about the tattooed fingers.
Frances:	I heard they can do this new laser treatment=
Trish:	=to get them off the fingers.
Frances:	off the fingers.
Trish:	Hey ...

These 5 staves of women's talk contain nearly as much talk as the 10 staves of all-male talk (22 turns-at-talk compared with 25). This is because the participants frequently sign simultaneously. (See Figure 12.1 for an illustration of simultaneous signing in the all-female group.) For example, in staves 1–2, three participants overlap as they work to establish who they mean by Pamela. It is obvious that the four women friends are not organising their talk according to a one-at-a-time model: if they were, they would be guilty of frequent violations of each other's right to a turn, yet no one protests and there is a notable absence of the recycling of overlapped speech which is found in talk where a speaker feels interrupted (cf. Sid's repair in example 1). In other words, the evidence of the conversation itself is that the four participants are enjoying their talk and do not experience the overlapping talk as interruptive. This is because the four participants are organising their talk in terms of a collaborative floor.

When a collaborative floor is established, all participants have equal rights to the floor and talk is viewed as a joint enterprise. Two key features of a collaborative floor are overlapping talk and the joint construction of utterances. Both features are predictable given that the floor is construed as being shared. In this brief extract there are many examples of overlap, where the women friends combine as signers and contribute to talk simultaneously. Some examples are minor; for example, in stave 4 Trish and Tanya both sign YES-RIGHT at the same time in response to Frances. Also minor is Frances' strategy in stave 2 of holding the sign HEY throughout most of Trish's utterance, a strategy which signals her presence in the collaborative floor but which is semantically undemanding. However, before Trish finishes this utterance, Frances signs SHE DIFFERENT HUSBAND TOMMY. This utterance introduces new information about Pamela Anderson and begins long before Trish's last word or syllable. Such overlap assumes a shared floor: it is underpinned by the assumption that participants at talk can attend to more than one thing at a time, but only if (and this is a crucial proviso) the contributions to talk have 'positive polarity' (Coates 1994). Where two chunks of talk occur simultaneously, they can be described as having positive polarity if the second chunk 'agrees with, confirms, repeats or extends the proposition expressed in the first chunk or makes a point on the same topic that demonstrates shared attitudes or beliefs' (Coates 1994: 185). Frances' turn at talk makes a point on the same topic that demonstrates a shared attitude to the topic, and therefore has positive polarity.

A further example of significant overlap can be seen in staves 3–4, where Frances signs HOW DIVORCE I-DUNNO at the same time as Tanya signs RIGHT YOU KNOW DIVORCED. These two utterances clearly have positive polarity: the two participants are here saying the same thing in different ways. Frances is saying she isn't sure whether Pamela Anderson is divorced, whereas Tanya is saying she thinks Pamela Anderson *is* divorced.

There is only one example of a jointly constructed utterance in this brief extract (we shall discuss others later). In stave 5, Frances and Trish collaborate to say that there is a new laser treatment which removes tattoos from fingers. Frances begins the utterance, Trish completes it (though Frances signals her continued involvement by holding the sign LASER) and then Frances acknowledges Trish's contribution by repeating the sign OFF-FINGERS. This pattern of repetition is very common in the Deaf talk we have collected, and parallels exactly what is found in hearing conversation (Coates 1996a, 1997b). Typical examples from English conversation are the following (from Coates 1996a: 141):

(3) [*discussion of what happens if someone is absent from a group*]

Helen:	they won't be so=		=yes yes/
Jen:		=homogeneous=	

(4) [*discussion of Christmas play at local primary school*]

Karen:	once those cameras start flashing particularly with the infants=
Pat:	

Karen:		=it puts them off=	
Pat:	=it puts them off=		=yeah/

In both these examples, two speakers combine to construct an utterance, and in both cases the speaker who initiated the utterance says something to indicate her acceptance of what the second speaker has added. This can be by giving a minimal response such as *yes* (as in example 3), or by repeating the final words of the utterance (example 4). In example 4, Karen's repetition of Pat's words is in its turn accepted by Pat with the minimal response *yeah.*

The collaborative floor in Deaf friends' talk

In the preceding section we have analysed two brief extracts, one from an all-male conversation and one from an all-female conversation. In terms of turn-taking, the extract from the men's conversation can be analysed in terms of a single floor, that is, a floor which participants hold one-at-a-time. This finding accords with assumptions made by researchers about the organisation of signed conversation (see discussion in section on 'Turn-taking in conversation' above), and also with research into the talk of hearing men (see Chapter 6, this volume).

The extract from the Deaf women's conversation, however, could not be analysed in terms of a single floor. The conversational participants organised their talk in terms of a collaborative floor, that is, a floor which is shared by all participants. This finding constitutes a challenge to the claim that signers will only sign if they are sure their addressee(s) can see them. It also challenges the claim that a basic rule of Deaf talk is that addressees maintain their gaze on the (solo) signer. 'When deaf signers are conversing, the receiver tends to look at the sender's face. Eye movements that do occur tend to be small excursions about the signer's face' (Siple 1978: 96). But if two signers are signing simultaneously, what do addressees do? Do they choose to focus on one signer's face, while using peripheral vision to maintain a sense of what the other signer is saying?

Research investigating the role of peripheral vision in sign language perception (for example, Siple 1978; Swisher et al. 1989) indicates enhanced peripheral vision for Deaf native signers. This finding is clearly relevant to our finding that Deaf interactants are able to organise their talk in terms of a collaborative model. Swisher et al. (1989) found that signers in experimental circumstances were able to perceive single sign utterances articulated at 61 to 77 degrees in the periphery with a mean accuracy of 68 per cent. They point out that extra information perceived in the periphery can allow addressees to monitor the rest of the group while maintaining the gaze on the current signer (or signers). Certainly there were many occasions in our data when the next-door neighbour of a signer turned to that signer and nodded agreement to the signer when the signer was looking across the floor at the opposite participants. The nod contribution was thus made in a 90-degree periphery.

In this section we shall examine another brief extract from the women's talk, to consolidate our claim that a collaborative floor is in operation in these conversations. We shall provide evidence that signers sign even when there is clear evidence that no one is attending to them. We shall then examine a further extract from the men's talk to show that they too can organise their talk collaboratively.

The next extract from the Deaf women's conversation is about school and teachers. Nancy has just finished a story about a maths teacher who was good at explaining maths but who wore dirty clothes, was a heavy smoker and drinker and smelled terrible. She ends her story with the words 'he was a funny man, and he was a maths teacher'. The conversation continues as follows:

(5) **Teachers**

1								
TA:	INTERESTING		MATHS		YOU-SEE			
TR:	WELL NOW		INTERESTING———					
N:			YOU-SEE	IT'S-STRANGE		HE CLEVER BUT CRAP		
F:								
2								
TA:								
TR:		HEY	HEY———		ME-TOO	ART TEACHER	SIMILAR	
N:	MAKE	YOU	WONDER	WHY				
F:		HOW-MANY———		WHAT				
3								
TA:								
TR:	SIMILAR	———	YES-BUT SIMILAR———		OH-YES	SIMILAR	ODD CLOTHES	
N:	HAVE	((xxx))	CLOTHES	ART THEIRS	MEANS	THAT		
F:								
4								
TA:		YES-RIGHT I AGREE		YOU	HOW	YOU?		
TR:	ART	ODD———		CLOTHING				
N:				ODD			<laughs—	
F:					SAME	YOU	ODD	
5								
TA:	THAT'S-WHY	ODD						
TR:			ME ———		GET-OUT-OF-IT ———		ME	ART —
N:	———>							
F:		YOU	BEFORE	YOU	ART	SCHOOL	YOU — MEAN	
6								
TA			UGH		TRUE ———			
TR:		<shakes head>	NOT-REALLY BUT DEAF		HEY! DEAF ONLY			
N:		<shakes head>						
F:	((XXX))							

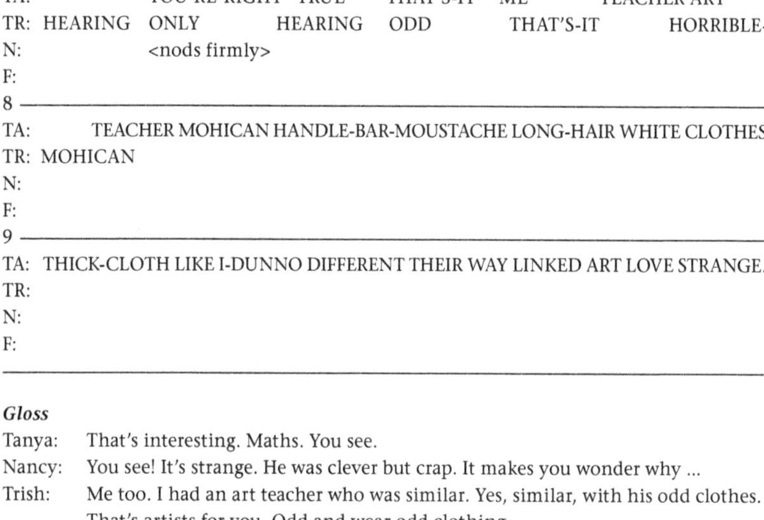

7

TA: YOU'RE-RIGHT TRUE THAT'S-IT ME TEACHER ART
TR: HEARING ONLY HEARING ODD THAT'S-IT HORRIBLE-
N: <nods firmly>
F:

8

TA: TEACHER MOHICAN HANDLE-BAR-MOUSTACHE LONG-HAIR WHITE CLOTHES
TR: MOHICAN
N:
F:

9

TA: THICK-CLOTH LIKE I-DUNNO DIFFERENT THEIR WAY LINKED ART LOVE STRANGE.
TR:
N:
F:

Gloss

Tanya: That's interesting. Maths. You see.
Nancy: You see! It's strange. He was clever but crap. It makes you wonder why ...
Trish: Me too. I had an art teacher who was similar. Yes, similar, with his odd clothes. That's artists for you. Odd and wear odd clothing.
Frances: Odd like you then, Trish.
Tanya: Yes, that's why you're odd.
Frances: You went to art school, didn't you Trish?
Trish: Yes, I did art but I left.
Frances: <comments not clearly visible>
Trish: Not really, but he was deaf. Hey, that's the point, he was deaf. Only the hearing teachers were odd.
Tanya: Yes, you're right, that's true. I had an art teacher=
Trish: =with a horrible mohican cut
Tanya: Yes, he had a mohican cut and a handle-bar moustache. He had long hair and wore white clothes of some thick cloth. I dunno. There's something different about art teachers. It must be because of their love of art. They are very strange.

This extract is full of overlap: participants share the floor in complex ways to construct talk jointly. In several places, three participants are signing simultaneously, and all four women contribute to this topic. Overlaps involve minimal responses, repetition, as well as more complex polyphonic (Chafe 1997) talk. We will look briefly at each of these kinds of overlap.

Minimal responses have a particular function when a collaborative floor is in operation and occur more frequently than in a single floor. This is because, once the conversational floor is construed as occupied by all participants, participants have an obligation to signal their continued presence in, and acceptance of, the shared floor. This extract contains several examples, as we would predict: OH-YES (stave 3),

YES-RIGHT (stave 4), I-AGREE (stave 4) and YOU'RE-RIGHT (stave 7), as well as nodding and shaking of heads (staves 6 and 7). Laughter (stave 4) is another way for participants to signal their presence in the collaborative floor.

In terms of repetition, particular signs are repeated throughout this topic (extending well beyond this extract), for example, ODD and STRANGE, which emphasise the women's unanimity about the odd ways that art teachers dress. Later, after this extract, Tanya suggests that Trish should sell her pictures, and Nancy echoes this with SELL-THEM a few words later. Supportive repetition of this kind occurs very frequently in our data. In a discussion of the apparently sham marriage of two pop stars, Trish signs SEPARATE-BEDS and Nancy immediately signs SEPARATE-BEDS. Later, talking about where her brother lives, Nancy signs BOSTON, Trish says OH NEAR NEW-YORK, and Nancy immediately signs NEW-YORK. In a further example, when Tanya asks whether the others have heard the news about the Euro-Tunnel, Nancy immediately signs FIRE before Tanya signs FIRE, and Frances then signs FIRE.

This pattern of lexical repetition seems to us to serve two functions. First, it means that talk is textually cohesive (Halliday and Hasan 1976); through the repetition of words and phrases, participants bind their turns together. Second, it has a particular function in relation to the joint construction of utterances, which tend to consist of three parts: an initial chunk, contributed by Speaker A, a chunk which adds to the first chunk in a syntactically and semantically appropriate way, contributed by Speaker B, and finally a chunk which repeats all or part of the second chunk (Speaker A). Lexical repetition as the third part of this three-part sequence signals a speaker's acceptance of another speaker's contribution. In the passage above (stave 7), Tanya says 'I had an art teacher' (ME TEACHER ART) and Trish adds a post-modifying phrase 'with a horrible Mohican cut' (HORRIBLE-MOHICAN). This is picked up by Tanya (TEACHER MOHICAN), who repeats the sign MOHICAN. We saw the same pattern in example (1) (with the repetition of OFF-FINGERS), and this pattern is also responsible for the repetition of FIRE in the sequence described in the last paragraph. In hearing conversation, collaborative completions are as likely to be accepted by a minimal response from the first speaker (see example 3), but in Deaf conversation, the norm is for a sign (or signs) involved in the completion to be repeated.

Example (5) also contains many examples of polyphonic talk, that is, talk where individual signers make substantive contributions simultaneously (e.g. stave 1, stave 3, stave 4, stave 5). In stave 7, Tanya's and

Trish's contributions occur simultaneously as they jointly say that it was only the hearing teachers who were odd and then move on to focus on Tanya's art teacher. Their jointly constructed utterance about Tanya's art teacher's horrible haircut itself involves overlap. Clearly, their contributions have positive polarity. Moreover, Trish's contribution not only functions to strengthen the picture of the odd teacher, but also testifies to her friendship with Tanya, through demonstrating the extent of their shared knowledge.

The three extracts we have looked at illustrate two culturally approved ways of getting attention: first, the waving of a hand in the line of sight of the person or people with whom the signer wants eye contact (glossed here as HEY), and, second, tapping either the shoulder or the knee (see particularly example 2). However, there are also many occasions when the signers just launch in with their contributions and expect (or hope) that the others will watch eventually. There are two key strategies associated with this 'launching in'. Signers may keep repeating the sign until they have established eye contact with somebody, or they may hold the sign until they get attention. In spoken language, a speaker cannot hold a word, but rather must repeat it for the same effect. A signer can continue a sign for some time, either by simply holding the handshape, or by repeating the movement of the sign. We can see examples of signs being held or repeated throughout example (5). Siple (1978) demonstrated that signs viewed more peripherally all contain more redundant elements than signs nearer to the visual focus. Repetition of signs or maintaining the sign for longer can both increase redundancy. In our view, the redundancy which characterises this extract suggests that participants are operating on the basis that peripheral vision will play an important part in their processing of the ongoing talk.

Occasionally, signers will launch in with contributions which nobody attends to (as examination of our video-tapes shows). This clearly violates the claims made by Mather (1996) for formal talk. At one point in the women's talk, for example, Tanya signs YOU'RE-RIGHT while everyone else is focused on Trish. It is possible that signers contributing when no one is looking are working with an assumption that they will be seen in peripheral vision. However, because of the way the signers were obliged to sit in this particular situation, Tanya could not guarantee she would be seen. It is more likely that this phenomenon (of launching in without a guarantee of being seen) is evidence to confirm the existence of a collaborative floor. As we have argued in our analysis of minimal responses, participants in a collaborative floor have an obligation to signal their presence in the floor. Joining in is what talk is about.

Talk of this kind can be likened to a jam session, with friends meeting 'for the spontaneous and improvisatory performance of talk, for their own enjoyment' (Coates 1996a: 118–119). Tanya signs YOU'RE-RIGHT as much to feel that she is part of the group as to make a contribution of any significance.

It is not the case that only women signers use a collaborative floor. While male signers seem to prefer a one-at-a-time floor, this occasionally mutates into a collaborative floor. The following very brief extract illustrates this; it follows on directly from example (1) above.

(6) **Ronaldo** *(continued)*

1 ———
R:
J:
N: THAT'S TERRIBLE. GREAT <touches S>. I HEAR LOOK BECAUSE BEEN SHAGGING
S:

2 ———
R:
J: OH! <points to N & S> WORLD CUP CAMERA-
N: GIRLFRIEND WITH HIM ——— WHY LOOK
S: WHY? ——— <points to J ———

3 ———
R:
J: ZOOM-IN HER. HORRIBLE WOMAN!
N: CAMERA. BUT THAT I THINK EVERYONE LAUGH. THAT'S
S: ———> OH! <taps N's arm———

4 ———
R:
J: <starts to point, then chews nail>
N: WHY WITH HER. WHY HAVE NOW. FUNNY. THAT. FUNNY.
S: ——> WHY? ALWAYS WITH GIRLFRIEND. I REMEMBER. SHE UGLY.

5 ———
R:
J:
N:
S: I REMEMBER SHE LOOK HORRIBLE. READ SUN NEWSPAPER. HORRIBLE PICTURE. OH!

6 ———
R: MONEY MONEY. I HEARD IT'S FOR MONEY.
J: <nods> RIGHT <nods>
N: NOT-MARRIED. RIGHT
S: RIGHT

7 ———
R:
J: I-SAW. LOOK LIKE
N:
S: <waves> BUT RONALDO SHIT-UGLY TOO. BIG-EARS. BALD BIG-EARS———

8 ———————————————————————————

R: I-WONDER———————— ALLOWED SEX TOO-MUCH RUIN-HIM
J: DONKEY SHAVEN-HEADED DONKEY
N: BUCK-TEETH
S: ——— <laughs> DONKEY!

———————————————————————————

Gloss

Nick:	I hear they've been arguing because he's been shagging. His girlfriend's with him. They've been arguing.
James:	Oh, in the World Cup, the camera was focused on her. Horrible woman.
Nick:	But that's- I think everyone was laughing. That's why she's here now.
Sid:	Why's he always with his girlfriend? I remember, she's ugly.
Nick:	That's funny, that's funny.
Sid:	I remember she looked horrible. I read it in the Sun newspaper. Horrible picture.
Robert:	Money. Money. I heard it's for the money.
J, S, N:	Right
Sid:	But Ronaldo's shit-ugly too. Big ears, bald.
James:	I saw. He looks like a donkey – a shaven-headed donkey!
Robert:	I wonder if it's all that shagging – too much sex has ruined him.

In this brief stretch of conversation, the four friends switch from a single, one-at-a-time floor to a collaborative floor. Turns are short, there is lots of overlap, and the talk about Ronaldo is a joint production. The last two staves (staves 7 and 8) are a good example of the way signers can collaborate in the construction of talk. The proposition that Ronaldo's girlfriend is ugly has already been accepted (stave 4), and in stave 7 Sid states BUT RONALDO SHIT-UGLY TOO. The remainder of the extract consists of the four friends embroidering on the theme of Ronaldo's ugliness: he is described as BALD, as having BIG EARS and BUCK-TEETH, and as LOOKING-LIKE-A-DONKEY. These descriptions are provided by Sid, James and Nick, and their signing overlaps. At the same time as adding new information, the signers also repeat key points: James expands DONKEY into SHAVEN-HEADED DONKEY, and Sid echoes DONKEY. While these three are absorbed in this polyphonic description of Ronaldo, Robert adds the comment I-WONDER------------ALLOWED SEX TOO-MUCH RUIN-HIM (roughly meaning 'I wonder if it's all that shagging – too much sex has ruined him'). His contribution overlaps contributions from all the others. The use of the collaborative floor here arises at a point in conversation where the four friends become excited about a topic, and where they are not so much saying anything new as constructing variations on a theme.

Conclusions

Researchers in the field of Deaf Studies have until now assumed that signed conversation would inevitably involve a one-at-a-time floor. (The assumption is nowhere spelt out explicitly, but underpins all work to date in the area.) This assumption has arisen from a preoccupation with formal talk, and particularly from a preoccupation with classroom talk. Clearly, in a classroom it is important for a teacher to have the attention of all pupils before speaking, and in the Deaf classroom having the pupils' attention is signalled by the pupils looking at the teacher. However, this highly structured, asymmetrical situation is very different from the informality and symmetry of friendly talk.

Our analysis of several hours of data collected from groups of Deaf friends suggests that signers are not restricted to a one-at-a-time mode of talking, but that signers can and do take advantage of a collaborative floor. One reason that this finding should not be viewed as surprising is that where participants at talk are friends and equals, a norm of cooperation stronger than that invoked by Grice (1975) will be invoked. Participants will assume, all other things being equal, that they are all attending to each other at all times, even though at any given time the gaze has to be directed at one signer rather than another. After all, participants in friendly talk have chosen to spend time with each other and have chosen to spend this time talking (two facts that are not necessarily true of participants in a classroom).

Our observations of groups of signers tell us that the speaker or speakers holding the floor can usually see more than one person in a single visual field. It is the task of addressees to maintain eye contact with speakers, while speakers will keep a regular eye on addressees, but may look away from them at times. This pattern of eye contact is also found in hearing conversation. But what it means for Deaf participants in conversation is that, if they want to make a contribution to talk, they cannot guarantee being seen by anyone other than the current speaker or speakers. The evidence of our data is that speakers may take the risk of not being seen, because in a collaborative floor the importance of taking part overrides that concern. In other words, participating in talk sometimes has priority over being seen.

Our analysis also suggests that, while signers have the choice of either a one-at-a-time floor or a collaborative floor, female signers are far more likely than male signers to choose a collaborative floor. The men friends we recorded did at times shift from a one-at-a-time mode of talk to an all-in-together mode but, as Cameron (1997) has pointed out in her analysis of the talk of American college students, male speakers may exploit more cooperative modes of talk while simultaneously performing 'the same old gendered script' (Cameron 1997: 62). In example (6), the Deaf male friends adopt a collaborative floor, but their choice of topic (football), their delight in making insulting remarks about Ronaldo and his girlfriend, and their use of taboo language all reinforce their masculine identity.

In conclusion, it seems that speakers, whether Deaf or hearing, have access to two modes of conversational organisation: the single floor, where the floor is held by one speaker at a time, and the collaborative floor, where the floor is shared by all participants. This was first recognised for hearing conversationalists by Edelsky in her ground-breaking paper of 1981. Interestingly, Edelsky argued that those engaged in research on turn-taking had mistakenly assumed a norm of one-at-a-time because they depended too heavily on data from dyads and on data from formal situations such as classrooms (Edelsky 1981 [1993: 201]).[5] This mistaken assumption has been replicated in studies of Deaf interaction for exactly the same reasons, we would argue. Moreover, researchers into spoken interaction also assumed that a one-at-a-time system was inevitable because 'simultaneous talk would not permit much communication (Meltzer et al 1971) since it is potentially unhearable (Jefferson 1973)' (Edelsky 1981 [1993: 201]). This inference was replicated in Deaf Studies, where researchers assumed that simultaneous signing would not permit much communication because it is potentially unseeable.

In fact, as Edelsky demonstrated for hearing conversation, and as we have demonstrated in this chapter for Deaf conversation, participants at talk can attend to more than one source of talk at a time, whether sound-based or visual. In fact, Swisher et al.'s conclusion that 'peripheral vision may be linguistically and communicatively useful for deaf people' (1989: 99) seems to be an under-statement. Furthermore, being heard or being seen is sometimes less important than taking part. Participating in a collaborative floor provides 'high levels of communicative satisfaction (interest, a sense of "we"-ness, excitement, fun, etc)' (Edelsky 1981 [1993: 221]).

Deaf interactants have certain advantages over hearing interactants when it comes to polyphonic talk. First, as we have said, signs can be held for a considerable time, unlike words, and they can also be repeated over and over, a strategy that does not have a parallel in hearing conversation. Second, it seems likely that overlapping speech creates interference (noise) for speakers in monitoring their own speech while listening to others, whereas overlapping signing does not create visual noise. Third, as our discussion of peripheral vision has pointed out, signers are able to see far more than might be realised. In other words, perhaps it is not so surprising to discover the collaborative floor being used in Deaf interaction. Just like hearing friends, Deaf friends, especially women friends, exploit the potential of the collaborative floor to construct talk jointly. They accept the risk of (occasionally) making contributions which are not seen by others because this risk is outweighed by the capacity of polyphonic talk to symbolise solidarity and connection. This is clearly salient in talk among friends. Further research will establish whether or not the collaborative floor is drawn on by Deaf interactants in other, more formal contexts.

Appendix: Transcription Conventions

1. Words representing signs are given in upper case, e.g. PLAY, HORRIBLE.
2. Additional actions or comments in the analysis are described in English in lowercase, bounded by <>, e.g. <nods> or <taps N's arm>. They are not representations of language used by the signers.
3. Where more than one English word is needed to translate a single sign, the several English words are joined by hyphens, e.g. YOUR'RE-RIGHT, BIG-EARS or TOO-MUCH. It should not be assumed that these several words appear in any order as part of the sign, nor that the sign is necessarily any longer than a sign that requires fewer English words to translate. The sign that they gloss is a single sign, with multiple morphemes being articulated simultaneously through use of specific handshapes, location and movement of the sign.
4. The word 'HEY' has been used to translate the wave that is used to get another signer's attention. The wave has no other semantic content.
5. It is possible to hold the articulation of a sign (or at least its final element) indefinitely – in a way that a spoken word cannot be held. Where this happens, a line indicates that the same sign is held for the duration of the period covered by the line, e.g. when Robert signs I-WONDER (in example 6) this sign is also held while Nick makes the remark about the SHAVEN-HEAD. Where the sign gloss is repeated, the sign was repeated, rather than held, e.g. SIMILAR SIMILAR.

Notes

1. Special thanks are due to Rachel Sutton-Spence for giving me permission to reproduce our paper here. An earlier version of this chapter was given at a

research seminar at the University of Roehampton. We are grateful to participants at that seminar for their questions and comments, as well as to Joanna Thornborrow, Nik Coupland, Allan Bell and two anonymous referees for helpful suggestions on the written version for the *Journal of Sociolinguistics.*

2. Following the convention adopted by Woodward (1972), the word 'Deaf' is used here to refer to signing members of the Deaf community. This contrasts with 'deaf', which is used to refer to people with a hearing loss but who may not necessarily be members of the Deaf community.
3. We will follow here the convention adopted by sign language researchers such as Baker (1977) and Mather (1996) to extend the use of the word 'speaker' to refer to a person who is signing, even though they are not 'speaking' in the usual sense of the word. 'Speaker' should be interpreted here to mean a person participating in the conversational floor, no matter what their language modality. Similarly, 'talking' is used to refer to any conversational act, irrespective of language modality.
4. We would like to put on record our gratitude to those who took part in this research. We would also like to thank Joseph Collins, Kate Clements and Richard Smith for their technical help with the split-screen recording.
5. Edelsky's paper was originally published in 1981 in *Language in Society*, and later reprinted in a 1993 collection of papers edited by Deborah Tannen. Page references are to the 1993 version.

Part IV

Language and Gender – Changing Theoretical Frameworks

13
The Rise and Fall (and Rise) of Mars and Venus in Language and Gender Research [2009]

In this chapter,[1] I look at the ways conceptualisations of gender have changed over the last 35 years and explore the ways in which this has impacted on language and gender research. Ideas of gender have shifted as competing social scientific theories have come in and out of fashion; moreover, sociolinguists have been slow to pay attention to these theories. But I shall argue in this chapter that just as significant for linguistic research has been the myth of Mars and Venus. By the 'Mars and Venus myth', I mean the popular idea that people can be divided unproblematically into two groups known as 'women' and 'men'. The human tendency to think in terms of binary oppositions can be traced back to the works of Aristotle (384–322 BC). His Table of Opposites listed binaries such as In–Out and Odd–Even, as well as Male–Female, and was hugely influential on subsequent thinking.

Evidence of the power of this myth was the phenomenal success of John Gray's book *Men Are from Mars, Women Are from Venus*, first published in 1992. In his introduction, Gray claimed, 'Not only do men and women communicate differently but they think, feel, perceive, react, respond, love, need and appreciate differently. They almost seem to be from different planets, speaking different languages and needing different nourishment' (1992: 5). His premise – that women and men 'almost seem to be from different planets' – is ludicrous, and his claim that women and men speak different languages is patently untrue. But millions of people bought the book and claimed to find it helpful in their relationships. The book clearly tapped into something important in Western consciousness.

Twenty years later, language and gender researchers are well aware of the dangers of binary thinking, but even so we need to acknowledge the fact that myths are highly functional: they help us to deal with the complexity of everyday life. The Mars and Venus myth encapsulates the fact that divisions between women and men, between the feminine and the masculine, are fundamental to the operation of contemporary societies; all societies promote communities of practice in which norms of femininity and masculinity are established. Children learn to take their place in society as apprentice women or apprentice men, and one of the ways they learn to 'do' femininity or masculinity is through language. As a result, in all societies, certain linguistic forms, certain linguistic strategies become marked for gender. Gender may be indexed directly or indirectly through the use of these linguistic markers (Ochs 1992).

My aim in this chapter is to look at some of these linguistic markers, and to show how sociolinguists have focused on different markers at different times, as interest in different aspects of language has evolved and as different theoretical frameworks have evolved to make sense of the linguistic patterns found. At the same time, I want to show how the Mars and Venus myth has waxed and waned over time in language and gender research, and how this waxing and waning fits with changing ideas of gender. This chapter will demonstrate that the label 'language and gender' covers a wide range of research; what all this research has in common is that it deals with language and its relationship to the social variable gender. At the risk of presenting an over-tidy picture, I will summarise the way language and gender research has developed, dividing my summary into three sections which correspond with three phases in language and gender research:

- The first will discuss language and gender research in the 1970s and early 1980s.
- The second will focus on the 1980s and 1990s, an era when the Mars and Venus myth was at its height.
- The third will explore the waning of the Mars and Venus myth in the face of challenges from post-modern critiques of binaries and essentialism.

(These dates are, of course, only approximate – there were no neat cut-offs between one phase and the next, but rather lots of overlap.)

These three phases correspond with changing conceptualisations of gender. In the first phase, gender was conceptualised in biological terms, with the binary expressed as male–female. In the second phase, gender was conceptualised in cultural terms, with the binary expressed as masculine–feminine. In the third phase, binaries have been deconstructed, with gender expressed as multiple (multiple masculinities and multiple femininities). At the same time, there has been a queering of gender, with a new understanding that gender and sexuality are inextricably linked.

Phase 1 (1970s and 1980s)

In the early years of language and gender study (that is, in the early 1970s), the term used by sociolinguists to refer to what we now call 'gender' was 'sex'. In linguistics, the term 'gender' was reserved for 'a grammatical category used for the analysis of word classes [such as nouns and adjectives] displaying such contrasts as masculine/feminine/neuter, animate/inanimate, etc.' (Crystal 1980: 158). Linguistic analysis of 'language and sex' was oriented to the binary *male–female*, a binary based on biology rather than culture. For example, Peter Trudgill, who carried out research on social class stratification in Norwich in the 1970s, observed that there were some interesting links between 'sex' and pronunciation. In 1972, he published an article called 'Sex, Covert Prestige and Linguistic Change in the Urban British English of Norwich', and later in a chapter in his 1983 book, he says, 'we present some data which illustrate quite clearly the phenomenon of sex differentiation in language in one variety of British English' (1983: 169). My early publications also refer to 'sex' rather than 'gender'. The subtitle of the first edition of *Women, Men and Language* (1986) was *A Sociolinguistic Account of Sex Differences in Language*, and the subtitle of the book I co-edited with Deborah Cameron in 1989 (*Women in Their Speech Communities*) was *New Perspectives on Language and Sex*.[2]

There was growing interest in the subject of language and 'sex differences': it became very popular with students and, as a result, from the mid-1970s, most sociolinguistics courses included the topic. Unfortunately, the word's ambiguity could lead to misunderstanding: on a British Council trip to Bulgaria in the 1980s I gave a public lecture at Sofia University on 'Language and Sex', which drew a huge audience, many of whom had come for the wrong reasons!

Early sociolinguistic research exploring the role of 'sex' in language use adopted a quantitative approach. This seems in retrospect an inevitable first step, as Linguistics was a new academic discipline, trying to position itself as a science in order to acquire some of the prestige attached to scientific subjects. Sociolinguistics had to try extra hard, as it explicitly brings human beings and social life into the linguistic picture, so a quantitative approach fitted better with idea of 'linguistic science'. Researchers looked for correlations between linguistic variables and certain groups of people – for example, working-class speakers or Black adolescents. Results were presented in the form of graphs and tables and histograms, with statistical tests to show whether a finding was significant or not.

At this stage, sociolinguistic research followed linguistics in concentrating on three levels of language: pronunciation, grammar and lexis. Quantitative sociolinguistic research discovered 'sex' differences in all of these (see, for example, Labov 1972a; Trudgill 1974; Macaulay 1977; Milroy and Milroy 1978; Romaine 1978; Cheshire 1982; Newbrook 1982; Nichols 1983; Eisikovits 1988). One striking thing to come out of this research was the finding that men tend to prefer non-standard forms of language, where women tend to prefer more standard forms. This pattern was originally discovered in relation to social class differences in speech, with middle-class speakers tending to choose prestigious forms, as opposed to working-class speakers, who were observed to choose non-standard forms. To account for this pattern, Labov coined the term 'covert prestige' (1966: 108), arguing that there must be 'an equal and opposing prestige for informal, working-class speech – a covert prestige enforcing this speech pattern'. It began to be evident that there must also be 'an equal and opposing prestige' for the speech of many men.

For his research on Norwich English, Trudgill recorded and analysed the speech of a large number of Norwich residents involving five different social class groups, ranging from upper middle to lower working class. In most cases, men had lower (where lower means more non-standard) scores than women from the same social class group. He also carried out a test to find out how speakers judged their own speech, and discovered a tendency for men to exaggerate the extent to which they used non-standard forms. He was able to demonstrate convincingly that, when asked to report on their own usage, male informants were more likely to under-report (that is, to claim they used non-standard forms more than they actually did) and female informants to over-report (that is, to claim they used more standard forms than they actually did). 'This, then, is the objective evidence which demonstrates that male speakers, at least in Norwich, are at a subconscious or perhaps simply private level very favourably disposed towards non-standard speech forms. ... Privately and subconsciously, a large number of male speakers are more concerned with acquiring prestige of the covert sort and with signalling group solidarity than with obtaining social status...' (Trudgill 1983: 177).

Trudgill's analysis of language use in Norwich is a clear demonstration that use of the vernacular (that is, non-standard forms of language) seems to be associated not only with working-class speakers, but also with *male* speakers. Janet Holmes has suggested that this finding could be considered a 'strong contender for the status of a sociolinguistic universal tendency' (1998: 473).

The examples below illustrate sociolinguistic variation in pronunciation in different regions of Britain.

(i) Norwich: (ng), e.g. *hopping, skipping*
- female speakers more likely to use the standard variant /ɪŋ/
- male speakers more likely to use the non-standard variant /ən/

(Trudgill 1974)

(ii) Glasgow: (glottal stop), e.g. *butter, kettle*
- female speakers more likely to use the standard variant /t/ intervocalically
- male speakers more like to use the non-standard variant, the glottal stop, intervocalically

(Macaulay 1977)

(iii) West Wirral: (a), e.g. *bath, grass*
- female speakers more likely to use the standard variant /ɑ:/
- male speakers more likely to use the nonstandard variant /æ/

(Newbrook 1982)

The same pattern has been found in relation to grammatical variables. Each of the non-standard variants given below was used more frequently by male speakers than by female speakers.

(iv) Reading, England
- non-standard *-s*
  e.g. *we goes shopping on Saturdays*
- non-standard *was*
  e.g. *you was with me, wasn't you?*
- non-standard *what*
  e.g. *there's a knob what you turn*

(Cheshire 1982)

(v) Sydney, Australia
- non-standard past tense forms
  e.g. *he woke up an' seen something*
- multiple negation
  e.g. *they don't say nothing*
- invariable *don't*
  e.g. *Mum don't have to do nothing*

(Eisikovits 1988)

But it should be noted that researchers began to be aware that the sociolinguistic situation was more complex than the above examples might suggest. Jenny Cheshire, for example, who studied the language of girls and boys in Reading, compared the usage of girls who adhere to vernacular norms such as stealing and playing truant from school, and the usage of those she labelled 'good girls', who did not adhere to these norms. She found that the 'good girls' used non-standard *was* and non-standard *-s* far less than the other girls. Moreover, *ain't* functioned as a marker of vernacular loyalty for the girls but not for the boys. As Cheshire says, 'different linguistic features are used in different ways by boys and girls' (1982: 110), with speakers exploiting the system differentially.

Below is a brief extract from a conversation involving four young men, to show how these variables interact in spontaneous speech. (These four friends recorded themselves one evening in Manchester while they were drinking beer and eating a take-away curry.)

(1)
George: we was playing naked football the other night, like it was only about half eleven, er-
Chaz: play that often, do you?
George: well I was- in our pants like, we were only kicking it about back I live off
Chaz: what, in your duds or wi' fuck all?
(Gough and Edwards 1998: 417)

Note the non-standard grammar (*we was playing*), the non-standard lexis (*duds*), the use of taboo words (*fuck all*). We can also assume the speakers used Manchester pronunciation, so, for example, the first vowel in *other* and the vowel in *duds* would be pronounced as /ʊ/. This demonstrates that young men in Manchester, like male speakers in Norwich, are 'very favourably disposed toward non-standard speech forms' (Trudgill 1983: 177). Contemporary analysts, however, would be less likely to claim that this behaviour occurs 'at a subconscious or perhaps simply private level' and would be more likely to see it as a straightforward performance of masculinity.

Phase 2 (1980s and 1990s)

During the late 1980s and early 1990s, sociolinguists were re-positioning themselves as social scientists rather than (pure) scientists. We began to pay more attention to the 'socio' element in sociolinguistics (though we were still shamefully ignorant of the work of significant figures in the social sciences, as Joshua Fishman pointed out at Sociolinguistics Symposium 8 in London in 1990).

One social scientific theory that had a big influence on the development of language and gender research was feminist theory. Second-wave feminists adopted a binary approach and talked unequivocally about 'women' and 'men' as they worked to expose the inequalities normalised under patriarchy (see Lakoff 1975; Miller and Swift 1977; Zimmerman and West 1975). The term 'gender' began to be used as part of feminist theory in the early 1970s (see Millett 1970; Firestone 1970; Greer 1970), and its widespread use in the social sciences eventually impinged on sociolinguists. There was a recognition among researchers working in what is now unproblematically called 'language and gender' that a distinction needed to be made between 'sex', which is biological, and 'gender', which is cultural. Gender is not dependent on biology but is acquired through a process of acculturation. So the key binary was now masculine–feminine, rather than male–female.

During the 1980s, language and gender researchers began to work within a theoretical framework called the 'difference' or 'Two Cultures' model, the two cultures being women and men. A hugely influential paper published at this time was Maltz and Borker's (1982) article 'A Cultural Approach to Male-Female Communication', which argued that the same-sex groups in which children play lead to gender-differentiated language practices. If we think of the planets in the Mars and Venus image standing for subcultures, then we can see why research on language and gender at this time was so in tune with John Gray's book, even though as academics we were dismissive of it. The idea of linguistic differences arising simply from boys and girls growing up in different subcultures may seem simplistic now, but the Two Cultures approach was a breakthrough. It allowed researchers – in particular feminist researchers – to show the strengths of linguistic strategies characteristic of women and to celebrate women's ways of talking. Before the adoption of the Two Cultures approach, the prevailing theoretical framework slid very easily into a *deficit* model, that is, a way of interpreting the linguistic facts which represented men's language as the norm and women's language as deviant. The new approach, which treated women and men as culturally different, allowed women's language to be looked at in its own right, rather than as a faulty version of 'normal' language, that is, men's language.

Sociolinguists in the 1980s and 1990s increasingly turned their attention away from pronunciation and grammar and focused instead on conversation and on the conversational strategies adopted by speakers in everyday talk. This research has found gender differences in a large range of features, such as the ones listed here:

- minimal responses
- hedges
- tag questions
- questions
- commands and directives
- swearing and taboo language
- compliments

Research during this phase focused on talk in single-sex groups, rather than on talk in mixed groups. For example, Goodwin's (1980, 1990) work on the talk of children in a Philadelphia street shows that the children habitually chose to play in same-sex groups (though she is able to show how girls' talk changes when they play with the boys – Goodwin 1988). Barrie Thorne (1993) carried out research into children's social and linguistic practices in the school playground and again found that girls and boys usually played in same-sex groups but also engaged in 'borderwork' when they interacted with each other in ways which emphasised opposition. In my own research, I have focused on same-sex friendship groups (Coates 1996a, 2003a). Drawing on my database of spontaneous conversation, I conclude that all-female talk is characterised by the following:

- personal topics and gradual topic development
- frequent and well-placed minimal responses
- frequent use of hedges (linked to topic)
- questions (rarely information-seeking)
- collaborative turn-taking strategies (jam sessions)

This contrasts with what has been found in all-male talk. All-male talk is characterised by:

- more impersonal topics
- abrupt topic shifts
- few hedges
- information-seeking questions

- one-at-a-time turn-taking patterns
- monologues and playing the expert
- verbal sparring

For reasons of space, I will look at just three of these conversational strategies, topic choice, hedging, and turn-taking, and will compare the findings for all-male and all-female groups.

Topic choice

Below are examples of four topic sequences from friendly conversation in same-sex groups. Two are from all-female conversation and two from all-male conversation.

Topic sequence A (five women)
- mothers' funerals
- child abuse
- wives' loyalty to husbands
- the Yorkshire Ripper case
- fear of men

Topic sequence B (three women)
- holidays
- skiing
- rabbits
- children's piano lessons
- musical instruments
- relationships

Topic sequence C (three men discuss the 1960s):
- Bob Dylan
- revolution and why it hasn't happened in Britain
- Marxism
- students today

Topic sequence D (two men)
- the merits of Burger King versus McDonald's
- mobile phones
- work and plans for the future
- computers

Topic sequence A, from a conversation which took place between five women friends, comes from an intense conversation involving sensitive topics, with much self-disclosure. Topics lead seamlessly on from one another, with a focus on mothers and mother-blaming developing into an over-arching theme of problems relating to men. Topic sequence B comes from a less intense conversation, but one that still deals with personal issues. The three friends share stories of their holidays, including a terrible skiing holiday that one of them had had with her sister. Talk about the school rabbit, brought home for half term, leads into talk about children and their piano lessons, and then musical instruments in general (with one of the friends disclosing that she cannot stand her husband's saxophone playing). The sequence closes with a discussion of relationships, in which all three speakers self-disclose. In both examples, topics are developed slowly and accretively, with participants building on each other's contributions and arriving at a consensus.

Topic sequences C and D come from all-male conversation. The topics in these two extracts are very different from those in sequences A and B. Male speakers in all-male groups tend to avoid self-disclosure and prefer to talk about more impersonal topics such as current affairs, cars or sport (see, for example, Tolson 1977; Seidler 1989; Jackson 1990; Jukes 1993; Connell 1995). In topic sequence C we see a highly cohesive sequence of topics, all to do with the social and political history of the 1960s. Example D, by contrast, illustrates the way men will jump from topic to topic: here, the two friends discuss the merits of Burger King compared with McDonald's, before shifting abruptly to the topic of mobile phones.

Hedges

The use of hedges is strongly linked to topic choice. One of the reasons women have been found to use hedges more frequently than men (see, for example, Preisler 1986; Coates 1987, 1989; Cameron et al. 1989; Holmes 1984, 1995) is that they choose to talk about more personal topics, sometimes very sensitive topics. The following examples from all-female conversation illustrate this (hedges are underlined):

(2) [*talking about an old friend she's recently bumped into*]
she looks very <u>sort of</u> um – <u>kind of</u> matronly <u>really</u>

(3) [*talking about the incestuous family*]
<u>I mean I think</u> it was your theory <u>wasn't it?</u> that- that it runs in families?

(4) [*topic = police appeals at time of Yorkshire Ripper case*]
oh god yes <u>well I mean</u> we were living in Yorkshire at the time and I – <u>I mean</u>
I . <u>I mean</u> I did/ I <u>sort of</u> thought <u>well could</u> it be John?

In the first example, Meg chooses to talk about an old friend she's bumped into while out shopping. She is well aware that the adjective 'matronly' might not be seen as flattering, with its connotations of 'older' and 'overweight'. She needs to be careful since she does not want her friends to think this is the way she might talk about them behind their backs. She surrounds the adjective with hedges – *sort of, kind of, really* – and this, combined with her hesitation (*um*) makes her utterance very tentative and is designed to protect her own face as well as that of her addressees.

The second example is designed to mitigate the force of Mary's assertion that another member of the group had originally put forward this theory about the incestuous family. By using interrogative intonation and a tag question (*wasn't it?*), and by prefixing her words with the hedges *I think* and *I mean*, she makes it possible to retreat from this assertion if necessary.

The third example is a very good example of how hedges are typically found where a sensitive topic is being discussed. Here, the five friends are talking about the Yorkshire Ripper case, a case that had a big impact on some of them as they had links with Sheffield (where many of the murders took place). They reminisce about radio appeals made by the police to the public asking them to help them in the search for the serial killer. The police explicitly asked women listeners to consider whether any male member of their family could be the murderer. Sally bravely volunteers the information that she had forced herself to consider whether her partner, John, might be the wanted man. Not surprisingly, her utterance is full of hedges as well as hesitations, since she makes herself very vulnerable and needs to protect her own face, as well as that of her friends. But her self-disclosure leads to Meg telling the group that she too had forced herself to check her partner. Without using hedges, it would be impossible for speakers to make these kinds of disclosures, as they would make themselves too vulnerable.

Turn-taking

Carole Edelsky (1981) suggested that speakers can draw on two models of turn-taking in their everyday interactions: a one-at-a-time model and an alternative all-in-together model. She calls these two models the single, or singly developed, floor, and the collaborative, or collaboratively developed, floor. The main characteristic of the single floor is that one speaker speaks at a time: in other words, in a single floor speakers take turns to speak. By contrast, the defining characteristic of the collaborative floor is that the floor is potentially open to all participants simultaneously.

Male speakers engaged in friendly interaction seem to prefer a one-at-a-time floor (Edelsky 1981; Coates 1997b; Chapter 6, this volume). (This is, of course, the preferred floor in the public domain, in arenas such as business meetings, churches, law courts, Parliament.) In the informal all-male conversations I've recorded, I have found two typical patterns: serial monologues and verbal sparring.

(1) Serial monologues

Monologues – that is, stretches of conversation where one speaker holds the floor for a considerable time – are characteristic of men's talk. They seem to be associated with playing the expert. By 'playing the expert', I mean a kind of conversational game where participants take it in turns to hold the floor and to talk about a subject which they are an expert on. This is a game which seems to be played most commonly by male speakers; women, by contrast, avoid the role of expert in conversation. The following example comes from the conversation shown in list form as Topic sequence D. The conversation, involving two men friends having lunch together, ranges over a wide variety of topics, which tend to correlate with areas of expertise of the two friends, and means that they both get turns at being the expert, and turns at 'doing' a monologue. A brief extract from this conversation is given in example (5) below: Chris introduces the topic of mobile phones and proceeds to hold forth about mobile phone technology (minimal responses from Geoff in italics):

(5) 'Cos you know we've got BT internet at home (*mhm*) and I've set it up so that . um through the BT internet WAP portal so that Kate can read . her email that she gets . um on her phone (*oh right*) which is qui- which is quite useful if you're kinda not behind a computer but I was musing the other day on . on how funny it is that the sort of graphics you get on WAP phones now . is like you used to get on the ZX81 (*yeah*) and every- everything's having to adapt to that kind of LCSD based stuff (*that's right*) um computers have got to the point they've got to . and now they've gone all the way back with WAP technology.

This example illustrates very well how male speakers are happy to hold the floor for a considerable time. Note how this is achieved through the co-operation of the other speaker(s) present. In example (5), Geoff seems happy to be on the receiving end of Chris' monologue. His minimal responses function to show he is attending to what Chris is saying and to signal that he is content to go on listening. Note also the absence of hedges in this talk about a technical, non-emotional topic.

(2) Verbal sparring

The other pattern typically found in all-male friendly talk is verbal sparring. Sometimes men prefer a more cut-and-thrust style of talk, as in the two following examples. In the first, a group of English public school boys argue about whether a friend speaks French:

(6)
Julian: but the boy speaks French/
Henry: he does not/ . do you want this knife embedded in your face?/
Julian: do you want that tape-recorder inserted up your rectum?/
Henry: <LAUGHING> she'd get some pretty interesting sounds then/
Julian: yeah she would actually/

The second comes from a conversation involving a group of men working in a bakery in New Zealand; Sam and Ray disagree over whether apples are kept in cases or crates:

(7)
Ray: crate!
Sam: case!
Ray: what?
Sam: they come in cases Ray not crates
Ray: oh same thing if you must be picky over every one thing
Sam: just shut your fucking head Ray!
Ray: don't tell me to fuck off fuck (...)
Sam: I'll come over and shut yo-
Jim: yeah I'll have a crate of apples thanks [*laughingly using a thick-sounding voice*]
Ray: no fuck off Jim
Jim: a dozen ...
Dan: shitpicker! [*amused*]

(Pilkington 1998: 265)

Women, by contrast, seem to prefer a collaborative floor for friendly talk: the group takes priority over the individual, and the women's voices combine to construct a shared text. Chafe has described this kind of talk as 'polyphonic' (1994: 120ff); I have used another musical metaphor, describing the talk of women friends as a kind of jam session

(Coates 1996a: 117), a metaphor which draws attention to the spontaneous and improvisatory aspects of women's talk.

The three brief examples below (the first two from my database, the third from Pichler 2009) illustrate this kind of talk, though to give a true impression of collaborative talk, it would be necessary to give much longer extracts. (The examples are presented using stave notation: any word appearing vertically above or below any other word is to be read as occurring at the same time as that word. For more on transcription conventions, see pp. xiii–xv.)

(8) [*Pat tells Karen about her neighbour's attack of acute indigestion*]

P: he and his wife obviously thought he'd had a [heart attack/
K: [heart attack/

(9) [*talking about aging parents*]

Liz: and I mean it's a really weird situation because all

Sue: [you become a parent/ yeah/
Liz: of a sudden the [roles are all reversed/

(10) [*four teenage girls discuss a chat show they had seen where a man was boasting about his promiscuity*]

Nicky: he can't understand it when his girlfriends leave him because

Nicky: he says [it's in his genes] .hh [he says it's
Jane: [yeah he'll say you know] obvious[ly everyone

Nicky: natural for him to be] unfaithful
Jane: wants to do that]

As these examples demonstrate, simultaneous speech does not threaten comprehension, but on the contrary permits a more multi-layered development of topics. Sometimes two speakers will say the same thing at the same time (example 8), while at others different speakers will make different points (but on the same topic) simultaneously (examples 9 and 10).

These findings have led sociolinguists to make a distinction between two different conversational styles: one described as collaborative; the other as competitive. Jenny Cheshire and Peter Trudgill, for example, made the following claim:

> It seems clear that, other things being equal, women and men do have a preference for different conversational styles. Women – in most western societies at least – prefer a *collaborative speech style,* supporting other speakers and using language in a way that emphasizes their solidarity with the other person. Men, on the other hand, use a number of conversational strategies that can be described as a *competitive style,* stressing their own individuality and emphasizing the hierarchical relationships that they enter into with other people. (1998: 3)

This is a huge claim, and is obviously one that fits the Mars and Venus myth very well, in particular the idea that women and men can almost be said to be 'speaking different languages'. But does the sociolinguistic evidence support it? In the previous pages I have summarised some of the findings of research carried out on talk in same-sex groups, and this research suggests that all-female talk and all-male talk differ. But is it an over-simplification to describe all-male talk as competitive and all-female talk as cooperative? An understanding that these different ways of talking may share the goal of creating group solidarity suggests that it would be unwise to exaggerate male–female differences. However, even work which explores cooperation in all-male talk (e.g. Cameron 1997; Hewitt 1997) suggests that such cooperation either enables or accompanies competitive behaviour. Moreover, more recent research on all-female talk supports the claim that female speakers collaborate in the construction of talk: see, for example, Coates and Sutton-Spence (2001) on Deaf friends; Davies (2003) on all-female groups in the classroom in a Northern comprehensive school; Eppler (2009) on older bilingual Jewish refugees in London.

Phase 3: challenges at the turn of the century

The 1990s were the High Noon of Mars and Venus, and this period provided a context in which language and gender research flourished. The International Gender and Language Association (IGALA) was founded in 1999, and sociolinguistics conferences were inundated with papers on gender. In retrospect, the uncomplicated acceptance of the gender binary woman–man during this period seems a little naive. But what is important is that in this period language and gender research gained huge momentum – and also gained respectability in the academic world. This phase of research meant that women's – and girls' – ways of talking were analysed and celebrated, something which would have been unimaginable 10 years or so earlier.

But as the1990s progressed, challenges to the Mars and Venus myth began to come from several directions. The first challenge is the idea of gender as *plural*, an idea which completely undermines the Mars and Venus myth, which is intrinsically binary. By the turn of the century, in the academic world the idea of gender as plural was accepted: a more dynamic social constructionist approach had emerged which views gender as performative and as constantly 'in formation' (Butler 1990). It was now understood that, at any point in time, there will be a range of femininities and masculinities extant in a culture which differ in a variety of ways, such as class, sexual orientation, ethnicity, and age, as well as intersecting in complex ways.

The following examples provide a brief illustration of some of the masculinities currently available to be taken up by speakers; those shown here range from the laddish to the nerdy, from misogynistic to self-aggrandising. (All examples except (13) are taken from my database.)

(11) [*Rob tells a boastful story about ruining a customer's pornographic video*]
Rob: so I had to pluck up courage to tell him that I'd taped over his bloody pride and joy video tape with three hours <u>of MTV</u> <LAUGHING>
G and D: <LAUGHTER>

(12) [*Chris talking to Geoff about mobile phone technology*]
Chris: but I was musing the other day on . on how funny it is that the sort of graphics you get on WAP phones now . is like you used to get on the ZX81 (*yeah*) and every- everything's having to adapt to that kind of LCSD based stuff (*that's right*)

(13) [*four students in Manchester; George talks about a woman he claims he nearly went out with*]
George: she's got paps, big time
Dave: paps wi' the baps
George: she's got huge breasts ... they're just fuckin' huge, they are really big
Dave: dead 'eat in a bag a zeppelin race? [*laughter*]
Ewan: photo finish

(Gough and Edwards 1998: 422–3)

(14) [*Julian boasts to his friends about a sporting triumph*]
Julian: I did the most amazing left with this half-volley you will ever see

Female speakers similarly align themselves with a wide range of femininities. The following brief examples range from the caring to the bitchy, from the confident to the self-doubting:

(15) [*Sally talks understandingly about a friend who still trusts her ex-husband*]
Sally: I still think the most difficult thing is- is that when you've loved someone you- you half the time you forget their faults don't you?

(16) [*Meg tells a story showing her unconcealed pleasure at her ex-friend's son's failure to get a brilliant degree, despite his early promise*]
Meg: [Stan's] one of those few- one of the few people in the world that I feel deeply spiteful towards, and it's all to do with his son and my son ...

(17) [*Janet tells her friends about a recent job interview*]
Janet: I was really good in this interview because I was so unbothered about whether I got the job/

(18) [*Anna arrives late and explains why she is upset*]
Anna: I just had such a bad week/ and then my boss just stood in the office tonight and told me and his deputy that we're both crap managers basically/ [...] I get so angry at myself for crying/

The idea of multiple masculinities and femininities has proved very fruitful for sociolinguistic research, as the plethora of recent publications demonstrates (see, for example, Kosetzi and Polyzou 2009; Pichler 2009; Angouri 2011; Milani 2011; Luyt 2012; see also Chapters 3, 4 and 7, this volume).

The second challenge to binary thinking has come from Queer Linguistics. The first book to tackle this subject was an edited collection of papers entitled *Queerly Phrased* (Livia and Hall 1997), a book which had the subtitle *Language, Gender and Sexuality*. It had become increasingly apparent that gender and sexuality were intimately connected, to the extent that dominant forms of masculinity and femininity were heterosexual. Six years later, the first monograph devoted to the subject of language and sexuality appeared (Cameron and Kulick 2003). Queer Linguistics investigates 'the naturalising narratives of compulsory heterosexuality' (Butler 1990: 146), and examines how heterosexuality is 'actively produced in specific sociocultural contexts and situated interactions' (Cameron and Kulick 2003: 55).

Research on the language of gay, lesbian, bisexual and transsexual communities is at the heart of Queer Linguistics. Recent examples include studies of:

- British gay slang, known as *Polari* (Lucas 1997)
- the use of sexual insults by *hijras*, a class of transgendered individuals in India (Hall 1997)
- the language of Brazilian *travesti* (transvestite prostitutes) (Kulick 1998)

- the language of African American drag queens (Barrett 2006)
- lesbian bar talk in Tokyo (Abe 2004)

The notion of gender as fluid and multiple is intrinsic to queer linguistics, since binary categories like man–woman are unhelpful when studying communities like the ones listed above. For example, the point Barrett is making in his chapter on African American drag queens is that drag queens are *not* men who are acting like women, but men who are acting like drag queens.

Let's look in more detail at the last of the examples listed above, Abe's Tokyo study. The context for Abe's research was the two kinds of lesbian bar found in Tokyo: *rezubian* bars, for women who like women and are happy with their female body, and *onabe* bars, for women who are attracted to women but whose social and emotional identity is more masculine. Abe studied pronoun usage (among other things) in the talk taking place in these bars. The Japanese pronoun system can display the complexity of sexual identities in a way that English cannot: in Japanese, first-person pronouns are gendered, just like third-person pronouns in English (*he/she*). Abe found that three first-person pronouns – *jibun, watashi* and *boku* – were most commonly used in lesbian bars in Tokyo, and usage depended on which group the speaker identified with:

- *Onabe* use *jibun* (a reflexive pronoun associated with men in sports or the army).
- *Rezubian* use *watashi* (a pronoun available to both women and men).
- Transsexuals use *boku* (the masculine form).

But the same speaker can use multiple first-person forms depending on the context. So the following first-person pronouns, as well as those listed above, were all observed in the lesbian bars studied by Abe:

- *watashi* (form used by both women and men)
- *atashi* (standard form for women)
- *ore* (standard form used by men)
- *washi* (non-standard form used by men)
- *jibun* (reflexive form associated with men in sports or the army)

Research like this shows very clearly how constricting a binary approach can be. Here, all the people being studied are biologically women, but some identify as female and some as male. It would be all too easy to expect that first-person pronoun usage would correlate neatly with these two kinds of gay women, but, as we can see, this is not the case – the same speaker can use multiple forms, depending on context.

Case studies like this have been invaluable not only in breaking the stranglehold of simplistic understandings of gender but also in opening up research to non-English-speaking cultures.

Re-emerging binaries?

In the final part of this chapter, I want to assess where we are now. My title, 'The Rise and Fall (and Rise) of Mars and Venus', hints at the fact that the reality is more complex than a simple waxing and waning of the myth. Yes, the simple gender binary has been problematised and refined in various ways, and researchers working in the language and gender field are now more nuanced in their approach to gender. But this is not to say that binaries have disappeared. In fact, the evidence is that they are re-emerging.

One reason that binaries have not disappeared is because of the links between feminism and research to do with gender. Feminists in the past carried out research on language and gender with the aim of exposing inequalities between women and men. In the 1980s and early 1990s, research focusing on mixed talk in a variety of social contexts revealed asymmetrical patterns, with men's greater usage of certain strategies being associated with male dominance in conversation. The following are some examples of research showing conversational dominance in a range of contexts:

- in the classroom (e.g. Swann 1989)
- at the doctor's (e.g. West 1984b)
- in internet chat rooms (e.g. Herring et al. 1992)
- in the home (e.g. DeFrancisco 1991)

In the last ten years, there has been less research in this area as a result of the tension between the idea that 'woman' cannot be treated as a uniform social category and the continuing awareness that 'Gender relations are power relations' (Osmond and Thorne 1993: 593) and that 'women are still systematically discriminated against' (Mills 2003: 240).

Now, at the end of the first decade of the new century, there is a re-assertion of feminist goals. It is important that we feel able to appeal to the notion of 'woman' or 'man' without being accused of generalising or 'essentialising'; otherwise, how can patriarchy be challenged? Indeed, some researchers have begun to argue explicitly for a revival of feminist awareness in language and gender research (see Baxter 2003; McElhinny 2003; Swann 2003; Holmes 2007).

The re-assertion of the feminist project coincides with a new awareness of the role played by ideology in structuring society. There is a new understanding that the Mars and Venus myth corresponds with a social ideology of gender. Even though we now talk in terms of the fluidity and plurality of gender, we need to acknowledge the power of the social ideology of gender as dichotomous. Most people in most cultures align themselves with this ideology. Gender is seen as a simple mapping onto sex, and sex is construed as binary (male–female).

It is important to acknowledge the existence of prevailing ideologies of gender (see Cameron 2003; Talbot 2003). When speakers perform gender, they are inevitably influenced by the prevailing norms, even if they choose to resist them.

Ideologies of gender and language have varied over the last two hundred years, but one thing that is constant is 'the insistence that in any identifiable social group, women and men are *different*' (Cameron 2003: 452, italics in original). These ideologies of gender and language maintain gender distinctions and help to naturalise the idea that there are two 'opposite' sexes. Recent work in language and gender is increasingly paying attention to the ideologies of gender and language underpinning everyday interaction.

For example, Susan Ehrlich (2006) looks at the language used in a Canadian court room, in a trial about sexual assault, and shows how dominant ideologies of gender and of sexual behaviour make it very difficult for the woman complainant to be heard. A second example is research done by Sylvia Shaw (2006), who looked at the experience of women Members of Parliament in the UK. Women have trouble making themselves heard in Parliament, a problem arising from an ideology that still sees Parliament as a male arena and women as outsiders. Third, Jie Yang (2007) identifies a discourse which does important patriarchal work in China. This discourse includes a series of negative terms about women, reducing them to their mouths or tongues. In effect this discourse blames women's 'deviant' speaking styles for the serious social problem of domestic violence. This is a very nice example of why we still need to be able to call people 'women' and 'men'. The Chinese terms for women imply there are lots of different sorts of women with different (deviant) ways of speaking. But a feminist analysis makes clear that the true basis of violence against women is simply the fact that they are women.

Final words on Mars and Venus

What I have tried to do in this chapter is to show how binaries, in different ways and at different times, have shaped the way we understand the relationship between language and gender. Women and men do not come from different planets and they do not speak different languages. But with hindsight we can acknowledge that the Mars and Venus myth maps directly onto contemporary gender ideologies.

We now have a more sophisticated understanding of binaries and a more sophisticated understanding of gender. Even more importantly, we have come through the post-modern battles which threatened to make binaries taboo. While it is not true to say that there is now consensus, there is a sense that a more pragmatic approach needs to prevail. We can appeal to 'strategic essentialism' (Spivak 1987), that is, to the careful and temporary use of essentialism when the main goal is to expose discrimination against subaltern (subordinate) groups. In certain contexts, it may be strategically necessary to refer to categories such as 'women' and 'men', and to co-opt binaries as a tool in the feminist project.

Notes

1. This chapter was originally given as a lecture at Goldsmiths College, University of London. I am grateful to those who attended for their questions and comments. More importantly, I would like to thank Annabelle Mooney, Pia Pichler and Satori Soden for their invaluable comments and suggestions on earlier drafts of this chapter.
2. It should be noted that the preface to *Women in Their Speech Communities* (Coates and Cameron 1989: vi) states, 'This collection of papers is a contribution to the field of research on language and sex. Although "language and gender" might in some sense be more accurate, since we are dealing with a social rather than a biological category, the term *gender* has a technical meaning for linguists which has caused many writers to prefer the term *sex*.' Our inclusion of this sentence suggests that language and gender researchers were beginning to be self-conscious about the choice between 'sex' and 'gender'.

References

Abe, Hideko (2004) 'Lesbian bar talk in Shinjuku, Tokyo' in Shigeko Okamoto and Janet Shibamoto-Smith (eds) *Japanese Language, Gender and Ideology: Cultural Models and Real People*. Oxford: Oxford University Press.

Abrahams, Roger (1983) *The Man-of-Words in the West Indies: Performance and the Emergence of Creole Culture*. Baltimore: Johns Hopkins University Press.

Angouri, Jo (2011) '"We are in a masculine profession ...": constructing gender identities in a consortium of two multinational engineering companies', *Gender and Language*, 5 (2), 373–404.

Aries, Elizabeth (1976) 'Interaction patterns and themes of male, female and mixed groups', *Small Group Behaviour*, 7 (1), 7–18.

Aries, Elizabeth and Johnson, Fern (1983) 'Close friendship in adulthood: conversational conduct between same-sex friends', *Sex Roles*, 9 (12), 183–96.

Astedt-Kurki, Palvi, Isola, Arja, Tammentie, Tarja and Kervinen, Ulla (2001) 'Importance of humour to client-nurse relationships and clients' well-being', *International Journal of Nursing Practice*, 7 (2), 119–29.

Atkinson, Karen (1993) 'Co-operativity in all-female intergenerational talk', unpublished PhD thesis, Cardiff University.

Baker, Charlotte (1977) 'Regulators and turn-taking in American sign language discourse' in Lynn Friedman (ed.) *On the Other Hand*. New York: Academic Press.

Bakhtin, Mikael (1986) *Speech Genres and Other Late Essays*, ed. C. Emerson and M. Holmquist, trans. V.W. McGee. Austin: University of Texas Press.

Barker, D. (1988) 'Saving money and the world', *Guardian*, 11 November.

Barnes, Douglas (1971) 'Language and learning in the classroom', *Journal of Curriculum Studies*, 3 (1), 27–38.

Barrett, Rusty (1999) 'Indexing polyphonous identity in the speech of African American drag queens' in Mary Bucholtz et al. (eds) *Reinventing Identities*. Oxford: Oxford University Press, pp. 313–31.

Barrett, Rusty (2006) 'Supermodels of the world, unite! Political economy and the language of performance among African American drag queens' in Deborah Cameron and Don Kulick (eds) *The Language and Sexuality Reader*. London: Routledge, pp. 151–63.

Bateson, Gregory (1953) 'The position of humour in human communication' in H. von Foerster (ed.) *Cybernetics*, ninth conference. New York: Josiah Macey Jr. Foundation, pp. 1–47.

Bauman, R. (1986) *Story, Performance, and Event*. Cambridge: Cambridge University Press.

Baxter, Judith (2002) 'Jokers in the pack: why boys are more adept than girls at speaking in public settings', *Language and Education*, 16 (2), 81–96.

Baxter, Judith (2003) *Positioning Gender in Discourse: A Feminist Methodology*. London: Palgrave.

Baxter, Judith (2006a) 'Introduction' in J. Baxter (ed.) *Speaking Out: The Female Voice in Public Contexts*. London: Palgrave, pp. xiii–xviii.

Baxter, Judith (ed.) (2006b) *Speaking Out: The Female Voice in Public Contexts*. London: Palgrave.

Baxter, Judith (2010) *The Language of Female Leadership*. London: Palgrave.

Beckman, H.B. and Frankel, R.M. (1984) 'The effects of physician behaviour on the collection of data', *Annals of Internal Medicine*, 101, 692–96.

Belenky, M., Clinchy, B., Goldberger, N. and Tarule, J. (1986) *Women's Ways of Knowing*. New York: Basic Books.

Bell, Diane (1993) *Daughters of the Dreaming* (2nd edition). St Leonards, NSW: Allen and Unwin.

Benjamin, Jessica (1990) *The Bonds of Love*. London: Virago.

Benwell, Bethan (2002) 'Is there anything "new" about these lads? The construction of masculinity in men's magazines' in J. Sunderland and L. Litoselliti (eds) *Discourse Analysis and Gender Identity*. Amsterdam: John Benjamins, pp. 149–74.

Bourdieu, Pierre (1977) *Outline of a Theory of Practice*. Cambridge: Cambridge University Press.

Boxer, Diana and Cortes-Conde, Florencia (1997) 'From bonding to biting: conversational joking and identity display', *Journal of Pragmatics*, 27, 275–94.

Brown, Gillian (1977) *Listening to Spoken English*. London: Longman.

Brown, Lyn and Gilligan, Carol (1992) *Meeting at the Crossroads: Women's Psychology and Girls' Development*. Cambridge, MA: Harvard University Press.

Brown, Penelope and Levinson, Stephen (1987) *Politeness*. Cambridge: Cambridge University Press.

Bruner, Jerome (1990) 'Autobiography as self' in J. Bruner (ed.) *Acts of Meaning*. Cambridge, MA: Harvard University Press, pp. 33–66.

Bruner, Jerome (1991) 'The narrative construction of reality', *Critical Inquiry*, 18 (1), 1–21.

Bublitz, Wolfram (1988) *Supportive Fellow-Speakers and Cooperative Conversations*. Amsterdam: John Benjamins.

Bucholtz, Mary (2011) '"Why be normal?": language and identity practices in a community of nerd girls' in Jennifer Coates and Pia Pichler (eds) *Language and Gender: A Reader* (2nd edition). Oxford: Blackwell, pp. 224–35.

Bucholtz, Mary and Hall, Kira (2005) 'Identity and interaction: a socio-cultural linguistic approach', *Discourse Processes*, 7 (4–5), 585–614.

Butler, Judith (1990) *Gender Trouble: Feminism and the Subversion of Identity*. London: Routledge.

Cameron, Deborah (1992) *Feminism and Linguistic Theory* (2nd edition). London: Macmillan.

Cameron, D. (1997) 'Performing gender identity: young men's talk and the construction of heterosexual masculinity' in Sally Johnson and Ulrike H. Meinhof (eds) *Language and Masculinity*. Oxford: Blackwell, pp. 47–64.

Cameron, Deborah (2000) 'Styling the worker: gender and the commodification of language in the globalized service economy', *Journal of Sociolinguistics*, 4 (3), 323–47.

Cameron, Deborah (2003) 'Gender and language ideologies' in Janet Holmes and Miriam Meyerhoff (eds) *The Handbook of Language and Gender*. Oxford: Blackwell, pp. 447–67.

Cameron, Deborah and Kulick, Don (2003) *Language and Sexuality*. Cambridge: Cambridge University Press.

Cameron, Deborah and Kulick, Don (eds) (2006) *The Language and Sexuality Reader.* London: Routledge.

Cameron, Deborah, McAlinden, Fiona and O'Leary, Kathy (1989) 'Lakoff in context: the social and linguistic functions of tag questions' in Jennifer Coates and Deborah Cameron (eds) *Women in Their Speech Communities.* London: Longman, pp. 74–93.

Campbell, K. (1988) 'Master class', *Guardian,* 5 October, p. 16.

Campbell, K. and Jerry, C. (1988) 'Woman and speaker: a conflict in roles' in S.S. Brehm (ed.) *Seeing Female: Social Roles and Personal Lives.* New York: Greenwood Press.

Chafe, Wallace (1980) 'The deployment of consciousness in the production of narrative' in Wallace Chafe (ed.) *The Pear Stories: Cognitive, Cultural and Linguistic Aspects of Narrative Production.* Norwood, NJ: Ablex, pp. 9–50.

Chafe, W. (1994) *Discourse, Consciousness and Time: The Flow and Displacement of Conscious Experience in Speaking and Writing.* Chicago: University of Chicago Press.

Chafe, Wallace (1995) 'Polyphonic topic development', paper given at the Symposium on Conversation, University of New Mexico, Albuquerque, 12–14 July.

Chafe, Wallace (1997) 'Polyphonic topic development' in Talmy Givon (ed.) *Conversation: Cognitive, Communicative and Social Perspectives.* Philadelphia: John Benjamins, pp. 41–54.

Charteris-Black, Jonathan and Seale, Clive (2009) 'Men and emotion talk: evidence from the experience of illness', *Gender and Language,* 3 (1), 81–113.

Cheepen, Christine (1988) *The Predictability of Informal Conversation.* London: Pinter.

Cheshire, Jenny (1982) *Variation in an English Dialect.* Cambridge: Cambridge University Press.

Cheshire, Jenny and Trudgill, Peter (eds) (1998) *The Sociolinguistics Reader,* Vol. 2: *Gender and Discourse.* London: Arnold.

Coates, Jennifer (1986) *Women, Men and Language* (1st edition). London: Longman.

Coates, Jennifer (1987) 'Epistemic modality and spoken discourse', *Transactions of the Philological Society,* 85, 110–31.

Coates, Jennifer (1989) 'Gossip revisited: an analysis of all-female discourse' in Jennifer Coates and Deborah Cameron (eds) *Women in Their Speech Communities.* London: Longman, pp. 94–122 (reprinted in Jennifer Coates and Pia Pichler (eds) (2009) *Language and Gender: A Reader.* Oxford: Blackwell, pp. 199–223).

Coates, Jennifer (1991) 'Women's cooperative speech: a new kind of conversational duet?' in C. Uhlig and R. Zimmermann (eds) *Proceedings of the Anglistentag 1990 Marburg.* Tubingen: Max Niemeyer Verlag, pp. 296–311.

Coates, Jennifer (1993) *Women, Men and Language* (2nd edition). London: Longman.

Coates, Jennifer (1994) 'No gap, lots of overlap: turn-taking patterns in the talk of women friends' in David Graddol, Janet Maybin and Barry Stierer (eds) *Researching Language and Literacy in Social Context.* Clevedon, UK: Multilingual Matters, pp. 177–92.

Coates, Jennifer (1995a) 'Language, gender and career' in S. Mills (ed.) *Language and Gender: Interdisciplinary Perspectives*. London: Longman, pp. 13–30.

Coates, Jennifer (1995b) 'The expression of root and epistemic possibility in English' in Bas Aarts and Charles Meyer (eds) *The Verb in Contemporary English: Theory and Description*. Cambridge: Cambridge University Press, pp. 145–56.

Coates, Jennifer (1995c) 'The construction of a collaborative floor in women's friendly talk', paper given at the Symposium on Conversation, University of New Mexico, Albuquerque, 12–14 July.

Coates, Jennifer (1996a) *Women Talk: Conversation between Women Friends*. Oxford: Blackwell.

Coates, Jennifer (1996b) '"I just kept drinking and drinking and drinking": repetition and textual coherence' in J. Coates *Women Talk*. Oxford: Blackwell, pp. 203–31.

Coates, Jennifer (1996c) 'Women's stories: the role of narrative in friendly talk', inaugural lecture, Roehampton Institute, London.

Coates, Jennifer (1997a) 'One-at-a-time: the organisation of men's talk' in Sally Johnson and Ulrike Meinhof (eds) *Language and Masculinity*. Oxford: Blackwell, pp. 107–29.

Coates, Jennifer (1997b) 'The construction of a collaborative floor in women's friendly talk' in Talmy Givon (ed.) *Conversation: Cognitive, Communicative and Social Perspectives*. Philadelphia: John Benjamins, pp. 55–89.

Coates, Jennifer (1997c) 'Competing discourses of femininity' in Helga Kotthoff and Ruth Wodak (eds) *Communicating Gender in Context*. Amsterdam: John Benjamins, pp. 285–314.

Coates, Jennifer (ed.) (1998a) *Language and Gender: A Reader*. Oxford: Blackwell.

Coates, Jennifer (1998b) 'Women's friendships, women's talk' in Ruth Wodak (ed.) *Gender and Discourse*. London: Sage, pp. 245–62.

Coates, Jennifer (1999a) 'Women behaving badly: female speakers backstage', *Journal of Sociolinguistics*, 3 (1), 67–82.

Coates, Jennifer (1999b) 'Changing femininities: the talk of teenage girls' in Mary Bucholtz, A.C. Liang and L.A. Sutton (eds) *Reinventing Identities: The Gendered Self in Discourse*. Oxford: Oxford University Press, pp. 123–44.

Coates, Jennifer (2000) 'So I thought "Bollocks to it": men, stories and masculinities' in Janet Holmes (ed.) *Gendered Speech in Social Context*. Wellington, New Zealand: Victoria University Press, pp. 11–38.

Coates, Jennifer (2001) 'Pushing at the boundaries: the expression of alternative masculinities' in Janet Cotterill and Anne Ife (eds) *Language across Boundaries*. London: BAAL/Continuum, pp. 1–24.

Coates, Jennifer (2003a) *Men Talk: Stories in the Making of Masculinities*. Oxford: Blackwell.

Coates, Jennifer (2003b) '"She'd made sardines in aspic": women's stories, men's stories and the construction of gender' in *Men Talk*. Oxford: Blackwell, chapter 5.

Coates, Jennifer (2004) *Women, Men and Language* (3rd edition). London: Longman.

Coates, Jennifer (in press) 'Gender and humour in everyday conversation' in Delia Chiaro and Raffaella Baccolini (eds) *Gender and Humor: Interdisciplinary and International Perspectives*. London: Routledge.

Coates, Jennifer and Cameron, Deborah (eds) (1989) *Women in Their Speech Communities*. London: Longman.
Coates, Jennifer and Jordan, Mary Ellen (1997) 'Que(e)rying friendship: discourses of resistance and the construction of gendered subjectivity' in Anna Livia and Kira Hall (eds) *Queerly Phrased*. New York: Oxford University Press, pp. 214–32.
Coates, Jennifer and Pichler, Pia (eds) (2011) *Language and Gender: A Reader* (2nd edition). Oxford: Blackwell.
Coates, Jennifer and Sutton-Spence, Rachel (2001) 'Turn-taking patterns in Deaf friends' talk', *Journal of Sociolinguistics*, 4 (4), 507–29.
Cokely, David and Baker, Charlotte (1980) *American Sign Language*. Silver Spring, MD: T.J. Publishers.
Collins, Randall (1988) 'Theoretical continuities in Goffman's work' in Paul Drew and Anthony Wootton (eds) *Erving Goffman: Exploring the Interaction Order*. Cambridge: Polity Press, pp. 41–63.
Conley, John M. and O'Barr, William M. (2005) *Just Words: Law, Language and Power* (2nd edition). Chicago: University of Chicago Press.
Connell, R.W. (1995) *Masculinities*. Cambridge: Polity Press.
Cook-Gumperz, Jenny (1995) 'Reproducing the discourse of mothering: how gendered talk makes gendered lives' in Kira Hall and Mary Bucholtz (eds) *Gender Articulated: Language and the Socially Constructed Self*. London: Routledge, pp. 401–19.
Cook-Gumperz, Jenny (2001) 'Girls' oppositional stances: the interactional accomplishment of gender in nursery school and family life' in Bettina Baron and Helga Kotthoff (eds) *Gender in Interaction*. Amsterdam: John Benjamins, pp. 22–49.
Coupland, Nikolas, Garrett, Peter and Williams, Angie (2005) 'Narrative demands, cultural performance and evaluation: teenage boys' stories for their age-peers' in Joanna Thornborrow and Jennifer Coates (eds) *The Sociolinguistics of Narrative*. Amsterdam: John Benjamins, pp. 67–88.
Crawford, Mary (1995) *Talking Difference*. London: Sage.
Crawford, Mary (2003) 'Gender and humour in social context', *Journal of Pragmatics*, 5 (3), 1413–30.
Crawford, Mary and Gressley, Diane (1991) 'Creativity, caring and context: women's and men's accounts of humour preferences and practices', *Psychology of Women Quarterly*, 15, 217–31.
Crystal, David (1980) *A First Dictionary of Linguistics and Phonetics*. London: Andre Deutsch.
Curry, T. (1991) 'Fraternal bonding in the locker room: a pro-feminist analysis of talk about competition and women', *Sociology of Sport Journal*, 8, 119–35.
Daley, I. (1990) 'Some women confine themselves to the nursery pool of life', *Independent*, 20 December, p. 16.
Davidoff, Leonora and Hall, Catherine (1982) *Family Fortunes: Men and Women of the English Middle Classes 1780–1850*. London: Hutchinson.
Davidson, L.R. and Duberman, L. (1982) 'Friendship: communication and interactional patterns in same-sex dyads', *Sex Roles*, 8, 809–22.
Davies, Bronwyn (1989) 'The discursive production of the male/female dualism in school settings', *Oxford Review of Education*, 15 (3), 229–41.

Davies, Catherine Evans (2003) 'How English-learners joke with native speakers: an interactional sociolinguistic perspective on humor as collaborative discourse across cultures', *Journal of Pragmatics*, 35, 1361–85.

Davies, Julia (2003) 'Expressions of gender: an analysis of pupils' gendered discourse styles in small group classroom discussions', *Discourse & Society*, 14 (2), 115–32.

De Beauvoir, Simone (1988) *The Second Sex*, trans. H.M. Parshley. London: Picador.

DeFrancisco, Victoria (1991) 'The sounds of silence: how men silence women in marital relations', *Discourse & Society*, 2 (4), 413–24.

Dorval, Bruce (ed.) (1990) *Conversational Organisation and Its Development*. Norwood, NJ: Ablex.

Dunbar, R. (1996) *Grooming, Gossip and the Evolution of Language*. London: Faber and Faber.

DuPre, Athena (1998) *Humour and the Healing Arts*. Mahwah, NJ: Erlbaum.

Duranti, A. (1986) 'The audience as co-author: an introduction', *Text*, 6 (3), 239–47.

Eckert, Penelope (1993) 'Cooperative competition in adolescent "girl talk"' in Deborah Tannen (ed.) *Gender and Conversational Interaction*. Oxford: Oxford University Press, pp. 32–61.

Eckert, Penelope (1998) 'Gender and sociolinguistic variation' in Jennifer Coates (ed.) *Language and Gender: A Reader*. Oxford: Blackwell, pp. 64–75.

Edelsky, Carole (1981) 'Who's got the floor?' *Language in Society*, 10 (3), 383–421 (reprinted in Deborah Tannen (ed.) (1993) *Gender and Conversational Interaction*. Oxford: Oxford University Press, pp. 189–227).

Eder, Donna (1993) '"Go get ya a french": romantic and sexual teasing among adolescent girls' in Deborah Tannen (ed.) *Gender and Conversational Interaction*. Oxford: Oxford University Press, pp. 17–31.

Edley, Nigel and Wetherell, Margaret (1997) 'Jockeying for position: the construction of masculine identities', *Discourse & Society*, 8 (2), 203–17.

Ehrlich, Susan (2006) 'Trial discourse and judicial decision-making: constraining the boundaries of gendered identities' in Judith Baxter (ed.) *Speaking Out: The Female Voice in Public Contexts*. London: Palgrave, pp. 139–58.

Eisikovits, Edina (1988) 'Girl-talk/boy-talk: sex differences in adolescent speech' in P. Collins and D. Blair (eds) *Australian English*. Brisbane: University of Queensland Press, pp. 35–54 (reprinted in Jennifer Coates and Pia Pichler (eds) (2011) *Language and Gender: A Reader* (2nd edition). Oxford: Blackwell, pp. 38–48).

Eppler, Eva (2009) 'Four women, two codes and one (crowded) floor: the joint construction of a bilingual collaborative floor' in Pia Pichler and Eva Eppler (eds) *Gender and Spoken Interaction*. London: Palgrave, pp. 211–34.

Everts, Elisa (2003) 'Identifying a particular family humor style: a sociolinguistic discourse analysis', *Humor: International Journal of Humor Studies*, 16 (4), 369–412.

Facchinetti, Roberta, Krug, Manfred and Palmer, Frank (eds) (2003) *Modality in Contemporary English*. Berlin: Mouton de Gruyter.

Fairclough, Norman (1989) *Language and Power*. London: Longman.

Fairclough, Norman (1992) *Discourse and Social Change*. Cambridge: Polity Press.

Falk, Jane (1980) 'The conversational duet', *Proceedings of the 6th Annual Meeting of the Berkeley Linguistics Society*, 6, 507–14.

Firestone, Shulamith (1970) *The Dialectic of Sex*. New York: Morrow.

Fisher, S. (1991) 'A discourse of the social: medical talk/power talk/oppositional talk?' *Discourse & Society*, 2 (2), 157–82.

Ford, Cecilia E. (2008) *Women Speaking Up: Getting and Using Turns in Workplace Meetings*. New York: Palgrave Macmillan.

Foucault, Michel (1972) *The Archaeology of Knowledge and the Discourse on Language*. New York: Pantheon.

Frankel, R. (1983) 'The laying on of hands: aspects of the organisation of gaze, touch and talk in a medical encounter' in S. Fisher and A.D. Todd (eds) *The Social Organisation of Doctor-Patient Communication*. Washington, DC: Center for Applied Linguistics, pp. 19–54.

Frankel. R. (1991) 'Talking in interviews: a dispreference for patient-initiated questions in physician-patient encounters' in G. Psathas (ed.) *Interactional Competence*. New York: Irvington.

Frosh, Stephen, Phoenix, Ann and Pattman, Rob (2002) *Young Masculinities: Understanding Boys in Contemporary Society*. London: Palgrave.

Galloway Young, K. (1987) *Taleworlds and Storyrealms*. Lancaster: Kluwer Academic Publishers.

Gavey, Nicola (1989) 'Feminist poststructuralism and discourse analysis', *Psychology of Women Quarterly*, 13, 459–75.

Gibbs, Raymond W., Jr. (2000) 'Irony in talk among friends', *Metaphor and Symbol*, 15 (1–2), 5–27.

Gilligan, Carol (1982) *In a Different Voice*. Cambridge, MA: Harvard University Press.

Gilligan, C., Ward, J. and Taylor, J.M. (eds) (1988) *Mapping the Moral Domain*. Cambridge, MA: Harvard University Press.

Goffman, Erving (1971) *The Presentation of Self in Everyday Life*. Harmondsworth, UK: Penguin Books.

Goffman, Erving (1981) *Forms of Talk*. Oxford: Blackwell.

Goodwin, Charles (1986) 'Audience diversity, participation and interpretation', *Text*, 6 (3), 283–316.

Goodwin, Marjorie Harness (1980) 'Directive-response speech sequences in girls' and boys' task activities' in Sally McConnell-Ginet et al. (eds) *Women and Language in Literature and Society*. New York: Praeger, pp. 157–73.

Goodwin, Marjorie Harness (1988) 'Cooperation and competition across girls' play activities' in A.D. Todd and S. Fisher (eds) *Gender and Discourse: The Power of Talk*. Norwood, NJ: Ablex, pp. 55–94.

Goodwin, Marjorie Harness (1990) *He-Said-She-Said: Talk as Social Organisation among Black Children*. Bloomington: Indiana University Press.

Goodwin, Marjorie Harness (1992) 'Orchestrating participation in events: powerful talk among African American girls' in Kira Hall (ed.) *Locating Power: Proceedings of the 1992 Berkeley Women and Language Conference*. Berkeley, CA: Berkeley Women and Language Group, Linguistics Department, UC-Berkeley, pp. 182–96.

Goodwin, Marjorie Harness (1999) 'Constructing opposition within girls' games' in Mary Bucholtz, A.C. Liang and Laurel A. Sutton (eds) *Reinventing Identities: The Gendered Self in Discourse*. Oxford: Oxford University Press, pp. 388–409.

Goodwin, Marjorie Harness (2003) 'The relevance of ethnicity, class, and gender in children's peer negotiations' in Janet Holmes and Miriam Meyerhoff (eds) *The Handbook of Language and Gender*. Oxford: Blackwell, pp. 229–51.

Gough, Brendan (1998) 'Men and the discursive reproduction of sexism: repertoires of difference and equality', *Feminism and Psychology*, 8 (1), 25–49.

Gough, Brendan and Edwards, Gareth (1998) 'The beer talking: four lads, a carry out and the reproduction of masculinities', *The Sociological Review*, 46 (3), 409–35.

Gouldner, Helen and Strong, Mary Symons (1987) *Speaking of Friendship*. New York: Greenwood Press.

Graddol, David and Swann, Joan (1989) *Gender Voices*. Oxford: Basil Blackwell.

Gray, John (1992) *Men Are from Mars, Women Are from Venus*. London: Element Greenwood Press.

Greer, Germaine (1970) *The Female Eunuch*. London: Paladin.

Greif, Geoffrey (2009) *Buddy System: Understanding Male Friendships*. New York: Oxford University Press.

Grice H.P. (1975) 'Logic and conversation' in P. Cole and J.L. Morgan (eds) *Syntax and Semantics*, Vol. 3: *Speech Acts*. New York: Academic Press, pp. 41–58.

Griffin, Christine (1989) '"I'm not a woman's libber but ...": feminism, consciousness and identity' in S. Skevington and D. Baker (eds) *The Social Identity of Women*. London: Sage, pp. 173–93.

Haas, Adelaide (1979) 'Male and female spoken language differences: stereotypes and evidence', *Psychological Bulletin*, 86, 616–26.

Hall, C. (1985) 'Private persons versus public someones: class, gender and politics in England, 1780–1850' in C. Steedman, C. Urwin and V. Walkerdine (eds) *Language, Gender and Childhood*. London: Routledge and Kegan Paul, pp. 10–33.

Hall, Kira (1997) '"Go suck your husband's sugarcane!": hijras and the use of sexual insult' in Anna Livia and Kira Hall (eds) *Queerly Phrased: Language, Gender and Sexuality*. New York: Oxford University Press, pp. 430–60.

Halliday, M.A.K. (1973) *Explorations in the Function of Language*. London: Edward Arnold.

Halliday, M.A.K. and Hasan, Ruqaiya (1976) *Cohesion in English*. London: Longman.

Harris, Sandra (1984) 'Questions as a mode of control in magistrates' courts', *International Journal of the Sociology of Language*, 49, 5–27.

Hay, Jennifer (1995) 'Gender and humour: beyond a joke', unpublished MA dissertation, Victoria University of Wellington, New Zealand.

Hay, Jennifer (2000) 'Functions of humour in the conversations of men and women', *Journal of Pragmatics*, 32, 709–42.

Haywood, C. and Mac an Ghaill, M. (1997) 'A man in the making: sexual masculinities within changing training cultures', *The Sociological Review*, 45 (4), 576–90.

Herek, G.M. (1987) 'On heterosexual masculinity: some psychical consequences of the social construction of gender and sexuality' in Michael S. Kimmel (ed.) *Changing Men: New Directions in Research on Men and Masculinity*. London: Sage, pp. 68–82.

Herring, Susan, Johnson, Deborah and DiBenedetto, Tamra (1992) 'Participation in electronic discourse in a "feminist" field' in Kira Hall (ed.) *Locating Power: Proceedings of the 2nd Berkeley Women and Language Conference*. Berkeley:

Berkeley Women and Language Group, Linguistics Department, UC-Berkeley, pp. 250–62.

Hewitt, Roger (1997) '"Box-out" and "taxing"' in Sally Johnson and Ulrike Meinhof (eds) *Language and Masculinity*. Oxford: Blackwell, pp. 27–46.

Hey, Valerie (1996) *The Company She Keeps: An Ethnography of Girls' Friendship*. Buckingham, UK: Open University Press.

Hollway, Wendy (1983) 'Heterosexual sex: power and desire for the other' in Sue Cartledge and J. Ryan (eds) *Sex and Love: New Thoughts on Old Contradictions*. London: Women's Press, pp. 124–40.

Holmes, Janet (1984) 'Hedging your bets and sitting on the fence: some evidence for hedges as support structures', *Te Reo*, 27, 47–62.

Holmes, Janet (1995) *Women, Men and Politeness*. London: Longman.

Holmes, Janet (1998) 'Women's talk: the question of sociolinguistic universals' in Jennifer Coates (ed.) *Language and Gender: A Reader* (1st edition). Oxford: Blackwell, pp. 461–83.

Holmes, Janet (2000) 'Politeness, power and provocation: how humour functions in the workplace', *Discourse Studies*, 2 (2), 159–85.

Holmes, Janet (2006) *Gendered Talk at Work: Constructing Gender Identity through Workplace Discourse*. Oxford: Blackwell.

Holmes, Janet (2007) 'Social constructionism, postmodernism and feminist sociolinguistics', *Gender and Language*, 1, 51–65.

Holmes, Janet and Hay, Jennifer (2003) 'Humour as an ethnic boundary marker in New Zealand interaction', *Journal of Intercultural Studies*, 18 (2), 127–51.

Homes, Janet and Marra, Meredith (2002) 'Over the edge? Subversive humour between colleagues and friends', *Humor: International Journal of Humor Studies*, 15 (1), 65–87.

Holmes, Janet and Schnurr, Stephanie (2006) 'Doing "femininity" at work: more than just relational practice', *Journal of Sociolinguistics*, 10 (1), 31–51.

Holmes, Janet and Stubbe, Maria (2003) *Power and Politeness in the Workplace: A Sociolinguistic Analysis of Talk at Work*. London: Pearson.

Holmes, Janet, Marra, Meredith and Burns, Louise (2001) 'Women's humour in the workplace: a quantitative analysis', *Australian Journal of Communication*, 28 (1), 83–108.

Holmgreen, Lise-Lotte (2009) 'Metaphorically speaking: construction of gender and career in the Danish financial sector', *Gender and Language*, 3 (1), 1–32.

Jackson, David (1990) *Unmasking Masculinity*. London: Unwin Hyman.

Jefferson, Gail (1973) 'A case of precision timing in ordinary conversation: overlapped tag-positioned address terms in closing sequences', *Semiotica*, 9, 47–96.

Johnson, Anthony (1990) 'Couples talking: conversational duets and conversational style', paper given at Sociolinguistics Symposium 8, Roehampton Institute, London.

Johnson, Fern and Aries, Elizabeth (1983a) 'The talk of women friends', *Women's Studies International Forum*, 6 (4), 353–61.

Johnson, Fern and Aries, Elizabeth (1983b) 'Conversational patterns among same-sex pairs of late-adolescent close friends', *Journal of Genetic Psychology*, 142, 225–38.

Johnson, Sally (1997) 'Theorizing language and masculinity: a feminist perspective' in Sally Johnson and Ulrike H. Meinhof (eds) *Language and Masculinity*. Oxford: Blackwell, pp. 8–26.

Johnson, Sally and Finlay, Frank (1997) 'Do men gossip? An analysis of football talk on television' in Sally Johnson and Ulla H. Meinhof (eds) *Language and Masculinity*. Oxford: Blackwell, pp. 130–43.

Johnstone, Barbara (1990) *Stories, Community, and Place*. Bloomington: Indiana University Press.

Johnstone, Barbara (1993) 'Community and contest: Midwestern men and women creating their worlds in conversational storytelling' in Deborah Tannen (ed.) *Gender and Conversational Interaction*. Oxford: Oxford University Press, pp. 62–80.

Jones, Deborah (1980) 'Gossip: notes on women's oral culture' in Cheris Kramarae (ed.) *The Words and Voices of Women and Men*. Oxford: Pergamon Press, pp. 193–8.

Jordan, Rosan and Kalcik, Susan (eds) (1985) *Women's Folklore, Women's Culture*. Philadelphia: University of Pennsylvania Press.

Jukes, Adam (1993) *Why Men Hate Women*. London: Free Association Books.

Kalcik, Susan (1975) '"... like Ann's gynecologist or the time I was almost raped": personal narratives in women's rap groups' in C.R. Farrer (ed.) *Women and Folklore*. Austin: University of Texas Press, pp. 3–11.

Kaminer, Debra and Dixon, John (1995) 'The reproduction of masculinity: a discourse analysis of men's drinking talk', *South African Journal of Psychology*, 25 (3), 168–74.

Kehily, Mary Jane and Nayak, Anoop (1997) '"Lads and laughter": humour and the production of heterosexual hierarchies', *Gender and Education*, 9 (1), 69–87.

Kerby, Anthony (1991) *Narrative and the Self*. Bloomington: Indiana University Press.

Kiesling, Scott (2002) 'Playing the straight man: displaying and maintaining male heterosexuality in discourse' in Kathryn Campbell-Kibler et al. (eds) *Language and Sexuality: Contesting Meaning in Theory and Practice*. Stanford: CSLI Publications, pp. 2–10 (reprinted in Jennifer Coates and Pia Pichler (eds) (2011) *Language and Gender: A Reader*. Oxford: Blackwell).

Kimmel, Michael S. (2000) *The Gendered Society*. Oxford: Oxford University Press.

Kimmel, Michael S. (ed.) (1987) *Changing Men: New Directions in Research on Men and Masculinity*. London: Sage.

Kirshenblatt-Gimblett, B. (1974) 'The concept and varieties of narrative performance in East European Jewish culture' in R. Baumann and J. Scherzer (eds) *Explorations in the Ethnography of Speaking*. New York: Cambridge University Press, pp. 283–308.

Kosetzi, Konstantia and Polyzou, Alexandra (2009) '"The perfect man, the proper man": construals of masculinities in *Nitro*, a Greek men's lifestyle magazine – an exploratory study', *Gender and Language*, 3 (2), 143–80.

Kotthoff, Helga (2003) 'Responding to irony in different contexts: on cognition in conversation', *Journal of* Pragmatics, 35 (3), 1387–411.

Kramarae, Cheris (ed.) (1980) *The Words and Voices of Women and Men*. Oxford: Pergamon Press.

Kuiper, Koenraad (1991) 'Sporting formulae in New Zealand English: two models of male solidarity' in J. Cheshire (ed.) *English around the World*. Cambridge: Cambridge University Press, pp. 200–9.

Kuiper, Koenraad (1997) 'Sporting formulae in New Zealand English: two models of male solidarity' in Jennifer Coates (ed.) *Language and Gender: A Reader.* Oxford: Blackwell, pp. 285–94.

Kulick, Don (1998) *Travesti: Sex, Gender and Culture among Brazilian Transgendered Prostitutes.* Chicago: University of Chicago Press.

Labov, William (1966) *The Social Stratification of English in New York City.* Washington DC: Center for Applied Linguistics/Cambridge: Cambridge University Press.

Labov, William (1972a) *Language in the Inner City.* Philadelphia: University of Pennsylvania Press.

Labov, William (1972b) 'The transformation of experience in narrative syntax' in *Language in the Inner City.* Philadelphia: University of Pennsylvania Press, pp. 354–96.

Lakoff, Robin (1975) *Language and Woman's Place.* New York: Harper and Row.

Lee, David (1992) *Competing Discourses: Perspective and Ideology in Language.* London: Longman.

Le Guin, Ursula K. (1992) 'Some thoughts on narrative' in Ursula K. Le Guin *Dancing at the Edge of the World.* London: Paladin, pp. 37–45.

Linde, Charlotte (1993) *Life Stories: The Creation of Coherence.* New York: Oxford University Press.

Livia, Anna and Hall, Kira (eds) (1997) *Queerly Phrased: Language, Gender and Sexuality.* New York: Oxford University Press.

Looser, D. (1997) 'Bonds and barriers: language in a New Zealand prison', *The New Zealand English Journal*, 11, 46–54.

Lovenduski, J. (1989) 'Euro resolve', *Guardian*, 6 June, p. 17.

Lucas, Ian (1997) 'The color of his eyes' in Anna Livia and Kira Hall (eds) *Queerly Phrased.* Oxford: Oxford University Press, pp. 85–94.

Lucas, Ian (2006) 'The colour of his eyes: Polari and the Sisters of Perpetual Indulgence' in Deborah Cameron and Don Kulick (eds) *The Language and Sexuality Reader.* London: Routledge, pp. 85–94.

Luyt, Russell (2012) 'Constructing hegemonic masculinities in South Africa: the discourse and rhetoric of heteronormativity', *Gender and Language*, 6 (1), 47–78.

Macaulay, R.K.S. (1977) *Language, Social Class and Education.* Edinburgh: Edinburgh University Press.

Maltz, D. and Borker, R. (1982) 'A cultural approach to male-female miscommunication' in J. Gumperz (ed.) *Language and Social Identity.* Cambridge: Cambridge University Press, pp. 195–216.

Mather, Susan (1996) 'Initiation in visually constructed dialogue: reading books to three- to eight-year-old students who are deaf and hard-of-hearing' in Ceil Lucas (ed.) *Multicultural Aspects of Sociolinguistics in Deaf Communities.* Washington DC: Gallaudet University Press, pp. 109–31.

Maybin, Janet (1996) 'Story voices: the use of reported speech in 10–12 years olds' spontaneous narratives', *Current Issues in Language and Society*, 3 (1), 36–48.

McCabe, T. (1981) 'Girls and leisure' in A. Tomlinson (ed.) *Leisure and Social Control.* Brighton: Brighton Polytechnic, Chelsea School of Human Movement.

McElhinny, Bonnie (2005) 'Gender and the stories Pittsburgh police officers tell about using physical force' in Caroline Brettell and Carolyn Sargent (eds) *Gender in Cross-Cultural Perspective.* London: Pearson Prentice Hall, pp. 219–30.

Mehan, H. (1979) *Learning Lessons: Social Organisation in the Classroom*. Cambridge, MA: Harvard University Press.
Meinhof, Ulrike H. (1997) '"The most important event of my life": a comparison of male and female written narratives' in Sally Johnson and Ulrike H. Meinhof (eds) *Language and Masculinity*. Oxford: Blackwell, pp. 208–28.
Meltzer, Leo, Morris, William N. and Hayes, Donald P. (1971) 'Interruption outcomes and vocal amplitude: explorations in psychophysics', *Journal of Personality and Social Psychology*, 18 (3), 392–402.
Mendoza-Denton, Norma (1999) 'Turn-initial no: collaborative opposition among Latina adolescents' in Mary Bucholtz, A.C. Liang and Laurel A. Sutton (eds) *Reinventing Identities: The Gendered Self in Discourse*. Oxford: Oxford University Press, pp. 273–92.
Mendoza-Denton, Norma (2007) *Homegirls: Language and Cultural Practice among Latina Youth Gangs*. Boston: Wiley-Blackwell.
Menz, Florian and Al-Roubaie, Ali (2008) 'Interruptions, status and gender in medical interviews: the harder you brake, the longer it takes', *Discourse & Society*, 19 (5), 645–66.
Milani, Tommaso M. (2011) 'Introduction: re-casting language and masculinities', *Gender and Language*, 5 (2), 175–86.
Milani, Tommaso and Jonsson, Rickard (2011) 'Incomprehensible language? Language, ethnicity and heterosexual masculinity in a Swedish school', *Gender and Language*, 5 (2), 241–70.
Miller, Casey and Swift, Kate (1977) *Words and Women*. London: Victor Gollancz.
Miller, I.B. (1976) *Toward a New Psychology of Women*. Boston: Beacon Press.
Miller, J. Hillis (1990) 'Narrative' in F. Lentricchia and T. McLaughlin (eds) *Critical Terms for Literary Study*. Chicago: University of Chicago Press.
Miller, Stuart (1983) *Men and Friendship*. San Leandro, CA: Gateway Books.
Millett, Kate (1970) *Sexual Politics*. Urbana: University of Illinois Press.
Mills, Sara (2003) *Gender and Politeness*. Cambridge: Cambridge University Press.
Milroy, James and Milroy, Lesley (1978) 'Belfast: change and variation in an urban vernacular' in Peter Trudgill (ed.) *Sociolinguistic Patterns in British English*. London: Edward Arnold, pp. 19–36.
Milroy, Lesley (1987) *Observing and Analysing Natural Language*. Oxford: Blackwell.
Mishler, E.G. (1984) *The Discourse of Medicine: Dialectics of Medical Interviews*. Norwood, NJ: Ablex.
Moerman, Michael and Sacks, Harvey (1971) 'On "understanding" in the analysis of natural conversation', paper given at the 70th Annual Meeting of the American Anthropological Association (reprinted in M. Moerman (1988) *Talking Culture: Ethnography and Conversation Analysis*. Philadelphia: University of Pennsylvania Press).
Moore, B. (1993) *A Lexicon of Cadet Language*. Canberra: Australian National Dictionary Centre.
Mullany, Louise (2003) 'Identity and role construction: a sociolinguistic study of gender and discourse in management', unpublished PhD thesis, Nottingham Trent University.
Mullany, Louise (2007) *Gendered Discourse in the Professional Workplace*. London: Palgrave.

Nardi, Peter (ed.) (1992) *Men's Friendships: Research on Men and Masculinities*. London: Sage.

Nelson, Marie W. (1988) 'Women's ways: interactive patterns in predominantly female research teams' in Barbara Bate and Anita Taylor (eds) *Women Communicating*. Norwood, NJ: Ablex, pp. 199–232.

Newbrook, Mark (1982) 'Sociolinguistic reflexes of dialect interference in West Wirral', unpublished PhD thesis, Reading University.

Nichols, Patricia (1983) 'Linguistic options and choices for Black women in the rural South' in Barrie Thorne, Cheris Kramarae and Nancy Henley (eds) *Language, Gender and Society*. Rowley, MA: Newbury House, pp. 54–68.

Norrick, Neal (1993) *Conversational Joking: Humour in Everyday Talk*. Bloomington: Indiana University Press.

Norrick, Neal (2004) 'Humor, tellability and conarration in conversational storytelling', *Text*, 24 (1), 79–111.

Norrick, Neal (2005) 'Contextualising and recontextualising interlaced stories in conversation' in Joanna Thornborrow and Jennifer Coates (eds) *The Sociolinguistics of Narrative*. Amsterdam: John Benjamins, pp. 107–27.

Ochs, Elinor (1992) 'Indexing gender' in Alessandro Duranti and Charles Goodwin (eds) *Rethinking Context: Language as an Interactive Phenomenon*. Cambridge: Cambridge University Press, pp. 335–58.

O'Connor, Pat (1992) *Friendships between Women: A Critical Review*. London: Harvester Wheatsheaf.

Osmond, Marie W. and Thorne, Barrie (1993) 'Feminist theories: the social construction of gender in families and society' in Pauline Boss et al. (eds) *Sourcebook of Family Theories and Methods*. New York: Plenum, pp. 591–622.

Ostermann, Ana Cristina (2003) 'Communities of practice at work: gender, facework and the power of habitus at an all-female police station and a feminist crisis interventions centre in Brazil', *Discourse & Society*, 14 (4), 473–505.

O'Sullivan, Tim (1983) *Key Concepts in Communication*. London: Methuen.

Phillips, Jock (1996) *A Man's Country? The Image of the Pakeha Male – A History*. Auckland: Penguin.

Pichler, Pia (2009) *Talking Young Femininities*. London: Palgrave.

Pilkington, Jane (1998) '"Don't try and make out that I'm nice": the different strategies women and men use when gossiping' in Jennifer Coates (ed.) *Language and Gender: A Reader* (1st edition). Oxford: Blackwell, pp. 254–69.

Pipher, Mary Bray (1994) *Reviving Ophelia: Saving the Selves of Adolescent Girls*. New York: Putnam.

Pleck, J.H. (1975) 'Man to man: is brotherhood possible?' in N. Glazer-Malbin (ed.) *Old Family, New Family*. New York: Van Nostrand.

Pleck, Joseph H. (1995) 'Men's power with women, other men, and society: a men's movement analysis' in M.S. Kimmel and M.A. Messner (eds) *Men's Lives* (3rd edition). Boston: Allyn and Bacon, pp. 5–12.

Polanyi, Livia (1985) *Telling the American Story: A Structural and Cultural Analysis of Conversational Storytelling*. Norwood, NJ: Ablex.

Polanyi, Livia (1982a) 'Literary complexity in everyday storytelling' in D. Tannen (ed.) *Spoken and Written Language: Exploring Orality and Literacy*. Norwood, NJ: Ablex, pp. 155–70.

Preisler, Bent (1986) *Linguistic Sex Roles in Conversation*. Berlin/New York: Mouton de Gruyter.

Pujolar, Joan (1997) 'Masculinities in a multilingual setting' in Sally Johnson and Ulrike H. Meinhof (eds) *Language and Masculinity*. Oxford: Blackwell, pp. 86–106.

Purvis, June (1987) 'Social class, education and ideals of femininity in the nineteenth century' in Madeleine Arnot and Gaby Weiner (eds) *Gender and the Politics of Schooling*. London: Hutchinson, pp. 253–75.

Rampton, Ben (1995) *Crossing: Language and Ethnicity among Adolescents*. London: Longman.

Reid, Euan (1978) 'Social and stylistic variation in the speech of children: some evidence from Edinburgh' in Peter Trudgill (ed.) *Sociolinguistic Patterns in British English*. London: Edward Arnold, pp. 158–71.

Renold, E. (2000) '"Coming out": gender, (hetero) sexuality and the primary school', *Gender and Education*, 12, 309–26.

Reynolds, Katsue Akiba (1991) 'Female speakers of Japanese in transition' in S. Ide and N. McGloin (eds) *Aspects of Japanese Women's Language*. Tokyo: Kurosio, pp. 129–46.

Rich, Adrienne (1980) 'Compulsory heterosexuality and lesbian existence', *Signs*, 5 (4), 631–60 (reprinted in A. Snitow, C. Stansell and S. Thompson (eds) (1984) *Desire: The Politics of Sexuality*. London: Virago).

Romaine, Suzanne (1978) 'Postvocalic /r/ in Scottish English: sound change in progress?' in Peter Trudgill (ed.) *Sociolinguistic Patterns in British English*. London: Edward Arnold, pp. 144–57.

Roper, Michael and Tosh, John (eds) (1991) *Manful Assertions: Masculinities in Britain since 1800*. London: Routledge.

Rubin, Lilian (1985) *Just Friends: The Role of Friendship in Our Lives*. New York: Harper & Row.

Ruddick, Sara (1989) *Maternal Thinking: Towards a Politics of Peace*. London: Women's Press.

Ryave, A. (1978) 'On the achievement of a series of stories' in J. Schenkein (ed.) *Studies in the Organisation of Conversational Interaction*. New York: Academic Press, pp. 113–32.

Sacks, Harvey (1995) *Lectures on Conversation*, Vols. I and II, ed. Gail Jefferson. Oxford: Blackwell.

Sacks, Harvey, Schegloff, Emanuel A. and Jefferson, Gail (1974) 'A simplest systematics for the organisation of turn-taking in conversation', *Language*, 50, 696–735.

Scheibman, Joanne (1995) 'Two-at-a-time: the intimacy of simultaneous speech in sister talk', LGSO Working Papers, University of New Mexico Linguistics Department.

Segal, Lynn (1990) *Slow Motion: Changing Masculinities, Changing Men*. London: Virago.

Seidler, Victor (1989) *Rediscovering Masculinity: Reason, Language and Sexuality*. London: Routledge.

Seidler, Victor (1991) '"Personally speaking": experiencing a men's group' in V. Seidler (ed.) *The Achilles Heel Reader*. London: Routledge, pp. 45–63.

Shaw, Sylvia (2006) 'Governing by the rules? The female voice in parliamentary debates' in Judith Baxter (ed.) *Speaking Out: The Female Voice in Public Contexts*. London: Palgrave, pp. 81–102.

Shepherd, Jennifer (1997) 'Storytelling in conversational discourse: a collaborative model', unpublished PhD thesis, University of Birmingham.

Sherrod, D. (1987) 'The bonds of men: problems and possibilities in close male relationships' in H. Brod (ed.) *The Making of Masculinities*. Boston: Allen and Unwin, pp. 213–39.

Siple, Patricia (1978) 'Visual constraints for sign language communication', *Sign Language Studies*, 19, 95–110.

Smith, Sandra (1999) 'Adult-child interaction in a BSL nursery: getting children's attention', paper presented at European Science Foundation 'Intersign' Workshop on Sign Language Acquisition, London, September 1999. www.sign-lang.uni-hamburg.de\intersign

Smith, Sandra and Sutton-Spence, Rachel (2006) 'Adult-child interaction in a BSL nursery – getting their attention!' *Journal of Sign Language and Linguistics*, 8 (1–2), 133–54.

Spivak, Gayatri Chakravorti (1987) *In Other Worlds: Essays in Cultural Politics*. New York: Routledge.

Stubbs, Michael (1983) *Discourse Analysis*. Oxford: Blackwell.

Sullivan, T., Weinart, C. and Cudney, S. (2003) 'Management of chronic illness: voices of rural women', *Journal of Advanced Nursing*, 44 (6), 566–76.

Swann, Joan (1989) 'Talk control: an illustration from the classroom of problems in analysing male dominance in conversation' in J. Coates and D. Cameron (eds) *Women in Their Speech Communities*. London: Longman, pp. 123–40.

Swann, Joan (1992) *Girls, Boys and Language*. Oxford: Blackwell.

Swann, Joan (2003) 'Schooled language: language and gender in educational settings' in J. Holmes and M. Meyerhoff (eds) *The Handbook of Language and Gender*. Oxford: Blackwell, pp. 624–44.

Swisher, Virginia, Christie, Karen and Miller, Sandra (1989) 'The reception of signs in peripheral vision by deaf persons', *Sign Language Studies*, 63, 99–125.

Talbot, Mary (1992) '"I wish you'd stop interrupting me": interruptions and asymmetries in speaker-rights in equal encounters', *Journal of Pragmatics*, 18, 451–66.

Talbot, Mary (2003) 'Gender stereotypes: reproduction and challenge' in J. Holmes and M. Meyerhoff (eds) *The Handbook of Language and Gender*. Oxford: Blackwell, pp. 468–86.

Thorne, Barrie (1993) *Gender Play: Girls and Boys in School*. Buckingham, UK: Open University Press.

Thorne, Barrie and Henley, Nancy (eds) (1975) *Language and Sex: Difference and Dominance*. Rowley, MA: Newbury House.

Thorne, Barrie, Kramarae, Cheris and Henley, Nancy (eds) (1983) *Language, Gender and Society*. Rowley, MA: Newbury House.

Todd, A.D. (1983) 'A diagnosis of doctor-patient discourse in the prescription of contraception' in S. Fisher and A.D. Todd (eds) *The Social Organisation of Doctor-Patient Communication*. Washington DC: Center for Applied Linguistics, pp. 159–87.

Tolson, Andrew (1977) *The Limits of Masculinity*. London: Tavistock Publications.

Tomsen, S. (1997) 'A top night: social protest, masculinity and the culture of drinking violence', *British Journal of Criminology*, 37 (1), 90–102.

Troemel Ploetz, S. (1985) Women's conversational culture: rupturing patriarchal discourse', ROLIG-papir 36, Roskilde Universitetscenter, Denmark.

Trudgill, Peter (1972) 'Sex, covert prestige and linguistic change in the urban British English of Norwich', *Language in Society*, 1, 179–95.

Trudgill, Peter (1974) *The Social Differentiation of English in Norwich*. Cambridge: Cambridge University Press.

Trudgill, Peter (1983) *On Dialect: Social and Geographical Perspectives*. Oxford: Basil Blackwell.

Walsh, Clare (2001) *Gender and Discourse: Language and Power in Politics, the Church and Organisations*. London: Longman.

Walsh, Clare (2006) 'Gender and the genre of the broadcast political interview' in Judith Baxter (ed.) *Speaking Out: The Female Voice in Public Contexts*. Basingstoke, UK: Palgrave Macmillan, pp. 121–38.

Warnock, M. (1987) 'Why women are their own worst enemies', *Daily Telegraph*, 19 January, p. 10.

Weedon, Chris (1987) *Feminist Practice and Poststructuralist Theory*. Oxford: Blackwell.

West, Candace (1984a) 'When the doctor is a "lady"', *Symbolic Interaction*, 7, 87–106.

West, Candace (1984b) *Routine Complications: Troubles with Talk between Doctors and Patients*. Bloomington: Indiana University Press.

West, Candace (1990) 'Not just "doctors' orders": directive-response sequences in patients' visits to women and men physicians', *Discourse & Society*, 1 (1), 85–112.

West, C. and Frankel, Richard M. (1991) 'Miscommunication in medicine' in N. Coupland, H. Giles and I. Wiemann (eds) *'Miscommunication' and Problematic Talk*. London: Sage, pp. 166–94.

Wetherell, Margaret and Edley, Nigel (1998) 'Gender practices: steps in the analysis of men and masculinities' in Karen Henwood, Christine Griffiths, and Ann Phoenix (eds) *Standpoints and Differences: Essays in the Practice of Feminist Psychology*. London: Sage.

Wetherell, Margaret and Edley, Nigel (1999) 'Negotiating hegemonic masculinity: imaginary positions and psycho-discursive practices', *Feminism and Psychology*, 9 (3), 335–56.

Willott, S. and Griffin, C. (1997) '"Wham bam, am I a man?": unemployed men talk about masculinities', *Feminism and Psychology*, 7 (1), 107–28.

Wilson, John (1989) *On the Boundaries of Conversation*. Oxford: Pergamon Press.

Wood, J. (1984) 'Groping towards sexism: boys' sex talk' in Angela McRobbie and Mica Nava (eds) *Gender and Generation*. London: Macmillan, pp. 54–84.

Woodward, James (1972) 'Historical bases of American Sign Language' in Patricia Siple (ed.) *Understanding Language through Sign Language Research*. New York: Academic Press.

Wulff, Helena (1988) *Twenty Girls: Growing Up, Ethnicity and Excitement in a South London Microculture*, Stockholm Studies in Social Anthropology 21. Stockholm: Almqvist & Wiksell International.

Xie, Yu and Shauman, Kimberlee (2003) *Women in Science: Career Processes and Outcomes*. Cambridge, MA: Harvard University Press.

Yang, Jie (2007) 'Zuiqian "deficient mouth": discourse, gender and domestic violence in urban China', *Gender and Language*, 1 (1), 107–18.

Yocom, Margaret R. (1985) 'Woman to woman: fieldwork and the private sphere' in R. Jordan and S. Kalcik (eds) *Women's Folklore, Women's Culture*. Philadelphia: University of Pennsylvania Press, pp. 45–53.

Young, K. Galloway (1987) *Taleworlds and Storyrealms*. Lancaster: Kluwer Academic Publishers.

Zimmerman, Don and West, Candace (1975) 'Sex roles, interruptions and silences in conversation' in Barrie Thorne and Nancy Henley (eds) *Language and Sex: Difference and Dominance*. Rowley, MA: Newbury House, pp. 105–29.

Index

Printed and bound by CPI Group (UK) Ltd, Croydon, CR0 4YY